Y0-DBX-355

American Rabbi

AMERICAN RABBI

THE LIFE AND THOUGHT OF JACOB B. AGUS

Edited by Steven T. Katz

NEW YORK UNIVERSITY PRESS
New York and London

NEW YORK UNIVERSITY PRESS
New York and London

Library of Congress Cataloging-in-Publication Data
American rabbi : the life and thought of Jacob B. Agus / edited by
Steven T. Katz.
p. cm.
Includes bibliographical references.
ISBN 0-8147-4693-4
1. Agus, Jacob B. (Jacob Bernard), 1911–1986. 2. Rabbis—United
States—Biography. 3. Jewish scholars—United States—Biography.
4. Judaism—United States. I. Katz, Steven T., 1944–
BM755.A53A44 1996
296.8′342′092—dc20
[B] 96-44953
CIP

New York University Press books are printed on acid-free paper,
and their binding materials are chosen for strength and durability.

Manufactured in the United States of America

10 9 8 7 6 5 4 3 2 1

CONTENTS

PREFACE

Steven T. Katz

The present collection of original essays on the life and thought of Rabbi Jacob B. Agus was commissioned by the Rabbi Jacob B. Agus Foundation of Baltimore, Maryland. Along with this collection, a second volume, an anthology of selections from the voluminous writings of Rabbi Agus, has been created under the title *The Essential Agus: The Writings of Jacob B. Agus,* also edited by Steven T. Katz and published by New York University Press. The two publications are closely interconnected, with the selections in the anthology chosen by the authors of the essays contained in this volume to illuminate the particular subject matter with which they deal. Readers will benefit from consulting both works, though each stands on its own.

As the editor of both volumes, I would like to thank publicly all the contributors for their cooperation in this venture. I would also like to thank Robert Agus, the son of Rabbi Jacob Agus, who represented the Agus Foundation in the ongoing conversation that accompanied the various stages in the creation of these books.

CONTRIBUTORS

DAVID R. BLUMENTHAL is Jay and Leslie Cohen Professor of Judaic Studies at Emory University, Atlanta, Georgia.

ELLIOT N. DORFF is professor of philosophy at the University of Judaism, Los Angeles, California.

EUGENE J. FISHER is director of the Secretariat for Ecumenical and Interreligious Affairs of the National Conference of Bishops, Washington, D.C.

NEIL GILLMAN is Aaron Rabinowitz and Simon H. Rifkind Associate Professor of Jewish philosophy at the Jewish Theological Seminary of America, New York City, New York.

STEVEN T. KATZ is director of the Center for Judaic Studies and professor of religion at Boston University.

WILLIAM E. KAUFMAN is rabbi of Temple Beth El, Fall River, Massachusetts.

MILTON R. KONVITZ is professor emeritus at Cornell University, Ithaca, New York.

MARK LOEB is rabbi of Congregation Beth El, Baltimore, Maryland.

DAVID NOVAK is Edgar M. Bronfman Professor of Modern Judaic Studies at the University of Virginia, Charlottesville, Virginia and Vice President of the Union for Traditional Judaism.

NORTON D. SHARGEL is rabbi of the Jewish Community Center, Harrison, New York.

MORDECAI WAXMAN is rabbi of Temple Israel, Great Neck, New York.

American Rabbi

I
JACOB B. AGUS: AN INTRODUCTORY OVERVIEW

Steven T. Katz

LIFE

JACOB AGUS (Agushewitz) was born into a distinguished rabbinical family in the month of Heshvan 5671—corresponding to November 2, 1911—in the shtetl of Sislevitch (Swislocz), situated in the Grodno Dubornik region of Poland. Descended through both parents from distinguished rabbinical lines (his mother being a member of the Katznellenbogen family), the young Agus, one of a family of seven children—four boys and three girls—early on showed signs of intellectual and religious precocity. After receiving tutoring at home and in the local heder, he joined his older brothers, Irving and Haiim, as a student at the Mizrachi-linked Tachnemoni yeshiva in Bialystock. Here he continued his intensive talmudic and classical studies, winning high praise as an *illui* (a genius) from the faculty of the yeshiva, and also began to be exposed to the wide variety of Jewish lifestyles and intellectual positions—ranging from secularists and bundists to Hasidim—that existed among Eastern European Jews. Raised in an almost totally Jewish environment, he knew little Polish and had limited relations with the non-Jewish world.

In the mid-1920s, as economic and political conditions worsened in Poland, many members of the Jewish community of Sislevitch emigrated to Palestine. This migratory wave also included the Agushewitzes, who arrived in Palestine in 1925. Unfortunately, the economic conditions and the religious life of the *Yishuv,* the emerging Jewish community in the land of Israel, were not favorable, and the Agushewitz family, including Jacob, now sixteen, moved again in 1927. This time they traveled to America, where Jacob's father, R. Yehuda Leïb, had relocated one year earlier to fill the position of rabbi in an East Side New York synagogue. R. Yehuda Leib later became a *schochet* (ritual slaughterer).

The family settled in Boro Park (Brooklyn), and Jacob, who already was able to read and write in English at a high school level, attended the high school connected with Yeshiva University. This marked a turning point in his personal life, for in this American yeshiva not only did students pursue a talmudic curriculum but—on the ideological presumption that all true human knowledge, the whole of creation, reflected God's wondrous ways—they were also exposed to a wide variety of secular and scientific subjects. For the remainder of his life, Jacob Agus would adhere to this religious-philosophical model.

After completing high school, Jacob attended the recently established Yeshiva University, where he continued both his rabbinical and secular studies, distinguishing himself in the secular realm in the areas of mathematics and science. He was so good at chemistry that he was encouraged to attend courses in this subject at Columbia University, which he did. He even briefly flirted with the idea of graduate work in chemistry. However, his deepest commitment was to Jewish studies and to the Jewish people, and he therefore chose a rabbinical career. A favorite of the founder and president of Yeshiva University, R. Bernard Revel, and the outstanding student of R. Moshe Soloveitchik, the head of the rabbinical school, Agus received his rabbinical ordination *(smicha)* in 1933. After two further years of intensive rabbinical study, Agus received the traditional "Yadin Yadin" smicha in 1935, an ordination intended to place Agus on the same level as those rabbinical students who graduated from the European yeshivas and to enable him to act as a *Poseik* (halakic, or legal, decision maker).

While still at Yeshiva University, Agus also served as an assistant to R. Leo Jung, a distinguished member of the American Orthodox rabbinate. In this role, at R. Jung's request, he researched the basis for requiring a *mechitza* (a partition between men and women) in the synagogue and concluded that there was no firm biblical or rabbinical basis for this halakic requirement—an early sign of important decisions to come.

After graduation from Yeshiva University in 1935, Agus took his first full-time rabbinical position in Norfolk, Virginia. Here he began to learn the trade of an active pulpit rabbi while continuing his Jewish education. Foremost among his educational pursuits at this time was an intensive study of midrash (the rabbinic commentaries on the Bible), guided, via the mail, by Professor Louis Ginsberg of the (Conservative) Jewish Theological Seminary of America, the great authority on midrash.

Having satisfied himself that with this control of the vast midrashic material, along with his talmudic erudition, he had reached a sufficiently well-rounded knowledge of classical Jewish materials, Agus began to pursue further secular studies in a serious and concentrated way. Convinced that these pursuits required a more intensive academic environment, he left Norfolk in 1936 for Harvard University, where he enrolled in the graduate program in philosophy. At Harvard his two main teachers were Professor Harry A. Wolfson, a master student of the history of Jewish philosophy, and Professor Ernest Hocking, a metaphysician of distinction.

While in the Boston area, Agus paid his way by taking on a rabbinical position in Cambridge and continued his rabbinical learning with R. Joseph Soloveitchik, the son of his Yeshiva University mentor, with whom he quickly formed a close friendship. For several years, Agus and the younger Soloveitchik met weekly to study Maimonides' philosophical and rabbinical works, as well as to discuss a host of more contemporary theological and halakic issues.

It was also in Boston that Agus met his future wife, Miriam Shore, the daughter of Bernard Shore, a Lithuanian Jew who had immigrated to America and become a Boston businessman. The Aguses married in 1940, with R. Joseph Soloveitchik officiating.

Harvard, however, was not all joy. In this great center of learning Agus for the first time in his life encountered serious, even intense, criticism of traditional Judaism. In response, he decided to devote a good deal of his energy for the remainder of his life to explicating, disseminating, and defending the ethical and humanistic values embodied in the Jewish tradition, particularly as these values were interpreted by its intellectual and philosophical elites, beginning with the Prophets and running through Philo, Saadya, Maimonides; and such modern intellectual giants as Hermann Cohen and R. Abraham Isaac Kook. Agus' first step on this path was his doctoral dissertation, published in 1940 under the title *Modern Philosophies of Judaism,* which critically examined the thought of the influential German triumvirate of Hermann Cohen, Franz Rosenzweig, and Martin Buber, as well as the work of Mordecai Kaplan, who in 1934 had published the classic *Judaism as a Civilization* that established his reputation as the leading American Jewish thinker.

After receiving his doctorate from Harvard, and with the encouragement of R. Revel, who wished to strengthen the foundations of modern Orthodoxy in the Midwest, Agus accepted the post of rabbi at the Agudas Achim Congregation in Chicago. Though the congregation permitted mixed seating, it was still considered an Orthodox synagogue. In this freer midwestern environment, removed from the yeshiva world of his student days, the orthodoxy of Yeshiva University, and the intensity of Jewish Boston, Agus began to have doubts about the intellectual claims and dogmatic premises of Orthodox Judaism. In particular, he began to redefine the meaning of halakah and its relationship to reason and independent ethical norms. Encouraged in this direction by Chicago's leading Conservative rabbi, Solomon Goldman, and by the radical reconstructionism of Mordecai Kaplan, Agus had initiated the process of philosophical and theological reconceptualization that would define his increasingly revisionist and non-Orthodox thought.

In 1943, disenchanted with his Chicago pulpit, Agus accepted a call to Dayton, Ohio, where three small synagogues merged to form a liberal Orthodox congregation that became a Conservative congregation during his tenure. Given the proximity of Dayton to Cincinnati, he began an ongoing and cordial dialogue with the faculty and students of the Reform movement's Hebrew Union College (HUC). In particular, Agus became a colleague of R. Abraham Joshua Heschel, who had fled war-torn Europe and taken up a position at HUC. Like Agus, Heschel was the heir of a great rabbinical family and a master of all branches of classical Jewish and rabbinical learning, with a special affinity for the thought of Maimonides. Alienated from the "tone" of classical Reform, which still dominated HUC, Heschel became a regular visitor at the Agus home on Sabbaths and holidays. Agus and Heschel formed a lifelong intellectual and personal collaboration that later manifested itself in joint efforts to alter the curriculum and character of the Jewish Theological Seminary, whose faculty Heschel joined in 1945, and in common undertakings on behalf of Jewish–Christian dialogue and various political causes.

Because of this intensive rethinking of modern Jewish thought—and perhaps also as a consequence of his engagement with Heschel—Agus turned his attention to the thought of R. Abraham Isaac Kook, the remarkable mystical personality who had served as the first chief rabbi of modern Palestine after World War I. (Kook died in 1935.) The result was Agus' *Banner of Jerusalem,* published in 1946, which sought to explore Kook's neocabalistic, panentheistic notion of holiness *(kedusha),* that is, the doctrine that God's presence was suffused throughout creation and incarnated most concretely in the Jewish people, the land of Israel, and the Torah. Deeply impressed by Kook's intense spirituality and authentic mystical vision, Agus yearned to invigorate American Orthodoxy with something of the same visionary passion. Yet at the same time, his deep engagement with Kook's traditional cabalistic *Weltanschauung* persuaded Agus that this essentially medieval worldview was one he did not, and could not, share. Modern Judaism had need of much that Kook had to teach, but it required that Kook's lessons be made available through a different vehicle, in a form more suitable to the modern temperament.

At this point Agus still hoped he could achieve his goal of effecting meaningful religious and structural change within the parameters of the Orthodox community. Like Mordecai Kaplan, he now advocated the creation of a reconstituted, metadenominational Sanhedrin (supreme Jewish religious legislative body) that would possess the power to alter—to modernize—Jewish religious life and practice. Though several important members of the Orthodox rabbinate, including R. Leo Jung and R. Joseph Lookstein, apparently were sympathetic to this call in private, none, including R. Joseph Soloveitchik, would support it openly. This lack of support, as well as Agus' own increasingly expansive and universalist spiritual and intellectual odyssey—one that was ever more appreciative of Western, non-Jewish culture and ever more critical of what Agus took to be certain forms of Jewish parochialism and chauvinism—led him, after his failure to gather support for an agenda of change and halakic reform at the Orthodox Rabbinical Council of America (RCA) convention in 1944 and 1945, to break decisively with the organized Orthodox community and its institutions.

This repercussive decision also reflected his personal experience as a community rabbi in a relatively small midwestern town like Dayton; for here Agus faced several new challenges. First, he had to be the force behind the restructuring of three congregations into one new, cohesive synagogue. Second, he had to respond to the personal needs of a religiously diverse group of Jews. Third, in the face of the unfolding catastrophe that engulfed the Jews of Europe, he had to offer Jews of limited learning who were attracted by the seductive options of assimilated life in America a Judaism that was intellectually and spiritually meaningful. Moreover, to his surprise he had discovered that he derived great satisfaction from his duties as a congregational rabbi. He enjoyed presenting sermons and lectures to his congregants—tasks at which he became very proficient, having hired a voice teacher to help him refine his oral delivery—meeting their pastoral needs, and even being active in the day-to-day affairs of the synagogue management; for example, he was very involved in the architectural design of the new sanctuary.

Disaffected from the Orthodox rabbinical community, Agus officially broke with the RCA in 1946–1947 and joined the Conservative movement's Rabbinical Assembly. In this new context, by virtue of his rabbinical erudition, his Orthodox *smicha,* and the force of his personality, he became a powerful presence and an agent of change. Over and against the conservative force exerted by Chancellor Louis Finkelstein and the great Talmudist Saul Leiberman, who between them controlled the faculty of the Jewish Theological Seminary, which in turn dominated the procedural processes of the Conservative movement, Agus, in consort with like-minded Conservative rabbis such as Solomon Goldman, Robert Gordis, Morris Adler, Milton Steinberg, Ben Zion Bokser, and Theodore Friedman, argued for a more open and dynamic halakic process within the movement.

As a first major step in this direction, Agus proposed that the Law Committee of the Conservative movement be restructured into the Committee on Jewish Law and Standards (CJLS)—a change in more than name, the rationale for which is explained in his essays in *Guideposts in Modern Judaism.* He was, in turn, appointed to this committee (and to others) and remained a member of it for nearly forty years, until his death.

One of the earliest and best examples of his view on how the halakah should be interpreted is reflected in the important "Responsum on the Sabbath" that was issued by the Committee on Jewish Law and Standards in 1950. This responsum stated that the use of electricity was permitted on the Sabbath and that riding to and from the synagogue on the Sabbath was also permitted. The first decision was arrived at by use of the traditional halakic process, with one major exception, and the second was justified as a *takkanah* (a rabbinic enactment) responding to the "needs of the hour." Both instantiated Agus' view that a reverent and reasoned approach to change and the admission of where the halakah was lacking were required to revitalize Judaism in the contemporary world.

It should also be remembered that these decisions were embedded in a lengthy report that placed central emphasis on a proposed program to "revitalize sabbath observance"; this was not merely a call for radical change and a capitulation to modernity. The program was to consist of standards to be promulgated for all United Synagogue member synagogues to lift the levels of observance. In the late 1940s and early 1950s, observance by laypeople was extremely lax—few attended services, many worked, few had Friday evening dinners, and many Jewish communal organizations held events that violated the Sabbath and at which nonkosher food was served.

R. Agus, impelled by a drive for honesty and integrity, held it wrong to encourage people to attend the synagogue on the Sabbath, with the knowledge that many individuals would have to drive there, and then to insist that driving was an *averah* (a sin). In general, he thought that in keeping with modern sensibilities and the intellectual levels of congregants, the primary emphasis should be placed on encouraging mitzvot and not on alleging *averot.* The doing of each mitzvah was a good in itself and would lead to the doing of other mitzvot. This positive view, stressing the appropriate performance of mitzvot, is expressed in *Guideposts* and was an underlying principle of Agus' halakic decisions.

As a recognized halakist, Agus was also asked by the United Synagogue to defend the principle of mixed seating in two secular court cases—one in New Orleans and one in Cincinnati—both of which occurred in the early 1950s. In both cases a deceased person had left funds in his will to his synagogue on condition that the synagogue remain "traditional." At the time of the deaths, both synagogues had separate seating for men and women, but they did not have a halakically acceptable *mechitza.* In fact, by 1950 both congregations wanted to introduce mixed seating, a move that prompted a minority group of congregants to sue for the retention of separate seating on the grounds that mixed seating was a violation of the tradition.

In response, Agus pointed out that neither synagogue had a *mechitza* and yet each had been considered traditional in the eyes of the now-deceased donor. Therefore, one could argue that mixed seating was no less traditional than separate seating. He also explained the lack of any clear halakic basis for separate seating and the nature of change within the tradition.

To the Orthodox members of the Agudas ha-Rabbonim, the organization of European-trained rabbis, this was wholly unacceptable. They were engaged at the time in an effort to force all Orthodox synagogues to maintain a *mechitza* as a way of drawing a distinction between Orthodox and Conservative synagogues. In the early 1950s, under the aegis of R. Joseph Soloveitchik's Halachah Committee, the Rabbinical Council of America issued a statement that *mechitzas* were required.

The Agudas ha-Rabbonim went further and issued a ruling that prayer within a synagogue without a kosher *mechitza* was not permitted and would not fulfill a person's religious obligations. In this same ruling, they placed R. Agus in *herem* (excommunication) for teaching false ideas. Intermarriage with R. Agus and his immediate family was prohibited. It should be noted, however, that two of the *gedolai ha-dor* (recognized halakic authorities), R. Aharon Kitler and R. Moshe Feinstein, who were friends of R. Yehuda Leib A. Agushewitz, denied knowledge of and repudiated this action. Three other rabbis—Eisenstein, Groubard, and Greenfield—were also specifically placed in *herem*. However, several years later the leaders of the Agudas repudiated this document and claimed that it had never been properly executed.

In 1950, R. Agus accepted the position of rabbi at the newly formed Conservative congregation Beth El in Baltimore. A small congregation of some fifty families when he arrived, it grew over his three decades as its rabbi into a major congregation—so popular, in fact, that it had to restrict new memberships—and one of the premier Conservative synagogues in the United States.

In his role as community rabbi, Agus attended the daily morning minyan (prayer quorum), taught Mishnah or Talmud for ten to fifteen minutes to those who came, and always returned for the evening daily service as well. He visited the sick weekly, paid shivah (week-of-mourning) calls, attended committee meetings in the evenings, and met congregants at all hours. He gave serious forty-minute lectures to the men's club each week, and hundreds of men attended on a regular basis. He did oral book reviews for the sisterhood. Agus also started adult education institutes for the whole community, attended by thousands. He planned the curriculum for the Beth El schools and taught the post–bar mitzvah class. He produced a siddur (prayer book) for everyday use that allowed services to be of a moderate length. He also changed the content of the services for late Friday night, Saturday morning, and holidays in ways that retained the traditional core of the liturgy but made the services more aesthetically pleasing, intellectually challenging, and time-efficient. His approach to services included intellectual sermons and beautiful congregational singing—all in a two-hour package. Congregants came on time and participated.

As a consequence of all this effort, Beth El moved to new suburban surroundings in 1960, reopened its membership rolls, and grew to a congregation of more than fifteen hundred families. It was typical of Agus that in the construction of the new building he worked closely with the architects and designers to ensure that it would be both aesthetic and Jewishly pleasing.

Here a word needs to be said about Agus' view on the role of women in the synagogue. Consistent with his more general theological position, he felt that artificial barriers to the full participation of women should be eliminated. However, he cautioned that societal change must occur at a pace and in a manner that allowed people's sensibilities to evolve and new means of order and value-teaching to develop. He was very concerned that the family be strengthened, not weakened, and feared that a radical transformation rather than measured progress on the role of women would disrupt the family and social order. In line with this understanding, he established a bas mitzvah ceremony on Friday nights because the issue of a woman's receiving an *aliyah* (call to the Torah) had not yet been addressed by the Rabbinical Assembly. Once it was, and once the assembly's CJLS approved *aliyot* for women—with Agus' active support as a member of the committee—he instituted the practice at Beth El. Likewise, when the counting of women in the minyan was approved by the CJLS with Agus' endorsement, Beth El followed suit.

The issue of female rabbis proved more complex. Agus felt that the CJLS should address the subissues of women as judges, witnesses, and *shlichit tzibbur* (leaders of public prayer) before that of rabbi. For political reasons, the Jewish Theological Seminary addressed the issue by setting up a commission, whose report attempted to skirt these halakic issues. R. Agus was upset at the process—he thought the report was deliberately disingenuous in not addressing the other issues of status, since everyone knew that once ordained, women rabbis would perform all of the functions not addressed. Though he agreed with the result, he disagreed with the process. Therefore, in a move that surprised both the left and the right, he led a group of Rabbinical Assembly members in rejecting the report's recommendation.

During the 1950s, despite his congregational responsibilities, Agus continued his scholarly work. He was a regular contributor to a variety of Jewish periodicals, such as the *Menorah Journal, Judaism, Midstream,* and *The Reconstructionist,* and he served on several of their editorial boards. He also published on occasion in Hebrew journals. At the same time, he began to teach at Johns Hopkins University in an adjunct capacity, lecture at B'nai B'rith institutes, and speak at colleges and seminaries around the country. In 1959 he published his well-known study *The Evolution of Jewish Thought,* an outgrowth of his lectures.

During this period, Agus also took an active interest in national and international affairs. A firm supporter of Franklin D. Roosevelt during the 1930s and 1940s and a supporter of the creation of the United Nations, he distrusted socialism and hated communism. However, he believed in the necessity of moderate dialogue with the Soviet Union and supported public figures such as Adlai Stevenson who advocated a less belligerent relationship with the USSR. He was a significant opponent of Senator Joseph McCarthy and openly fought McCarthyism, testifying on behalf of individuals who were under suspicion, and he invited Professor Owen Lattimore of Johns Hopkins University to lecture at Beth El. Agus fought for the limitation of nuclear weapons, even for nuclear disarmament. He even disregarded a federal requirement that Beth El build a nuclear shelter, arguing that such an action legitimated the idea of nuclear war. He supported the Civil Rights movement and efforts to desegregate Baltimore, though he opposed affirmative action programs as unfair and had a visceral fear of black inner-city violence, which threatened many Jewish shopkeepers. He was an early and consistent opponent of the Vietnam War and supported the antiwar political positions of Senators Eugene McCarthy and George McGovern. In the 1970s, Agus was an active participant in an interfaith group started by Sargent Shriver to discuss the intersection of religion and politics.

Beginning in 1968, Agus, while continuing his rabbinical duties in Baltimore, accepted a joint appointment as professor of Rabbinic Civilization at the new Reconstructionist Rabbinical College (RRC) in Philadelphia and at Temple University. Though not a reconstructionist, Agus had a long-standing relationship with Mordecai Kaplan, the founder of the reconstructionist movement, and he respected what promised to be a serious and innovative rabbinical training program. Agus taught in this capacity until the end of the academic year in 1970, when he resigned from the RRC in a dispute over the curriculum and the amount of Talmud students should be required to learn. The faculty wanted to reduce the hours devoted to talmudic study, while Agus wanted to increase it. However, he retained his professorship at Temple University and continued to teach graduate courses at that institution until 1980, when he resigned and accepted an adjunct appointment at Dropsie College in Philadelphia. He held this position until 1985, when his health would no longer permit the heavy schedule of travel that professorship entailed. Agus also had served as visiting professor in 1966 at the Rabbinical Seminary in Buenos Aires, affiliated with the Jewish Theological Seminary of America.

In addition to formal teaching, R. Agus taught the members of the local rabbinate on numerous occasions over the years. When he first came to Baltimore, he assisted local Conservative and Reform rabbis on an informal basis. In later years he gave seminars to rabbis in the Baltimore-Washington area on a bimonthly basis. Agus came to be known as the "rabbi of the rabbis" in the Baltimore-Washington area, because rabbis from all denominations of Judaism came to him not only to learn but also for advice on both personal and halakic issues. While his teaching was well known, the personal contacts were in confidence. The rabbis did invite him to speak before their congregations on a regular basis; for example, for a number of years he was invited to give a series of four lectures as year as a part of the Sunday Scholar Series at Washington (Reform) Hebrew Congregation. Also, over the years students at the Ner Israel ultra-Orthodox yeshiva in Baltimore would come to see Agus at his house late at night to study Talmud. This study was kept secret because if it had become known, it would have resulted in the students' expulsion from Ner Israel.

Another environment in which Agus taught was Christian seminaries. He lectured at Woodstock (Maryland, Jesuit), Union Theological in New York City, and St. Mary's Seminary in Baltimore. St. Mary's is the largest school for Catholic priests in the United States and is under the direct supervision of the Vatican. R. Agus was the first nonpriest, let alone Jew, officially authorized by the Vatican to teach Catholic seminarians. He lectured on the Jewish background and content of the Gospels for over ten years on a regular basis.

During the 1960s and 1970s, Agus was also active in projects that cut across the lines of Jewish organizational life. For example, he became involved in the recently founded organization of Jewish academic scholars the Association for Jewish Studies, and helped to establish a Jewish Philosophical Society. He worked with the American Jewish Committee at both the local and the national level on various communal issues, with the Synagogue Council of America on Jewish-Christian issues, and with a host of Jewish communal agencies.

In 1979–1980, Agus became part of a group of fifteen rabbis—five Orthodox, five Conservative, and five Reform—that was put together by the leaders of the Rabbinical Council of America (Orthodox), the Rabbinical Assembly (Conservative), and the Central Committee of American Rabbis (Reform) and that met in secret for a number of years to explore issues of theology and practice. Much of the early work of this group was based on papers prepared by Agus. He was very interested in and excited by this undertaking, as it brought him back into contact with people from Yeshiva University, including R. Joseph Lookstein, an old mentor. He found significant areas of commonality among the movements and even harbored some optimism that his quest to create a viable religiously based Judaism for America would begin to move forward. Unfortunately, his illnesses and other factors aborted this effort.

From the 1950s, Agus likewise was active in the Jewish-Christian dialogue, in the hope of reducing anti-Semitism and helping to restructure the Christian understanding of Jews and Judaism. He worked closely with the American Jewish Committee in developing interfaith programs and was directly involved in relationships with Cardinal Bea that bore fruit in Vatican II. He worked with the National Council of Christians and Jews and actively participated in interfaith conversations, programs, and education at the local and state levels.

R. Agus became rabbi emeritus at Beth El in 1980. From 1980 to 1986, despite poor health, he continued his academic work, publishing his last book, *The Jewish Quest,* in 1983. He died on the twenty-third day of Elul, September 26, 1986.

THOUGHT

Despite all his rabbinical teaching and public roles, Jacob Agus is best known as an important Jewish thinker and student of Jewish thought. This scholarly activity, which spanned nearly half a century—beginning with his Harvard doctoral dissertation, which became his first book, *Modern Philosophies of Judaism* (1941)—covers an enormous historical and conceptual range, stretching from the biblical to the modern era. Nothing Jewish was alien to Agus, and his research and reflections involved talmudic, philosophical, and cabalistic sources, though quite clearly the philosophical material had pride of place.

In *Modern Philosophies of Judaism,* Agus undertook the task of explicating and criticizing the work of the great German Jewish thinkers Hermann Cohen, Franz Rosenzweig, and Martin Buber—Cohen and Rosenzweig being little known in America at the time—as well as the radical theology of Mordecai Kaplan. Among this group of seminal thinkers, Agus was attracted most especially to the work of Franz Rosenzweig: "The spirit which permeates his work perforce escapes analysis. And that spirit is great and bright, glowing with the fire of God" (209). In particular, Agus was drawn to Rosenzweig's nonliteral, nonpropositional theory of revelation, which, he argued, "will be found to accord with an enlightened view of tradition and with the ways of thinking of the earnestly critical modern mind" (350). Cohen he found too abstract, his conception of God too distant from "the pattern of religious emotion" (126). Buber, whom Agus saw as a mystic, according to the criteria of mystical experience set out by William James,[1] is criticized for his subjectivism—"Devotion uncontrolled by reason is a greater danger to society than selfishness, history proves abundantly. We find this truth scrawled all over the story of mankind, in letters of fire and blood" (276)—and for his rejection of rational, objective criteria in religious and ethical matters:

> Those of us, however, who are constrained to judge the value of these "inner calls" by external standards, may well feel uneasy at the total absence of the rational element in the decision advocated by Buber. If only we were certain that the call came from God! But, what if Satan should intervene instead! How are we to tell the voice of the "Eternal Thou" from that of the "demonic Thou?" (Is not Hitler, too, a mystic?)

Alternatively, Kaplan, though described as a rationalist and a pragmatist, is found wanting because of internal contradictions within the structure of his thought, the inability "to develop [his] own conception of God to the point where it could serve as the basis of a life of religion" (315), and an excessive nationalism that, if not carefully counterpoised by "a deep conviction in the reality of the universal value of ethics" (322), could lead to disastrous consequences.

But interestingly, beyond the systematic differences among his four subjects and his individual criticisms of their work, Agus found a common core in all of them. As distinctively Jewish thinkers, all were said to recognize that

> the moral law appears in consciousness as an absolute command, spurning all selfish and unworthy motives. It can only be understood on its own face value, as an objective law of action, deriving from the structure of reality. An essential part of ethical experience is the feeling that there is an outside source to our judgments of right and wrong, that the stamp of validity attaches to our apprehensions of the rightness and wrongness of things.
>
> This conviction is not only common to the philosophers discussed in this book; it constitutes the main vantage point of their respective philosophies. While they express this fluid intuition in radically different ways, they agree in founding their systems of thought upon it. (330).

This conviction was also Agus':

> The intuition of the objective validity of ethical values must be taken into consideration. In moments of intense moral fervor, we feel that rightness and wrongness are eternally fixed in the scheme of things; that it is not our own personal dictates and impulses that are the source of ethical feeling; that the sense of authority attaching to our ethical judgment is not derived either from the opinions of other men or from the unconscious influence of society; that the things we call "good" and "bad" are similarly designated by the Eternal One, Who stands outside of us and yet dwells within us, speaking through our mouths in moments of great, ethical exaltation.
>
> This intuition is the basis of my philosophy and religion. I believe it, not only because on many occasions it has come to me with dazzling clarity, but far more because this insight has been shared by the great thinkers of humanity, in particular, by the religious geniuses of Israel. (340–41)

All his later philosophical reflections are predicated on this religio-ethical premise.

Agus' second book, *Banner of Jerusalem: The Life, Times, and Thought of Abraham Isaac Kuk* (1946), intended as a complement to *Modern*

Philosophies of Judaism, on its face dealt with a surprising subject for Agus, given his modernizing sympathies, his reservations about nationalism—including certain formulations of Zionism—and his often severe criticisms of cabala; for Rav Kook (Kuk) (b. 1865; d. 1935), the first Ashkenazi chief rabbi of modern Palestine (1919–1935), was, vis-à-vis halakah, a traditional rabbinical figure, an ardent religious Zionist, and the most original and creative cabalist of the twentieth century. Yet Agus, who shared much in the way of biography with R. Kook, was drawn to Kook's profound spirituality, his intense religious passion, his concern for all Jews, his support of the rebirth of all types of Jewish life in the renewed land of Israel, his unwaveringly religious Zionism, his mystical embrace of all things as part of the divine life, his respect for the religious potential of all men. Kook, for example, had written:

> It was indeed proper that the whole content of holiness should have reference to humanity in general, for the perception of holiness is universal and the content of holiness, the bond between man and God, is independent of any nationality. This universal content would, in that event, have appeared for Jews in a special Jewish garment, but the wave of moral perversion that set in later in world history caused the elements of holiness to be forgotten among all men. And a new creation was made in Israel. . . . Nevertheless, there are still titans of the spirit who find the cosmic element in the root of Adam's soul, which still throbs in the heart of mankind generally.[2]

Agus also was drawn to Kook's intense effort "to meet the manifold challenges of modernism thru the deepening of piety and the inclusion therein of the new and aggressive values" (*Banner,* 20) and to what Agus described in the "Preface to the Second Edition" of *Banner of Jerusalem* (retitled *High Priest of Rebirth*) as Kook's "generous, outgoing humanism" (*High Priest,* ix):

> The ritual of Judaism is designed to replenish the mystical springs of idealism in human society. Loyalty to Israel, [Kook] taught, was wholly in accord with unalloyed faithfulness to humanism, since Israel was "the ideal essence of humanity." With all his intense nationalism, he never allowed himself to forget that the ultimate justification of nationalism consisted in the good that it might bring to the whole race of mankind. (*High Priest,* 240)

It is also most probable that Agus was drawn to R. Kook because he saw in various of R. Kook's halakic enactments a prototype for his own halakic reforms. Thus, for example, one feels the passion in Agus' reprise of Kook's creative stand on the question of the observance of *sh'ittah* (the biblical law that in the seventh year the land should not be cultivated or worked) in the fledgling agricultural settlements of the renewed Jewish community in Palestine. R. Kook, developing an earlier ruling, allowed for sale of the land to a gentile as a way of circumventing the strict rule that agricultural work cease during the "sabbatical year of the land." Despite intense opposition from many in the Orthodox community, Kook held firm, and his ruling was adopted by most of the religious agricultural settlements. Here is R. Agus' description of R. Kook's moral courage during and after this religious crisis:

> Aware of the undeserved abuse heaped upon him by many who sought to make partisan, political capital out of the affair, but, certain of the rightness of his position, he did not permit even a drop of rancor to enter his mind. As soon as the storm of controversy subsided, the Jewish world in Palestine and abroad recognized in him, not only a great Talmudic scholar, but one of the gentle saints in Israel. Almost despite himself, he became a central figure in world Jewry, the symbol of brave and adventurous leadership in Orthodox Judaism and the hero for thousands of young *yeshivah* students in every part of the globe. Those who maintained that Orthodox Judaism was not rigid and petrified, hopelessly caught in the paralyzing grip of ancient law and doctrine, were able to point to the rabbi of Jaffa as proof of the pliancy, adaptability and courage of genuine Orthodox leadership. (*High Priest,* 83)

For Agus, this type of religious leadership was required more generally within the Orthodox world; and in certain real ways he worked to effect, as he saw it, similar halakic transformations within the orbit of American Jewry. What Agus said of R. Kook might also be taken as the theme of Agus' own life's work:

> He transformed Orthodoxy by reviving the components of humanism and secular culture in the Jewish tradition. And he appealed to the secularists to appreciate and reverence the depths of mystery, out of which spring man's genuine values. He lived "on the boundary" between

> the sacred and the secular, between the mystique of particularism and the outreach of universalism. And it is to this boundary that we must find our way in every generation. (*High Priest,* xiii)

In 1954, R. Agus continued his significant publishing activity with a collection of essays titled *Guideposts in Modern Judaism.* In the opening essay, "The Impact of American Culture," Agus expressed his admiration for American liberalism, his strong (correct) belief that Zionism cannot be a substitute religion for American Jews—though critical of this vicarious Zionism and various political forms of Zionism, he was a Zionist and defended the basic concept of a Jewish state in the land of Israel—his (correct) view that anti-Semitism is receding as an important issue in forming Jewish identity in America, his (correct) view that ethnicity is declining as a factor in Jewish identity in America, and his judgment that religion in America is distinctively pragmatic in tone and value. The second, quite provocative essay is an extended review and critique of various trends in the modern branches of Judaism. Agus is, not surprisingly, a keen critic of all the various conceptual efforts that have been advanced to explain, justify, or alter Judaism in the modern period. His critical comments on the philosophy of halakah of his former close friend, Rav Joseph Soloveitchik, are notable (37–44), while his own sympathy for the Conservative movement is clear in his analysis of that movement's handling of halakic matters (133–37).

The third essay in *Guideposts,* "The Jewish Community," revolves around the seminal issue of nationalism, that is, how and in what sense Judaism is Zionism. In particular, the essay is critical of Ahad HaʿAm's and Mordecai Kaplan's cultural form of Zionism and of the classical Zionist doctrine, espoused by David Ben-Gurion, among others, of "the negation of the diaspora" *(shelilat ha-golah).* (Agus was critical of all purely secular forms of Zionism, all forms of Zionism that called for the "normalization" of the Jewish people, and all efforts to deny the legitimacy of the *golah*—Jewish life outside the land of Israel.) In America, Judaism must dominate the Jewish agenda as religion, not nationalism. The fourth essay, "Ends and Means of Jewish Life in America," originally published in the *Menorah Journal* in 1949, argues the same point but advances the argument by introducing an idea that henceforth would be central to Agus' general position on Jewish matters: what he calls the "meta-myth" and defines as "that indeterminate but all-too-real *plus* in the consciousness of Jewish difference, as it is reflected in the minds of both Jews and Gentiles" (*Guideposts,* 181). For non-Jews, this meta-myth manifests itself in the belief that

> the Jew is different in some mysterious manner. In the imagination of the untutored he may appear to be now partaking of divine qualities, now bordering on the diabolical, now superhuman in his tenacity, now subhuman in his spiteful determination to survive; but always, in some dim sense, the traditional stereotype of the Jew held by the Gentiles includes the apprehension of deep cosmic distinction from the rest of humanity.
>
> This feeling has been reflected in the mythological substructure of antisemitism from its very origins. (*Guideposts,* 181)

Both positive and negative aspects of Jewish-Gentile relationships over time—and here Agus includes both anti-Semitism and Zionism—have been directed, affected, and shaped by this belief. But Agus opposes this myth in all its forms. Instead, he again argues for optimism about the status of the Jew in America and for the centrality of the religious dimension in American Jewish life. Agus' moral idealism, his unceasing universalism, never wavers:

> The true Jewish way is to rise above the hatred by recognizing it as a universal evil, found in ourselves as well as in others, and to labor for its cure both within ourselves and in the total society of which we are a part.
>
> By cleaving to the spiritual interpretation of Jewish experience we provide a means for the non-religious among us to progress in the realm of the spirit through their Jewish identification. To be sure, we have now shown how the gulf in many men's minds between adherence to spiritual values and the convictions of religion may be bridged. There is in fact a plus of conviction in religious faith, with regard to the roots in eternity of spiritual values, which cannot be obtained by the cultivation of a humanist attitude alone. Spiritually minded people will still find congregational life the best means of continuing their own spiritual progress, through self-identification with Jewish experience in the religious interpretation, and by promoting its values in the social grouping of which they are a part. (*Guideposts,* 201)

This cardinal theme is further developed in "Building Our Future in America." While continuing to criticize the notion of a Jewish "mission," Agus here advocates what he calls "the concept of a 'creative minority,' " by which he means that the American Jewish community should emphasize "autonomy, on creativeness, [which] will cherish and foster whatever cultural and spiritual values are generated by every individual interpretation, every aspiration, within the community" (*Guideposts,* 213). That is to say:

> A "creative minority" is, first, a minority that senses its underlying and essential unity with the general population, even as it is conscious of its own distinguishing attributes. We are not as a lonely island, battered by the endless waves of the encircling ocean, but one of a chain of islands which form a solid continuous range beneath the raging, restless surface. Distinctive as our history and tradition are, they yet constitute a vital part of the realm of ideas and experience upon which American civilization is based. Thus we are part of Christian culture, though apart from it; and, even as we cherish and cultivate our own specific heritage, we must not ignore the massive historical reality, the "Judeo-Christian tradition," which forms the spiritual substratum of Western civilization.
>
> Secondly, a "creative minority" evolves new values for the general community, of which it is a part, out of the peculiar circumstances which set it apart. While not officiously seeking to lead or teach or preach, it expands the cultural horizons of the whole community by developing the implications of its unique position. In this sense the Jewish community, by faithfully tracing out the inner logic of its traditions and developing the implicit truths of its peculiar status, might unfold fresh insights for the guidance of the entire American nation.
>
> Thirdly, a "creative minority" is value-centered and oriented to the future. Neither exhausted by the elemental struggle for bare survival nor overcome by the great glory of the past, its face is turned toward the sunlight of spiritual growth. It refuses either to chafe vainly against the boundaries that enclose it or to look above them with Olympian detachment as if they did not exist. (*Guideposts,* 214–15)

The Jewish community will and should remain in America and can flourish here, if it works to maintain and enhance its religio-spiritual identity.

The remaining essays in *Guideposts* are more directly theological in nature, beginning with a two-part essay titled "A Reasoned Faith" and subtitled "The Idea of God." The first half of this essay tries, with considerable success, to establish the conceptual basis for a knowledge of God; the second half deals with God as known through our experience. Here Agus argues for the intuitionist position: "When we are face to face with a striking truth, an act of triumphant goodness or an event of surpassing beauty, we recognize the quality of time-transcending reality, as an immediate, direct experience, and we thrill to it as a fact, not merely a reasoned argument" (*Guideposts,* 257). The most important theological claim advanced in this essay, however, is that God is to be conceived of in personal rather than impersonal terms:

> Shall we think of Him in physical-philosophical terms such as Principle, Power, Absolute, Form or Cause, or shall we employ the personalistic-biblical terms of Father, the Merciful One, the Living God? Manifestly, the only concept which, in our experience constitutes the polar opposite to the concept of mechanical causation. Yet, God is not the Self or Soul of the universe, but, as the Kabbalists correctly pointed out, He is the Soul of the Soul, etc. of the universe. And we have no way of knowing how many links there be found in the spiritual chain of being. (*Guideposts,* 268).

The second theological paper deals with the absolutely essential and Jewishly unavoidable issue of "Torah Mi-Sinai," that is, the nature and claims of revelation. Rejecting the rejection of faith while affirming the authenticity of revelation, yet aware of the philosophical problems that the traditional, literalist notion of revelation has engendered in the modern world, Agus attempts to steer a middle ground that argues for the reality of nonpropositional revelation. God speaks to us in our ethical intuition, in our religious feeling (piety), and in moments of inspiration—our ethical intuitions being the most "objective" category (*Guideposts,* 288)—rather than in the literal legal and historical formulations of the Bible:

> Since revelation occurs between man and God, it is obviously unscientific and therefore untruthful to assume that the human or particular element is not felt in the content of revelation. Inevitably, the "Torah speaks the language of men," in all its finiteness, limitation and particular-

> ity. Thus, objectively, God's speech is not verbal expression; God's command is not a specific precept; God's behest is not the fire, clamor and whirlwind of dogmatic rivalries. (*Guideposts,* 291–92)

What makes Judaism distinctive—what makes Judaism, Judaism—is that it translates this encounter with God into legal categories—"the command of God" (296), the halakah:

> Halachah is for us the way in which God's word is progressively being shaped into ways of life. This view is in perfect harmony with our historical knowledge of the evolution of Halachah. The laws of Halachah were not only consciously ordained for the purpose of fostering the "normative" consciousness; they were also in part subconsciously evolved out of the inner religious drive, to translate "feeling" into "law." In this way, the regimen of Halachah made the observant Jew feel that the whole world was encompassed by the sway of Divine Law. (*Guideposts,* 297)

However, the halakah is, like all products of revelation, an admixture of human and divine elements:

> We must make it clear from the objective viewpoint that the revealed character of Jewish legislation refers to the general subconscious spritual drive which underlies the whole body of Halachah, not to the details of the Law. The vital fluid of the Torah-tree derives from the numinous soil of the Divine, but the actual contours of the branches and the leaves are the product of a variety of climatic and accidental causes. It is of the very essence of the reasoning process to recognize that the particular is accidental and contingent. . . . All that we can and do affirm is the Divine character of the principle of Halachah. From the viewpoint of history, we know that the Shulchan Aruch did not spring fullblown from the mind of Moses. It is the product of gradual evolution, in which diverse social and economic factors were conjoined with those of a purely religious character. (*Guideposts,* 298–99)

And the outcome of this complex, evolutionary, historical process, according to Agus' criteria, allows for change, modification, and innovation in the halakah—but not for the rejection of the Law itself, that is, a full denial of the category of halakah per se.

Agus then applies this understanding of the halakah in the next three essays, which are devoted, respectively, to (1) "Law in Conservative Judaism"; (2) "Laws as Standards"; and (3) "Pluralism in Law." He rightly recognizes the fundamental difference between his understanding of halakah (also that of the Conservative movement) and that of the Orthodox tradition. With honesty he acknowledges, "Manifestly, then, the Conservative movement cannot be described as falling within the limits of 'Halachah'—true Judaism. On the other hand, it does not reject 'Halachah' in the slightest in theory and it does not accept Halachah very largely in practice" (*Guideposts,* 310–11). Alternatively, he contends that, for the Conservative movement, "the present is more determinative than the past" (312); and therefore the movement must depend on the legitimacy of its own considered *takkanot* (rabbinical enactments), in order to modernize the halakah as it deems necessary. To aid in this process, Agus supported the creation of a modern Sanhedrin, empowered to make halakic change as necessary:

> I would therefore suggest the creation of a Synhedrin-Academy to consist of Jewish scholars and leaders in every field of culture and achievement, chosen from among the world-wide community of Israel. Meeting annually, this convocation of the best representatives of the spirit of Judaism would deal with the moral and spiritual problems of the land of Israel, of the Jewish people, and of humanity. Its discussions and decisions would, of course, not be binding upon the government of Israel, though it would no doubt take up for review and critical appraisal the moral issues involved in the debates and proceedings of the Kenesset.
>
> The discussions of the Synhedrin-Academy, constituting as they would a running commentary upon the varied problems of the Jew in particular and of man in general, would in time perhaps come to form a new Talmud, expressive of the best thought of our time. World Jewry, through its leading representatives, would be given the opportunity to think together, and to unfold the implications of Jewish tradition for the understanding of the crises of our own day and age. (*Guideposts,* 376–77)

Guideposts' collection of essays ends with two critical book reviews: the first of Mordecai Kaplan's *The Future of the American Jew* (New York, 1948), the second of *The Theology of Paul Tillich,* volume 1 in the Library of Living Theology (New York, 1953).

R. Agus' fourth major publication was *Evolution of Jewish Thought*

(1959). Growing out of a variety of teaching contexts, this study sets out to provide an educated review of the main historical stages of Jewish thought. It opens with chapters on the Bible and the Rabbinic period—including, interestingly, a chapter on "The Secession of Christianity" (chapter 4)—and then moves through "The Rise of Jewish Rationalism" (chapter 6), "The Decline of Rationalism" (chapter 7), Cabala (chapter 9), Hasidism (chapter 10), and "The Age of Reason." This last chapter analyzes the work of Baruch Spinoza and Moses Mendelssohn and the repercussive intellectual and political issues that arose from the debate over Jewish emancipation after the French Revolution. The specific character and the academic strengths and weaknesses of individual aspects of this long and fascinating history, as retold by Agus, are treated at length in several of the original essays that make up the chapters in this book. I would call attention not only to Agus' wide erudition and mastery of the entire range of rabbinical, philosophical, and cabalistic materials but, more important, to his methodological insight:

> In this volume, we propose to show that Judaism in nearly every age resembled an Oriental tapestry in the plenitude of colors and shades it embraced and unified. The comparative unity of law and custom concealed the great diversity of thought and sentiment. Within the authentic field of Jewish consciousness we recognize an unending struggle between the self-exaltation of romantic nationalism and the self-dedication of prophetism; between the austere appeal of ruthless rationality and the beguiling seduction of self-flattering sentiments; between the gentle charm of moralistic and pietistic devotions and the popular preference for routinized rites and doubt-proof dogmas. The mighty tensions within the soul of contemporary Western man were reflected faithfully and clearly in the currents and cross-currents of the historic stream of Judaism. (*Evolution,* 6)

In contradistinction to older, monolithic renderings of the Jewish past, Agus here expresses the most important insight generated by the best modern Jewish scholarship, namely, that Judaism is a "rich spectrum of colors ranging from the twilight moods of mysticism to the stark clarity of rationalism, from the lofty heights of universal idealism to the dark depths of collective 'sacred egoism' " (400).

Yet despite this diversity, this absence of a central authority, this tolerance of various intellectual approaches and understandings, there was an abiding "unity of the Jewish tradition." This lay

> in the text, the context and the emphasis of all schools in Judaism. The unity of a river consists of the bedrock and banks of the channels through which it flows, the intermingling of the tributaries in the course of its flow and the impetus of direction shared by its waters. In Judaism, the unity of source is the chain of sacred literature, the unity of bedrock is the social structure of Jewish life and the unity of impetus is the quest for the realization of the Godlike qualities of the human personality. The text is the series of sacred documents, the Pentateuch, Bible and Talmud, and all the varied books of the classical tradition. All interpreters of Judaism, as far as their ideas may range, return for inspiration and guidance to the same sacred books. There exists also the unifying code of conduct regulating worship, home ritual and everyday life. (*Evolution,* 413)

Despite Agus' desire to "modernize" central aspects of classical Judaism, he was too rooted in the rabbinical tradition to fail to understand (and to want) some residue of vital meaning and authority remaining in the canonical texts of the tradition and in the ongoing Jewish community.

However, with regard to the Jewish people, Judaism, and the Jewish community, Agus is quick to add—sensitive to the criticism regularly directed at Jews and Judaism, that they are "narrow-minded" and parochial in their interests and concerns—that Jews and Judaism need be neither of these things. In particular, he reinterprets the doctrine of Israel's chosenness, of the Jews as the "chosen people," in this way:

> Is it the intention of this concept that the people ought to be dedicated to the ideals of God, or does it mean that the life of the people is supremely important because the ideals of God are attached to it? The two alternatives do not appear to be mutually exclusive. Yet there is a real choice between the two attitudes in every concrete situation. In the one case the community acts as a "prophet-people," gauging its policies by means of universal, ethical principles and sacrificing its own temporal welfare for the sake of its ideals. In the other case the welfare of the nation itself is ranked as the supreme value and embraced with the wholeheartedness and totality of devotion that is characteristic of genuine piety. In effect the second alternative turns nationalism itself into a

> zealous religion and all universal ideals are accorded only secondary significance. The posture of a "prophet-people" is still assumed, but the ideals of prophecy are no longer the goal of the nation's existence and the measuring rod of its actions, only so much guise and disguise. (*Evolution,* 419–20)

Ever sensitive to the universal ethical implications of religious dogmas, Agus here once again deciphers the tradition in broad, humanistic, and nonexclusivist terms.

Agus' next major publication was his two-volume *The Meaning of Jewish History* (1963). This can fairly be described as an ideological history of the Jewish people from biblical times to the present. The concern of the narrative is to show the breadth and diversity of Jewish historical experience, its plural spiritual and political forms, while demythologizing its essential character. In the course of his exposition, Agus continually throws light on the dialectic between ethnic and universal loyalties in this history, arguing against the ethnic, mystical, romantic, and chauvinistic and for the ecumenical, rational, philosophical, and broadly humane elements within the tradition. The latter values and principles are to be our model and guide into the Jewish future.

Two historical cases discussed at some length are especially notable. The first, "The Jewish-Christian Schism," is of unusual interest because of Agus' long and profound involvement in Jewish-Christian dialogue. According to Agus, the missionizing success of Christianity was the result of two phenomena. One was the specific Christian resolution of the tension within Judaism between the Jewish people and others:

> First, the tension between the Jewish people and humanity. It is not true that the Christians were more universalist than the Jews, opening up the boon of salvation to all men, while the Jews sought to keep the Promise all to themselves. But it is true that Christianity was less *nation-centered* than Judaism. The fact is that within Pharisaic Judaism there was a powerful, liberal trend that aimed to disseminate the faith among the nations and that taught "the pious of the nations have a share in the world to come." There was also a tendency to take account of the monotheistic currents of piety, flowing beneath the surface trends of paganism. On the other hand, in the first two centuries, Christian thought was distinctly illiberal, discountenancing the belief that God reveals Himself in different ways to different peoples. Did not the Fathers consign the vast majority of mankind to per-

> dition and open the gates of paradise only to those who accepted their dogmas?
>
> Yet the Christian community was far better disposed for the winning of converts than the Jewish people, precisely because it was a church, not a historical-sociological group. The essential difference lay in the fact that the Christian community consisted of *individuals,* who gained or lost their own title to salvation. Anyone could enter and anyone could leave this "Israel of the spirit." The promise of salvation and the warning of damnation were directed to the individual. In Judaism, the individual could dissipate or enlarge his heritage, but the faith was still his heritage, as a member of "the people."
>
> In Christianity, the balance between the individual and the historic community was shattered by the rejection of "the people" as the focus of Divine concern. Any number of individual Jews could enter the Christian community, but "the people" as such was repudiated. (*Meaning,* 1:167–68)

The other phenomenon was the way in which the Church shattered the tension, inherent in Judaism, between prophecy and priesthood:

> The evolution of events was paradoxical. For in the beginning, it was the renewal of the mystical-ecstatic phase of prophecy that served as a substitute for the priestly concern with ritual. To become a Christian was to be baptized by the "Holy Spirit." (*Meaning,* 1:168)

The second case concerns the development of the Talmud. As a true *talmid chacham,* Agus knew his Talmud, and therefore his reflections on its creation, organization, and meaning—in light of his liberal philosophy of halakah—are full of theological interest. He does not disguise the narrow aspects of talmudic teaching—for example, regarding the difference between Israel and the nations—but he is at pains to indicate that the opposite tendencies are to be found in the Talmud as well. And he leaves no doubt as to where his preferences lie:

> Within the Talmud, the tension between humanism and ethnicism was continuous and unresolved. It was possible for Talmud-trained people to effect their own resolution of these conflicting trends, some magnifying the one aspect of the tradition and some emphasizing the other aspect. As we have noted previously, the masses of the people probably inclined

> toward the pole of ethnic pride and prejudice, while the saintly few thought in universal and humanistic terms. (*Meaning,* 1:222)

In the second volume of *The Meaning of Jewish History,* Agus takes his narrative forward into the medieval and modern eras. Of the two chapters on the medieval period, the first is a rather long essay on what might be called Jewish social history. It intelligently, and with considerable historical learning, seeks to explore the perplexing issue of Jewish survival in this hostile epoch. Agus rightly stresses that Jews were subjects, as well as objects, who took responsibility for their circumstances and acted to defend their interests and assure their collective survival. And Agus pays special attention to the role of messianism in this historical context (*Meaning,* 2:269–80). The second essay deals critically with what Agus calls "The Triumph of Subjectivism: Qabbalah." Agus is fundamentally unsympathetic to this tradition of esoteric speculation, which he describes in this way:

> While philosophy seeks to explain life in terms of the categories of *spirit*—logic, ethics, and esthetic harmony—Qabbalah aims to take account of man's existence, especially the destiny of the Jew, in terms of the categories of *life*—the rhythms of the Divine Being and the various emanations deriving from it. To the philosopher, all human history is ultimately reducible to mechanical forces and mathematical formulae. To the Qabbalist, all explanations are ultimately the narration of a series of events in the *Divine Pleroma* (the Emanations and Sefiroth), which stands between God and man. Yet Qabbalah is not altogether a reversion to pagan mythology, since the impetus of monotheism is still contained within it. The Qabbalist strains with all the powers of personality toward the dark, comforting shadows of insulated piety, but there is a desperate tension in his soul for he has been driven from the paradise of naivete by the subtle serpent of speculation.
>
> It is important to take a good look at the bizarre pattern of Qabbalistic speculations, for Qabbalah was not merely a temporary aberration of Medieval Jews. As a matter of fact, Qabbalah captured the Jewish mind at the end of the fifteenth century, at the very time when the diverse movements of Renaissance, Reformation, and Counter-Reformation were struggling for supremacy. Steadily through the sixteenth and eighteenth centuries, it dominated the minds of Jewish thinkers. (*Meaning,* 2:287–88)

Agus attributes the power and attraction of cabalistic thought to the oppressive situation in which Jews found themselves in the late medieval and early modern eras. Amid the brutality and persecution, cabala provided a "pious fantasy" that consoled the Jewish people while they waited "supinely for the Messiah" (289). Agus' understanding of cabala is not flattering, and there is more to be said about the nature of cabalistic teachings than Agus says, but he is certainly correct in his historical judgment that

> Qabbalah . . . aided the Jew in his struggle for survival under adverse conditions, but it also separated him from any intellectual-ethical communion with the emerging society of mankind. It provided an exciting mythology, elevating every Jewish custom and every nuance of the liturgy to the rank of a world-saving enterprise. At the same time, the speculative notions and the debris of ancient philosophical systems contained within its volumes offered substitute satisfactions to the insistent quest of the intellectuals. But these services of Qabbalah were purchased at the high price of deepening the isolation of the Jew. The ritual barriers were raised higher. Even more important, the division between Jew and Gentile was now universally assumed to be one of metaphysical substance and origin. It was no longer a matter of belief that separated the Jew from "the nations," but the fact that the Jewish souls were derived from the Divine Being, while the souls of the nations were sparks from the satanic *Pleroma* of shells, the so called "other side" *(Sitra Ahra)*. On this basis, there could not possibly be any kind of intellectual contact between Jews and Gentiles. (*Meaning,* 2:295)

In his treatment of the modern period, Agus begins by tracing the influence of cabala in Sabbatianism (seventeenth century) and Hasidism (eighteenth century). He then turns to the process of emancipation in Western Europe and retells the familiar tale of Spinoza; Mendelssohn; the Haskalah; the "Jewish question" before, during, and after the French Revolution; early Zionism; bundism; Napoleon; romanticism; Reform Judaism; Dubnow's "autonomism"; and the rise of modern anti-Semitism. Agus has read widely on all these matters, makes sober judgments (whether or not one agrees with all of them), and is, in general, a reliable guide to this complex historical development. What make the exercise interesting are Agus "opinionated" views on nearly every subject reviewed. He knows who the "good guys" and the "bad guys" are—and he has thought through the merits of the various ideological positions reported on.

In the "Epilogue," Agus discusses the rebirth of the State of Israel and the state of Jewish life in America. One must remark that the thirty-odd years since the publication of the *The Meaning of Jewish History* have shown Agus to be about half right in his view for the future of Arab–Israeli relations and of American Jewry—half right on the former because, while his insistence that peace was achievable has been proven true in the peace with Egypt, Jordan, and the accord with the Palestine Liberation Organization, his idealism that caused him to counsel:

> At this writing, we cannot foretell the course of Israel's development, nor can we outline a specific policy for immediate implementation. But this can be said with certainty, the moral health and the very life of Israel depend upon its finding ways to win over the Arabs. The task is not one of concluding pacts with the neighboring governments, but of achieving true *bonds of fraternity* with the Arab people. To this end, the Arabs within Israel's borders and those encamped on its periphery must be converted into a bridge of friendship between the two ancient peoples. By working for them and with them, smoldering hates can be transmuted into a new blaze of amity and unity (*Meaning,* 2:466)

still seems out of touch with the harsh mass situation on the ground.

Likewise, Agus' optimism vis-à-vis America was largely correct. The United States has proven to be a "golden land" of unlimited opportunities for Jews, especially in the last thirty years. Yet the corresponding erosion in commitment—to the identity and precepts of Judaism indicated most clearly by the rate of intermarriage—within the American Jewish community is unprecedented and threatens the very shape and enduring vitality of the community.

In 1966, Agus published his mature views on Jewish ethics in *The Vision and the Way.* Polarity again dominates his thought. Ethics is born of two sources, the intellect and feeling. Jewish ethics is notable, commendable, by virtue of the fact that it manages to hold these two "pillars" in creative tension. In consequence, the transrational vision which asserts that God is the source of all goodness and beyond human judgment is balanced by "the Way of justice and righteousness," that is, a rational, universal ethic which requires that ethical norms be subject to human investigation and judgment: "To believe in God, Who is beyond Nature and *unlike* all things, and, at the same time, to insist that the moral-rational Way, as it is manifest in the light of reason, is a revelation of His Will—this dual conviction establishes the central polarity in biblical religion" (*Vision and Way,* 33).

Agus traces this fruitful polarity through the main ethical categories of Jewish thought and life. He draws a rich picture of Jewish ethics from the talmudic texts that provide an image of an "Ideal Society"—with its concern for social justice, the poor, and the oppressed; its "massive philanthropic enterprises" (*Vision and Way,* 63); and its hope for messianic perfection, brought on by human deeds, at which time evil will be finally eradicated and the good vindicated—and an "Ideal Personality" (chapter 4) in which the moral "hero is the incarnation of the ideal(s)" (73), an heir of the prophets, a person who blends priestliness and the virtues of the "Disciple of the Wise" (78):

> Unlike the saint, he never forgets the claims of humanity—of family, of work, of innocent delights. He is aware of the "Evil Desire" and of the many ways in which it corrupts man's best intentions, but like the philosopher, he reveres the regenerative and intellectual qualities of human nature. (*Vision and Way,* 79)

In addition, Agus deciphers "The Virtue of Obedience," "The Infinite Dimension of Purity," "The Ethics of Self-Realization," and "Freedom and Determinism." For each topic, he presents the tradition in its variety, its strengths and limits. In sum, the book is, through his extensive quotation of primary materials mainly an anthology of rabbinical doctrines on the good life, compiled by a master anthologizer.

In regard to the contemporary situation in comparative historical perspective, Agus makes the important observation that

> looking at the total spectrum of Jewish ethics, one sees that the popular notion, that the Law governs every question in Judaism, is a fallacy. As has been pointed out, there were indeed times when nearly all creative principles were locked into the rigid categories of an all-embracing law that was presumed to be God-given. But *pan-halachism* is more characteristic of extremist Orthodoxy in the modern period than of the premodern tradition. In the Talmud the cast-iron logic of legalism was balanced by several factors—the projection of an ethical domain "beyond the law" *(lifnim mishurat hadin),* the recognition of the validity of

> the mores and morals of civilized humanity *(derech eretz),* and by the mystical or philosophical notions that were cultivated in esoteric circles. As late as the sixteenth century, when the Shulhan Aruch was codified, the realm of Perfection beyond the Law was cultivated in pietistic and mystical literature. (*Vision and Way,* 321)

He goes on to argue:

> An analysis of the inner dynamics of Jewish ethics does not reveal a monolithic philosophy of life. It is possible to resolve the tension between the Vision and the Way by choosing any one of many positions within the ethical-religious polarity. Tolerance of differences is a marked characteristic of rabbinic discussions—"these and these are the words of the Living God." A broad consensus on any one issue may emerge at any one time, but we can hardly dignify any one synthesis as being the Jewish, or the "normative" one. (*Vision and Way,* 324)

Once again, Agus calls for a rational, nonracial, non-"in-group" ethic. Such an inclusive ethic includes a concern for the world order, the search for international justice, disarmament, the end of nuclear weapons, and support for the United Nations so as to mitigate conflict and prevent new crimes against humanity.

Tradition and Dialogue, published in 1971, continued Agus' reflections on a variety of contemporary issues. Here the essays concern the Jewish-Christian dialogue; Agus' ongoing dialogue with Arnold Toynbee over the continuing vitality of Judaism (for Toynbee's change of opinion regarding Judaism, due to Agus' influence, see volume 12 of Toynbee's *A Study of History: Reconsiderations,* which includes two essays by Agus published as an appendix); his response to the "God is Dead" movement, in two sympathetic but critical essays collected under the heading "Dialogue with the New Atheists"; a variety of issues identified as "Dialogue with Secular Ideologies"; and last, ten essays on internal Jewish matters, ranging from "The Prophet in Modern Hebrew Literature" to "The Concept of Israel" and "Assimilation, Integration, Segregation: The Road to the Future."

What strikes one in reading these diverse pieces is the breadth of Agus' Jewish learning. Not only are biblical, talmudic, medieval, and modern sources critically evaluated, but Hebrew poets such as Hayim Nahum Bialik and the modern Hebrew authors Saul Tchernichovsky,

J. H. Brenner, and Uri Zvi Greenberg are engaged in a serious and informed way.

In 1978, Agus published his next to last book, *Jewish Identity in an Age of Ideologies.* This is a sustained effort both to situate the Jew and Judaism vis-à-vis the most important European ideologies of the past two hundred years and to view these ideologies from a Jewish perspective. He begins with Mendelssohn and the issue of Jewish-Christian relations in the age of Enlightenment. He then reviews Immanuel Kant's hostility toward Judaism and the efforts by Jewish Kantians such as Moritz Lazarus, Hermann Cohen, and Leo Baeck to bring about some rapprochement between Kantianism and Judaism. He considers the attitude of the German romantics toward religion, Judaism, and religious reform, including a critique of Jewish "romantics," that is, those who deprecate the role of reason in the religious life, such as Samuel David Luzzatto (1800–1865) and, in Agus' controversial view, Samson Raphael Hirsch (1808–1888). In chapter 4, titled "Are the Jews 'Ahistorical'?" Agus takes up a critical dialogue with G. W. F. Hegel's historicism and three Jewish responses thereto by, respectively, Samuel Hirsch (1815–1889), Solomon Formstecher (1808–1889), and Nahman Krochmal (1785–1840). Hirsch and Formstecher tried to meet Hegel's criticism of Judaism by calling for the internal reform of Judaism. Krochmal, a far deeper thinker, tried to respond to Hegel by denying the applicability of the Hegelian system to Judaism; that is, he argued, in contradistinction to Hegel's systemic claims, that Judaism is *not* subject to the normal laws of national development and decay that govern other nations. Other schools and movements dealt with by Agus are nationalism; socialism in its various forms, namely, bundism and Marxism; Zionism; racism in its myriad forms; Bergsonian vitalism; Jewish existentialism (Buber and Rosenzweig); biblical criticism; Barthianism (Karl Barth [1886–1968]); and Toynbeeism (Arnold Toynbee). In every instance Agus is a serious and respectful critic; in every dialogue he makes the case for a liberal, humanistic, nonromantic Judaism, shorn of the meta-myth of Jewish being. Though one can differ with Agus' various judgments, one can never ignore or dismiss them. In the end, he has accomplished what he set out to achieve in this work: to view Judaism from both within and without as it struggles with modernity.

Agus' last work, a collection of theological essays, was published in 1983 under the title *The Jewish Quest.* "The Jewish Quest," he tells us, "is to make oneself and the world fit for the indwelling of the Divine

Presence; theologically speaking, it is a yearning for the 'kingdom of heaven' " (vii). Here familiar themes are taken up, clarified, and deepened: America and the Jewish people, Jewish self-definition, classicism and romanticism, the meta-myth, Zionism, holism, nonliteral revelation, Jewish ethics, Judaism and the world community, Maimonides' philosophical rationalism, the defense of Conservative Judaism, the foundations for a modern revision of the halakah, anti-Semitism, and various aspects of the Jewish-Christian dialogue. To the end Agus was sober, cautious, yet hopeful; opposed to fanaticism of all sorts; an enemy of Jewish "self-mythification," of "biblical claims of singularity and uniqueness," of "the seductive fantasies of self-glorification" (*Jewish Quest,* 10); suspicious of messianic and self-serving metaphysical claims; and intensely committed to a demanding ethical vision that united all peoples.

Agus' philosophical and theological corpus can, in summation, be seen as extensive, consequential, and provocative. Perhaps best characterized as a neo-Maimonidean, Agus belongs to the long chain of Jewish rationalists that includes Philo, Saadya, Maimonides, and Mendelssohn, and which has been more recently represented so brilliantly by Hermann Cohen. Like Cohen, of whom he wrote admiringly, Agus held firm to the conviction that Judaism was explicable and defensible in universal rational and ethical terms. Possessing their own deep spiritual integrity, the classical sources of Judaism embodied a profoundly humane moral vision that was both philosophically compelling and metaphysically attractive. Those who, out of religious frustration or a failure of philosophical nerve, seek to turn away from rational analysis and criteria in their deconstruction of Judaism and its God do a serious disservice to the intellectual and spiritual tradition they seek to excavate and defend. Here is the ground of Agus' sharp disagreement with Buber's dialogical philosophy and his reservations about the work of Abraham Joshua Heschel and other contemporary religious existentialists. Agus admired their religious intentions but faulted their method and logic.

Agus was not a stranger to religious feelings or deep traditional religious commitments; but he held that these necessary aspects of the religious life must be regulated by constraints that only reason could supply. Thus, for example, though a longtime colleague of Mordecai Kaplan, he was critical of Kaplan's reconstructionist views, not only because they lacked grounding in the traditional halakic and intellectual sources of Judaism but also because Kaplan's systematic revision of Judaism along functionalist anthropological and sociological lines was spiritually impoverished and impoverishing. God, for Agus, had to be more than "the power that makes for salvation"; Jewish behavior had to be more than sociologically defined "sancta," and the obligations of Torah and halakah more than pragmatic initiatives and psychological panaceas. Indeed, it was this tension, this firmly held belief in the necessity of holding onto a more traditional spirituality, that led Agus to admire the genuine mystical personality of Rev Kook, even though he was profoundly critical of the cabalistic *Weltanschauung* that defined Kook's entire thought world. Kook's spirituality, his sense of the presence of the Living God, attracted Agus—not least because he shared the same openness to the numinous.

Agus' rationalism also separated him from all forms of romanticism, the most important modern Jewish manifestations of this inclination being found in certain versions of Zionism. Here, while defining himself as a supporter and defender of the Jewish right to a national state, Agus' outspoken criticism of aspects of American Zionism—that is, nationalism as a substitute for authentic religious commitment—made him many enemies. In arguing for this position, he manifested an attitude close to the intellectual-spiritual stance that had been struck by Franz Rosenzweig, though Rosenzweig was writing in the 1920s, before the Shoah and the creation of the modern State of Israel. Like Rosenzweig, and unlike Buber, Agus was suspicious of all forms of nationalism, including Jewish nationalism. I believe his stance vis-à-vis the State of Israel was too critical and that he was too optimistic with regard to both the future of Jewish life in the diaspora, especially in America, and Israeli-Arab relations, but he was certainly right to warn of the pseudomessianic temptations that the creation of a renewed Jewish state, and especially Jewish victory in 1967, has spawned. The State of Israel need not be the messianic state for it to be Jewishly necessary, legitimate, and worthy of our unwavering, though not uncritical, support.

If Agus had serious reservations about the systematic work of other nineteenth- or twentieth-century Jewish thinkers and movements, he shared, in a broad sense, their call for halakic revision. This he did on ethical and rational grounds—and here especially he becomes a "modern" thinker among the pantheon of modern thinkers, stretching from the early reformers to certain contemporary feminists. However, even in this area of fundamental concern, his approach was distinctive. As a true *talmid chacham,* he demanded that the halakic changes he supported be undertaken in a way consistent with the spirit of the halakic process as he understood it. In consequence, he was considered too conservative and traditional for many of his Conservative rabbinical (and other) contemporaries, while for the Orthodox (and certain members of the Jewish Theological Seminary hierarchy) he was too radical.

Agus was also distinctively modern in his openness to interreligious dialogue. Almost all major Jewish thinkers of the twentieth century—for example, Baeck, Rosenzweig, Buber, and Heschel—have significantly involved themselves in reevaluating the relationship of Judaism and Christianity. Jacob Agus did likewise. Given his universal ethical norms and broad humanistic concerns, this is in no way surprising. Agus assumed that all people shared certain basic values, which were then individually expressed in the world's differing religious traditions. It was this dialectic between the universal and the particular that lay at the base of his deep, personal engagement in this area and that energized his theological conversation with such dialogue partners as Arnold Toynbee, Cardinal Bea, and Baltimore's Catholic hierarchy. Then too, like many Jewish thinkers before him—Philo, Maimonides, Mendelssohn, Cohen, and Rosenzweig—his participation in ecumenical dialogue was not free of apologetic concerns; that is, he sought to defend Judaism against its detractors and to share its spiritual and intellectual resources with others on the assumption that non-Jews could benefit from its distinctive wisdom.

Taken altogether, Agus pursued his own unique, quite American modernizing vision, which ardently sought to remain in touch with the wellsprings of the rabbinical tradition while being open to the intellectual and moral currents of his own time.

CONCLUSION

The individual essays in the present volume and the selections from R. Agus' own writings in the new companion volume, titled *The Essential Agus: The Writings of R. Jacob B. Agus* (New York: New York University Press, 1996), consider the main aspects of Agus' life and work in more detail. They flesh out the broad and repercussive themes adumbrated in a schematic way in this Introduction. And taken as a whole, they present a broad and substantial picture of a remarkable American rabbi and scholar. One does not have to agree with all of Agus' views—I, for one, disagree with aspects of his writings on Zionism, nonpropositional revelation, the Torah, the vitality and future of Conservative Judaism, and the basis for revising (or not revising) the halakah in our time—but one has to admire his commitment to the Jewish people everywhere, his profound and unwavering spirituality, his continual reminders of the very real dangers of pseudomessianism and misplaced romantic zeal, his devotion to "Talmud Torah" in all of its guises, his personal piety, his willingness to take politically and religiously unpopular stands, his defense of such men as Owen Lattimore and Arnold Toynbee, his consistent faith in reason, his erudition in Western philosophy, and his tenacious ethical humanism, which knew no ethnic or racial boundaries. In sum, much of the best of Jewish and Western tradition was incarnated in a *yeshiva bocher* from Sislevitch. May his memory be for a blessing.

NOTES

1. William James, *Varieties of Religious Experience* (New York, 1958), 292–93.
2. Jacob B. Agus, *High Priest of Rebirth* (New York, 1972), 154–55; hereafter cited as *High Priest*. This book is the retitled second edition of *Banner of Jerusalem*.

2
JACOB B. AGUS: A PERSONAL PORTRAIT

Norton D. Shargel

IN THE EARLY 1950s a young professor delivered a lecture before Congregation Beth Abraham United in Dayton, Ohio. After the talk, a member approached him. "I miss Rabbi Agus," said the man. "When he was here I attended services every Friday evening, *shabbos* morning and holiday. Even though I didn't understand a thing, I felt that he was saying something important."[1] Physically Jacob Agus was a small man, yet his moral and intellectual stature were such that, throughout his long career, he conveyed to the simplest congregant a message of high seriousness and inestimable value.

Yaakov Dov Agushewitz was born in Sislowitz, Poland, on November 8, 1911. The Jewish inhabitants of this shtetl were "Litvaks"; the family came from a long line of distinguished rabbis. Yaakov Dov's mother, Baila Devorah Beresnitsky, was descended from the Katzenellenbogen family, which traced its lineage back to the Maharam of Padua, R. Meir Katzenellenbogen (fifteenth century), and even to Rashi (eleventh century), and included Rabbi Yom Tov Lipmann Heller, the Tosfot Yom Tov, author of a sixteenth-century commentary on the Mishnah. Yaakov Dov's father, Rabbi Yehudah Leib Agushewitz, was a rabbi's son, a grandson of Rav Eli, the Grodner Rov. He had studied at his grandfather's yeshiva and was a classmate of Rabbi Moshe Feinstein, receiving his *semikha* from R. Shneur Zalman Pines, the father of Rabbi Aaron Kotler.

Yaakov Dov was one of eight children.[2] Although all were talented and bright, some exceedingly so, "Yankel" was regarded as the family *ilui*. In childhood he had a weak constitution and nearly succumbed to typhoid fever, which took the life of his younger sister. He was a favorite of both parents and they pampered him, thereby instilling in the young lad a sense of self-assurance that would stand him in good stead when he would later challenge Orthodox dogmatism, Conservative equivocation, and lay opponents in and out of his congregation.

After early studies at home and in the ḥeder, he attended the Tachkemoni Yeshiva in Bialystock, a Mizrachi-type yeshiva that added the study of Hebrew and Tanakh to the traditional study of Talmud. Compared with Sislowitz, Bialystock was a big city; there Jacob had the opportunity to meet different kinds of Jews. Occasionally he and his brothers were pursued by militant Hasidic youths, who had learned that the Agushewitz brothers were descendants of Rabbi Ezekiel Katzenellenbogen; in the eighteenth century, Katzenellenbogens had supported the Vilna Gaon's attacks on Shneur Zalman of Liadi, the founder of the Lubavitch dynasty.

Yaakov Agushewitz was raised in a traditional environment where his heroes were Abraham, Moses, and the great rabbis of the time. When Yaakov Dov was ten years old, one such hero, Rabbi Yisrael Meir Hakohen (1838–1933), the preeminent Jewish sage of his time (known as the Ḥafetz Ḥayim), visited Bialystok. Thousands of people, mostly women, waited for the rabbi to arrive at the train station. When the Hafetz Hayim emerged from the train, young Yaakov Dov was astonished at his tiny size. He stood transfixed as the great rabbi, annoyed by the attention, ran swiftly to a waiting car. Later that day, when Yankel heard the Hafetz Hayim speak at the yeshiva, he was more impressed by the aura of his personality than by his words.[3]

Before World War I the Agushewitz family was quite prosperous, the owners of tanneries and real properties, and their life was regulated by the patterns of traditional European Jewish piety. Traveling on a train after a brief vacation on Rosh Hodesh Nisan, little Yankel feared that the whistle of the locomotive and the clacking of the rails would prevent him from hearing the shofar announce the coming of the Messiah! In later years Jacob used the story of his Nisan train trip to illustrate the powerful sense of messianic imminence even among intellectual Lithuanian Jews.[4]

Jacob's father, Yehudah Leib, was an ardent admirer of the Malbim, Meir Loeb ben Jehiel Michael (1809–1879), one of the outstanding traditional European rabbis of the nineteenth century. Using the Malbim's commentary on Daniel as his guide, Yehudah Leib was convinced that 1925 would bring the expected Messiah.[5] Driven by the devastation and pogroms of postwar Poland, the Agushewitz family left the country in that year. Yehudah Leib traveled to America while his wife and children journeyed to Palestine. After a brief and unsuccessful career as a rabbi and businessman in New York, Yehudah Leib became a *shohet.* The plan was for him to accumulate enough capital to join his family in Eretz Yisrael.

For Yaakov, those two years in Palestine served as an antidote to his father's enthusiasm for the coming of the Messiah. First, the family was shocked by the primitive conditions they found in the Palestine of the 1920s. Then their plan to build a series of fruit orchards in the area now known as Ramat Gan was frustrated. Finally, the family became entangled in legal problems over the land they had acquired. After two years the Agushewitz family left Palestine for New York and a reunion with the head of the family.

In 1927 the family settled in Boro Park. Jacob's education continued in the Yeshiva High School, Yeshiva College, and the Rabbi Isaac Elchanan Theological Seminary (RIETS). He excelled in all subjects, especially math, chemistry, and history. He enrolled in graduate chemistry courses at Columbia University and for a while considered a doctoral program in science. But as the situation of European Jewry worsened, Jacob opted for full-time Jewish studies. While still pondering this decision, he became assistant to Rabbi Leo Jung at the Jewish Center in Manhattan. At Rabbi Jung's request, he researched the halakhic basis for the *meḥitza,* the partition between men and women required in Orthodox synagogues. The young student concluded that there was no firm basis for this requirement and that it could be removed, provided that leading rabbis agree. There was a plan to send a letter to rabbinic authorities abroad, asking for their opinion on this question, but because of the unsettling conditions in Europe at the time the letter was never sent.

Rabbi Moshe Soloveichik, the Rosh Yeshiva, and Dr. Bernard Revel, president of Yeshiva University, persuaded the brilliant student to continue his studies there for an additional two years. From 1933 to 1935, Jacob studied the Talmud Yerushalmi and texts of the *Shulhan Arukh,* intended to put him on a par with European-trained rabbis so that he could serve as a *Posek,* a religious decisor.

Agushewitz's first pulpit was in Norfolk, Virginia, where he was known as the Orthodox rabbi who refused to shake hands with women.[6] But he was restless to continue his studies and, as Jacob Agus, enrolled at Harvard University to study the philosophy of religion.[7] His mentors at Harvard were Harry Austryn Wolfson and William Ernest Hocking. Young Agus' first encounter with Wolfson was amusing. Having read Wolfson's writings, he imagined him to be tall, dignified, and austere. As Jacob sat in the lecture hall, a diminutive, middle-aged man, somewhat unkempt, entered the room, went directly to the window, and tried to open it. The little man had very little success until the window flew open and he nearly fell out. Certainly, Jacob thought, this was a new janitor, not yet familiar with the work. The "janitor" turned out to be the illustrious Professor Wolfson![8]

Thus began a friendship that lasted until Wolfson's death some forty years later. Agus regarded Wolfson as one of the proverbial hidden righteous men, who devoted his entire life to scholarship and quiet contemplation. Jacob would visit Wolfson in a drab, dusty study located in the basement of Harvard's Weidner Library. Wolfson would not leave the cubicle even during those suffocatingly hot summers before the age of air conditioning. Nevertheless, he received the greatest scholars of the generation in that unattractive, dusty basement room. To give him relief from summer heat, Jacob Agus would take Wolfson for a ride in his automobile. After a short period of respite and good conversation, the professor would insist on returning to his study.[9]

It was at Harvard that Agus was exposed to the virulent anti-Semitism that, he soon realized, remained an integral part of the Western intellectual tradition. In the 1930s, moreover, political anti-Semitism was widespread and palpable. This is how a German Bible professor expounded on the Hebrew prophets:

> Prophecy was the greatest achievement of the Semitic spirit. The Jews expressed their genius in the institution of prophecy where the prophet comes to feel that God enters him. Now the Semitic genius is an acquisitive one. It always tries to build itself up and to acquire more and more things. Therefore, Semites are very good at amassing things—property, dollars, gold. So when they direct themselves to spirituality their acquiring nature makes them want to build God up within themselves. They want to take God within them. The mystics, however, are different from the Hebrew prophets. The mystics are the expression of

> the Aryan genius. The Aryans care little about acquiring things. Aryans are filled with faith and love. They want to surrender and to yield to the beauty and the majesty of the Lord. So the mystic feels that he gives up his own being and surrenders to the mighty stream of Divinity and of creative energy that comes from God. This is the difference between Hebrew prophecy and Christian mysticism.[10]

On hearing racist expositions such as this one uttered in a calm, professorial style, Jacob's face was "aflame with embarrassment."[11] There and then he resolved to take on the challenge of intellectual anti-Semitism. His model became Harry A. Wolfson, the solitary Jewish academic who sallied forth in scholarly refutation of these attacks. Wolfson suggested that medieval Western philosophy began with Philo and ended with Spinoza and that basic Christian theological concepts such as the Virgin Birth and the Trinity are rooted in Judaism. Jacob Agus accepted Wolfson's suppositions and, in his own words, became a "little David," willing to take on Goliaths wherever he encountered them.[12]

Nevertheless, Agus chose a different path from Wolfson's; for forty-six years he served as a pulpit rabbi. In explanation Agus recounted that Philo of Alexandria had once fled to the wilderness in search of God but soon returned to the community; he realized that a Jew finds the Divine not in isolation but in the congregation of Israel. Agus offered the same explanation of his great hero Maimonides. Like the Rambam, Agus embraced what he called "two poles"—the "pole of books" and the "pole of life." He always strove to hold them in tension, though by nature he was more inclined to study and contemplation.[13]

While still a graduate student in Cambridge, Massachusetts (1936–1940), Jacob accepted the pulpit of Temple Ashkenaz, a small Orthodox congregation. At that time a delegation from the Aggudas Harabbonim came to him and offered him membership. The Aggudas Harabbonim consisted of the most outstanding European rabbis of the generation, who were not inclined to admit graduates of American yeshivas because of the lower U.S. standards of study and mastery of rabbinic texts. The invitation was an exceptional honor, indicating great respect for Agus' scholarship. Nevertheless, the young rabbi declined the invitation, shocking the Aggudah with the statement that he was not able to affirm the Orthodox belief in the traditional doctrine of "Torah le-Moshe mi-Sinai" which held that the written and oral Torahs were given in full and complete form from God to Moses at Sinai.[14] This indicates that Agus' renunciation of Orthodoxy, at least on an intellectual plane, predated his formal break with the Orthodox establishment. In later years he would claim that Dr. Bernard Revel, who had been grooming him for leadership in the Orthodox world, already discerned his changing perspective.[15]

It was during his graduate school years that Agus met Miriam Shore, the daughter of businessman Bernard Shore, an observant Jew and an ardent admirer of R. Joseph Baer Soloveichik. Miriam was a beautiful young woman and a graduate of the Boston Hebrew Teacher's College. The *mesader kidushin* at Jacob and Miriam's wedding was R. Joseph Soloveichik. After breaking the glass, the speeches began, with young rabbis and rabbinic students outdoing one another in displays of knowledge. The celebration concluded with music and social dancing.[16]

During Agus' Cambridge years, he met regularly with Rabbi Soloveichik to study the philosophy of Moses Maimonides. Clean-shaven and educated at a German university, Soloveichik at the time was experiencing opposition from ultra-Orthodox Boston Jews. Agus was one of the people who recommended Soloveichik for a teaching position at RIETS.[17]

Jacob Agus was awarded the Ph.D. in 1940; the following year, his doctoral dissertation was published under the title *Modern Philosophies of Judaism*. Although Agus was more than eligible for a university position, virtually none existed in Jewish fields. Dr. Revel urged him to carry the banner of Yeshiva University to Chicago as a full-time rabbi. Agus forthwith accepted a rabbinic post at the Agudas Achim North Shore Congregation, a traditional synagogue that was affiliated with Orthodoxy but tolerated mixed seating. While in Chicago, he conducted classes in Mishnah and Talmud, frequently teaching in Yiddish.[18]

Bernard Revel's premature death prevented him from attending Rabbi Agus' installation. His death was a bitter blow to the young rabbi, who believed that he and Dr. Revel possessed a shared vision. Revel's successor, Rabbi Samuel Belkin (another yeshiva *baḥur* from Sislowitz), allied himself with right-wing elements and rejected the halakhic reforms that Jacob had hoped to pioneer.

In 1942, the Aguses and their infant son, Zalman, moved to Dayton, Ohio. There the young rabbi assumed the pulpit of Beth Abraham United, a merger of three synagogues, two Orthodox and one Conservative. During their stay in Dayton (1942–1950), two more children,

Edna and Robert, were born. The Aguses immersed themselves in the task of building a viable and modern congregation out of many diverse elements. Jacob attended minyan services daily and was a devoted and effective pastor. During the war years, he conducted a weekly radio program that brought him an audience beyond the Jewish community.[19] Before the construction of a new synagogue in the postwar period, Jacob had the responsibility, during the High Holy Days, of conducting services in two locations. The first was a converted house; the second, a traditional shul in the old area of town that had an *ezrat nashim,* a balcony seating area reserved for women.[20]

In addition to her household duties and responsibilities as *rebetzin,* Miriam served as principal of the synagogue religious school.[21] Dayton's proximity to Cincinnati brought Agus into contact with the Hebrew Union College (HUC) faculty and other leaders of Reform Judaism. He lectured frequently at HUC and throughout the area. In the early 1940s, Abraham Joshua Heschel was a member of that faculty, lonely and uncomfortable in the Reform environment. Heschel was a frequent Sabbath guest at the Agus home and in later years maintained that he owed his sanity to Miriam's warmth and Jacob's intellectual companionship.[22] In the 1950s, Agus and Heschel would renew their friendship when they served together as scholars-in-residence at the Jewish Laymen's Summer Institutes at Camp Wohelo (Waynesboro, Pennsylvania).

Heschel must have been helpful to Agus as well, for during the Dayton years, Jacob turned his attention to Jewish mysticism. He read through all the major classics of Hasidic literature and in 1946 published his second major book, *The Banner of Jerusalem,* a study of the religious philosophy of Rabbi Abraham Isaac Kuk. This was followed by studies on the logic of the kabbalah and other aspects of Jewish mysticism.[23]

Agus did not abandon his own religious quest. At the Orthodox Rabbinical Council of America convention in 1945–1946, Jacob presented a paper on halakhic reform, but it was rejected. This prompted him to sever his connection to American Orthodoxy and affiliate with the Conservative movement. He joined the Conservative Rabbinical Assembly in 1947 and soon found a place on its Law Committee. Agus positioned himself on the left flank of the movement and coauthored the controversial *teshuva* that permitted riding to the synagogue on the Sabbath (1950).[24]

Helping Agus to ease the transition was one of American Judaism's most important thinkers, Rabbi Solomon Goldman of Chicago's Anshe

Emet Synagogue. Agus was drawn to Goldman's attempt to mold a new type of American rabbi who could balance spiritual depth and rootedness in Jewish tradition with Western philosophy, psychology, and literature. To achieve such a synthesis was no easy task. Goldman applied himself diligently to it, and Agus emulated his example.

Agus respected Goldman's integrity and his refusal to stoop to the vulgarity of the mob. In a lecture on Solomon Goldman, Agus later commented, "The American rabbi can be the most hypocritical person in the community. He can be the most empty-headed person in the community. Because if he conceives his task to be that of flattering the community and repeating their clichés for them, and embellishing the accepted vulgar opinions with beautiful rhetoric, then he becomes the servant of the mob and he becomes the symbol of the hypocrisy and the vulgarity that prevails in the community."[25] Like his mentor, Jacob Agus chose the high road.

That road would take him to Baltimore, Maryland. In 1950 the Conservative presence in that city was very weak. Chizuk Amuno Congregation was a founding member of the United Synagogue, yet it had retained the staid Germanic forms of its illustrious past and had only recently adopted mixed seating. The other Baltimore congregation, headed by a graduate of the Jewish Theological Seminary, was Beth Tefillah, but its rabbi, the scholarly Samuel Rosenblatt, refused to join the Conservative camp. The early 1950s was the time when the Conservative movement became the largest American Jewish religious movement, and Baltimore was a major Jewish community, numbering close to ninety thousand Jews. When some fifty families dissatisfied with Beth Tefillah approached Solomon Goldman seeking his advice, Goldman seized the opportunity to fill the vacuum. He suggested that they form an unequivocally Conservative congregation and recommended Jacob Agus as their spiritual leader.

In September 1950, Agus moved his family to Baltimore and began a steady process of congregation building. He did not attract people like the Dayton man who did not understand him, but many others who were willing to listen to his Sabbath morning sermons—never more than fifteen minutes long—and to learn. As in Dayton, Rabbi Agus vigorously attended to his pastoral duties. After the daily morning minyan, his office was open to the congregation. He was never too busy to offer words of comfort to the sick and the bereaved. Late mornings were devoted to hospital visits, funerals, and shiva calls; evenings were often taken up with meetings; afternoons were dedicated to scholarship.

In the early years Agus taught a course at the Baltimore Hebrew College. He took special interest in college students who continued their Jewish studies while pursuing degrees at Johns Hopkins University (where I studied) and Goucher College. A few of us gravitated to Beth El Congregation on Sabbath mornings and the Agus home on Sabbath afternoons. At his home we found tea and graciousness, but no small talk. Agus took interest in our studies and proffered guidance, but conversation inevitably focused on the books he was reading and the issues he was contemplating. With great tenderness, he would read excerpts from a work in progress. His writings, he indicated, were as dear to him as his deeply beloved children.

To those of us interested in philosophy, Agus represented the rationalist position, yet he also allowed space for the emotional side of life. He loved to quote the historian Edward Leckey, who found the most beautiful times of day to be dawn and dusk. "That is when you have the greatest beauty on the horizon. The light of the sun is reason; the darkness, emotion. Only when the two are balanced do you have the true beauty of the sunset."[26]

Surprisingly, Agus was drawn to Henri Bergson, the late romantic who reveled in intuition and popularized the term *élan vital.* Indeed, Agus was critical of this philosopher who gave primacy to feeling over reflection and who suggested that the Christian mystics advanced beyond the Hebrew prophets. But at the same time, Agus insisted that Bergson represented the true Jewish ideal, represented by Bergson's attack on materialism and his insistence on the reality of the spirit. There was a political element as well: Bergson's earlier writings were the inspiration for the precursors of fascism, but his last book, *Two Sources of Morality and Religion,* was, in Agus' opinion, a defense of democracy and a repudiation of fascism and tribalistic primitivism.[27]

If Agus mistrusted romantic religion, his own emotional side emerged when he spoke of his love of God. He prayed three times a day; when not attending minyan services at Beth El, he davened with sincere fervor at home. He also sought communion with God through sustained reflection. In response to the critics who called him a cold rationalist, this adherent of Maimonides insisted, "A great rationalist is also a mystic, for rationalism carried to its ultimate and mysticism carried to its ultimate coalesce and become one."[28]

William Kaufman, a rabbi trained in philosophy, wrote about Agus in his book on contemporary Jewish thinkers.[29] To me it seemed Kaufman expressed surprise that the rationalist Agus was a "believer" in the traditional sense, that his view of God was untainted by the atheism and cynicism characteristic of other contemporary thinkers. When I confronted Rabbi Agus with Kaufman's observation, he responded in an oblique fashion. He told me that as a believer, he found himself in good company; the greatest minds have accepted belief in God. He was, he said, proud to be in the company of Saadia, Maimonides, and Moses Mendelssohn.

Jacob Agus found spiritual refreshment on Sabbath afternoons when he devoted time to former students and younger colleagues who shared his interests. A sense of serenity reigned over the Agus home. Jacob would cast loving glances at his children. He adored his youngest child, Debby, born in Baltimore, and proudly displayed her accomplishments.[30] With David Novak, a philosophically trained, younger rabbinic colleague, Jacob Agus established a warm relationship, despite the fact that the two men represented opposite extremes of the Conservative spectrum. Jacob played with Novak's children and conducted lengthy and thoughtful conversations with their father.[31]

Jacob Agus was not a man to waste time. While Miriam would dress for an evening out, he would settle down in his study with a pad and paper. When he would come home from the synagogue in the afternoon, he would sit on a sofa, cover his face with a towel, and, after a brief period of meditation and reflection, resume his tasks.[32]

"I have always believed in Goethe's dictum that great thoughts are inspired by the outdoors," Agus once told me. From 1958 onward, the Agus family vacationed at Loon Lake in the Adirondack Mountains of New York. Surrounding the lake were buildings that had once comprised a flourishing kosher resort. When the hotel closed, the buildings were sold off. Jacob and his brother Chaim purchased large houses that became the summer gathering place of their extended family. In the earlier years, Jacob and Miriam played golf and tennis and even went square dancing. But there was also time for study, reflection, and writing. Rowing alone on the lake in the afternoons provided a daily opportunity for meditation and communion with nature. From a screened porch overlooking the lake, Jacob wrote articles and prepared books for publication.

At Loon Lake there was companionship as well. Shabbat morning services were conducted in a small synagogue that catered to observant residents of the summer community. Shabbat afternoons were dedicated to study with rabbinic colleagues.

After the vacation Agus would return to Baltimore, refreshed and ready to do battle for dearly held principles. In the early and mid-1950s he took on the Orthodox establishment; in the late 1950s and early 1960s, he came to grips with Arnold Toynbee.

In 1953 the Board of Trustees of Adath Israel Congregation in Cincinnati, Ohio, voted in favor of "optional family seating," that is, they permitted mixed seating in the sanctuary, with a portion reserved for those who wished to sit separately.[33] Although Adath Israel was affiliated with the United Synagogue from its inception and had never belonged to any Orthodox association, a minority contested this decision and took the matter to court. Orthodox leaders eagerly represented the minority.

The Rabbinical Assembly of America, the organization of Conservative rabbis, asked Agus to travel to Cincinnati as an expert witness. Ohio Supreme Court Justice Davies, who presided over the trial, insisted that no reporters be present. Rabbi Joseph B. Soloveichik, Agus' friend from Cambridge, and Rabbi Eliezer Silver of Cincinnati represented the opposite position. When they pronounced mixed seating "against the Torah," Rabbi Agus challenged them to indicate the chapter and verse stating the prohibition. Rabbi Soloveichik produced an eighth-century text that interpreted a verse in Deuteronomy to mean that because women are "indecent," they should not be seen by men in a sacred service. Rabbi Agus convinced the judge that the text reflected the setting of Muslim areas, where women generally were veiled, and that in the modern Western world this statement was anachronistic. His line of reasoning convinced the judge to rule in favor of the Conservative position.[34] The leaders of the Aggudas Harabbonim and Yeshiva University were furious. When they realized that the case was going against them, they revoked Jacob Agus' ordination and sent a telegram to the court announcing the decision. Unimpressed by this desperate action, the judge closed the case.

In 1957, Rabbi Agus and Rabbi David Aronson of Minneapolis

testified at a similar court case in New Orleans, Louisiana. This time the Orthodox position was upheld, but it was reversed on appeal.[35]

Soon after the second court case the Aggudas Harabbonim, which had solicited Agus' membership in the early 1940s, visited its revenge by excommunicating him. Yet Agus learned of the writ of *ḥerem* only through an article in the *National Jewish Post*. Defiantly, Rabbi Agus read the text of the ban before members of his congregation:

> Conservative Rabbis and the Conservative Movement created by them are a sect of freethinkers and, like the Sadducees, Karaites, and Reform Jews, are to be regarded as heretics, and they may not be trusted as witnesses, nor may their oaths be taken. It is not permitted to trust them with rabbinic functions and instructions. In particular, one may not trust them with the performances of marriages, and certainly not with the arrangement of Gittin.

Agus was not the only rabbi denounced in this document, which continued:

> After an investigation we have found that the following rabbis possess false ideas and that they speak and write words which lead people away from the Orthodox faith. They are Rabbis Eisenstein of Chicago, Graubart and his Beth Din, Agus from Baltimore, and Greenfeld from Indianapolis. With these aforementioned rabbis it is not permitted to intermarry.[36]

To his congregation Rabbi Agus remarked, "I have nothing against these people. They do what they think is best. While we should tolerate the intolerant, we should not tolerate intolerance."[37]

Agus realized that the *ḥerem* was not so much a personal vendetta as an attack on the Conservative movement. For him it was divisive, posing a danger for the future of American Jewry. He offered to debate any rabbi on any question: "To come along with the sword of the *ḥerem* and to say you separate one community from the other and declare that they may not intermarry is to bring back the spirit of the Middle Ages in this twentieth century. I think all of us should do our very best not to allow this to happen."[38]

This diminutive David also took on the intellectuals of the Gentile world. During the 1950s, Agus was reading deeply in the philosophy of history.[39] After studying Arnold Toynbee's *Study of History,* Agus initiated a dialogue with the professor that continued for many years. Toynbee's scornful references to Jews and Judaism had given him the reputation of an anti-Semite. Dr. Agus never accepted this view, common among Jews.[40] He understood Toynbee as a product of the Western intellectual tradition and a victim of an inherited bias. Agus' Harvard experience had convinced him that were he to engage fair-minded scholars in rational discourse, he would be able to modify their views. Ensuing exchanges in the university, he believed, would result in favorable political consequences as well.

To his congregation he explained the problem of dealing with the intellectual detractors of Judaism:

> At Harvard, I discovered a paradox—a paradox that I have been trying to explain all these years. On the one hand, there were mountains of anti-Jewish prejudice hanging upon that campus, a campus which was the most liberal in the United States and certainly the most enlightened. It was the soul of America. On the other hand, there was a certain openness, a certain willingness really to know and to understand what Jewish life was all about. On the one hand, there was a certain kind of antisemitism, something subtle and refined, not crude and vulgar. But without that subtle antisemitism, the vulgar antisemitism of the streets would have been impossible.[41]

Beth El Congregation made Baltimore news headlines in December 1960, when Rabbi Agus suggested Professor Toynbee as a guest lecturer for his congregation. Baltimore Jewry was enraged. Phone calls poured in with warnings of demonstrations and even a bomb threat. Although Agus was alarmed at these developments, he refused to withdraw the invitation. Instead of bringing Toynbee to Beth El, however, he arranged a meeting in his own home. At that time the Agus family had just moved to a location near the newly completed synagogue building in suburban Baltimore. Although the house was completed, the street was still unpaved, with inadequate drainage. The evening began with near disaster: a stream of water from melting snow seeped through heating ducts into the Agus living room. Fortunately, one of Beth El's leaders dashed out of the house to fetch a water pump, thus preventing the living room from turning into a lake.[42]

About one hundred people crowded into the Agus home, among

them congregational leaders, intellectuals, and college professors. For nearly two hours a riveting discussion took place.[43] Professor Toynbee was deeply respectful of Rabbi Agus and his guests, and the atmosphere was cordial. Johns Hopkins University professor William Foxwell Albright, the world-renowned archaeologist and Biblicist, challenged Toynbee with a passionate defense of Zionism, and Toynbee responded graciously and without rancor.

Agus' debate with Toynbee was not in vain. In 1961, Toynbee published his twelfth volume of the *Study of History,* titled *Reconsiderations.* In it he quoted generously from Agus' writings, acknowledging his cogent critique and stating that he was prepared to reevaluate his own findings. At the end of the book he reprinted, in full, three essays written by Agus: "The Use of the Term 'Fossil'," "The Notion of Uniqueness," and "The Prophetic Element in Judaism."

In another project to educate both Jews and Christians in the enduring worth of Judaism, Agus edited a series of reprints that encompassed forty-one Jewish classics of the medieval and modern period.[44]

Another effort at Jewish defense was Agus' enthusiastic participation in the Jewish–Christian dialogue. Agus was a trailblazer. He met with Cardinal Bea; he responded to Cardinal Danielou; he taught courses at St. Mary's Seminary and Woodstock Seminary; he participated in workshops, retreats, and dialogues.[45] Before Catholics and mainline and evangelical Protestants, he presented Judaism as the core and substance of Christianity.[46] He argued the New Testament was not an anti-Semitic work but a totally Jewish creation, reflecting Jewish ideas of the first century C.E. What were anti-Semitic, he insisted, were subsequent editorializing and interpretations; they introduced the teachings of contempt that have caused so much damage. Agus also encouraged other congregational rabbis to pursue Jewish–Christian dialogue and accepted invitations to address Christians in their own communities.[47]

Agus' prolific research and writing, his debates with scholars and church leaders, his teaching at seminaries and secular universities, his participation at institutes and retreats—all these precluded an intimate involvement in the daily operation of his congregation. In a twenty-fifth anniversary speech at Beth El, Dr. Agus acknowledged the members' forbearance:

> It was here at Beth El that I encountered the best lay leadership ever. I found my hands upheld in a manner which astonishes other congrega-

tions. For they say, "How could you find the time to write so many books? To attend so many institutes? To write so many articles?" I tell them that my people here at Beth El have taken pride in these tasks and these achievements, and therefore, I could do it."[48]

There is no doubt that the leaders of Beth El admired Rabbi Agus, basked in reflected glory, and protected him from the complaints of members who would have preferred a rabbi more involved in minute details of congregational life. Agus was equally blessed with the unstinting support of the Beth El staff: cantor, administrators and their assistants, assistant rabbis, and principals.[49] The fact that he came to a synagogue of fifty families and retired from a congregation of fifteen hundred offers testimony to an exceptionally well-run institution.

That Agus was also an effective pastor was brought home to me during a time of personal crisis. In 1979 my father lay on his deathbed. I was deeply shaken at the sight of a once vigorous and active man disintegrating from a galloping cancer. In a discussion at this time, Rabbi Agus told me that the greatest lesson a person can learn in life is how to face death with dignity and equanimity. He reminded me of victims of the Holocaust who died courageously—family members holding hands and sustaining one another. After this conversation I found the courage to face my father and speak openly about his condition. He told me with complete candor that he was not afraid of death. He had lived a good life. He was grateful for every minute, and he was prepared for the end. That conversation lingers in my mind and always comforts me.

Just seven years later, Rabbi Agus himself succumbed to a terrible cancer. I remember a time shortly before his death; I was waiting for an elevator at the Jewish Theological Seminary with my wife when the door opened and Jacob Agus emerged. Having accepted an invitation to speak at a conference, he had come alone by train from Baltimore. He seemed weak and disoriented. Baila and I escorted him to his hotel room, and we did not leave until we were certain he was comfortable. The next day he delivered his scheduled talk with the usual verve and enthusiasm and without any notes. He died a few months later.[50]

Some time earlier, in a lecture at Temple University, Agus had contrasted Baruch Spinoza with Franz Rosenzweig, to the detriment of the latter. Rosenzweig, reacting against the tradition of Maimonides, Agus noted, began his great work *The Star of Redemption* with these words:

"With the fear of death, all things begin." Spinoza, following Maimonides, said the opposite: "With the love of life, all things begin." For Agus, "Only sick-minded people think of death; healthy-minded people think of life, of joy." Jacob Agus faced death courageously, still filled with the joy of life and learning.[51]

GOING AGAINST THE GRAIN

With his beloved Maimonides as a model, Jacob Agus both participated in Jewish communal life and stepped back from it to analyze it.[52] The analysis can be found in his eight books and many articles. Other important vehicles of his thinking were the series of lectures he delivered at Beth El on Sunday mornings over a period of thirty years and other informal talks. In addition, he would present book reviews, to Beth El Sisterhood and other groups, that covered such widely divergent titles as Alexander Werth's *Russia At War,* William Golding's *The Spire,* Hugh Joseph Schonfield's *The Passover Plot,* Arthur Koestler's *The Thirteenth Tribe,* Bernard Malamud's *The Fixer,* Maurice Samuel's *Blood Accusation: The Beilus Trail.* Agus even reviewed popular movies with Jewish content and moral themes.[53] Congregants and other Baltimoreans who attended these lectures received an education unparalleled among synagogue laypeople.[54] The very informality of these addresses allowed for the free flow of Agus' iconoclastic ideas.

The "idols" that Jacob Agus set out to break can be subsumed under the following categories: American Zionism and the negation of the Diaspora; traditional interpretations of Jewish history and Jewish apologetics; the Jewish religious establishment; and the cold war mentality of America at mid-century.

If Maimonides was Agus' model, the prophets of Israel were his guide. "They [the prophets] did not have an easy time. Virtually every one of them had to go against the current most of the time."[55] Agus embraced Toynbee precisely because he understood the professor's philosophy of history in spiritual, prophetic terms. In the 1960 meeting at his house, he introduced Toynbee with the following words:

> It is possible to see the whole of history as a machine designed by God. This is the way people who interpret everything as happening by the hand of God in a literal way see it. It's possible to see the whole of history as a machine of reason, a machine of man; that is the way it was

> seen in the nineteenth century. It is possible to view history in the categories of biology. This, I believe, is the most dangerous way because it is the most seductive. . . .
>
> Our guest sees it [history] as a spiritual texture. Development consists in the unity that the mind and the soul impose, rather than in the manner in which a living being grows. The spirit can be understood, and by being understood it can be overcome, and therefore growth consists in the power to rise above oneself. And the dangers to growth, the things which stop growth, are the tendencies of people to fall in love with themselves. I consider the greatest heroes of the Bible to be the prophets. The essence of prophecy consists in the capacity or the passion to overleap oneself, to criticize one's faith, to criticize one's people, in the light of the deeper realities of one's faith, in the light of the deeper realities of one's people. It is this basic insight that our guest has laid down at the foundation of his entire interpretation of history.[56]

Two motives lay behind Agus' embrace of Arnold Toynbee. The first was the rabbi's lifelong aspiration to make Judaism intellectually respectable. In the 1950s, Toynbee's philosophy of history reigned supreme over the English-speaking world. For this reason Agus was driven to make a place for Judaism in Toynbee's philosophy, not in an apologetic fashion but by examining the rich heritage of postbiblical Jewish history and thought as he saw it. Second, Agus shared Toynbee's hatred of nationalism and ethnocentrism. This conviction informed his most controversial stance, his unrelenting criticism of Israel and the American Jewish establishment that supported it.

Agus' critique of Israel can be traced to three factors. In all likelihood, the first was the personal disappointment he had felt, as an extremely religious and idealistic adolescent, at the gap between the reality of life in the *Yishuv* (the new Jewish settlement) and his romantic and eschatological visions of the land of Israel. The second dates back to Agus' friendship with Solomon Goldman, his Baltimore congregation's founding guide. The third was ideological and philosophical.

In a lecture at Beth El, Agus reported Goldman's experience as president of the World Zionist Organization. He recounted how the older rabbi had revealed to him a deep frustration with the hollowness of the American Zionist leadership:

> I happen to be familiar with the fight he [Goldman] had on his hands when he became president of the Zionist organization; for at that time I,

> too, was part of the inner circle. . . . To see the hollowness and hypocrisy of Jewish leadership at the top is the worst experience that can come to a person. And he had it in the last years of his life.[57]

Many rabbis, Agus pointed out, forgot their calling when they enmeshed themselves in Jewish politics, but in his view, Solomon Goldman was not among them:

> His presidency was distinguished by the fact that when he was a rabbi, he was a political leader. And when he was a political leader, he was a rabbi. Many a rabbi who became the head of the Zionist movement ceased to be a rabbi. He became a "politician," a realistic politician, a man who will act and talk like any other politician; a man who only knows the gain of the moment; a man who, when he steps down from the *bima,* is no longer a rabbi but a rough-and-tumble politician. Nothing has been worse in Jewish life than to see rabbis divest themselves of the principles of Judaism the moment they enter upon the scene of politics and still use the title "rabbi" in defense of the most vicious policies that no prophet or no rabbi of the past would ever have endorsed.[58]

It was, indeed, some of the principles underlying the young Jewish state that constituted the third reason for Agus' position. From his family's run-ins with striking tannery workers and from his hostility to materialist and secular philosophies, Agus developed a distaste for the socialist ideas embraced by David Ben-Gurion and other founders of Israel. The fact that these leaders were neutral at best toward religion—and at worst, hostile—increased Agus' disapproval. Equally important was his objection to parochial nationalism, grounded in *volk*-ish ideas: "ethnic, blood-based, political and militant."[59] Those Israelis who championed this type of nationalism, Agus suggested, encouraged policies that were anything but prophetic: for example, eye-for-an-eye retaliation against terrorism and the marginalization of the Arab population.

There was another dimension to his attitude toward Zionism: his embrace of universalism. Agus acknowledged Zionism's rootedness in classical Judaism but saw it as a thing of the past. His goal was to absorb Zionism within Judaism, rather than the other way around. In a lecture series delivered at Beth El, titled "What's Right about Zionism?" he mentioned a conversation with Professor Mordecai Kaplan.[60] Agus had asked the older man why he didn't acknowledge that contemporary American Jews need Judaism more than Zionism; Kaplan responded that if he were to do this, he would lose his audience. Agus had no patience for this kind of reply. "He [Kaplan] preferred to be misunderstood by everybody and listened to than to be understood by a few, if that would have involved criticism by some."[61]

At the same time, Agus reminded his congregation of admirable aspects of Zionism, for example, the thought of A. D. Gordon, Ahad Ha-am, Rav Kuk, and the dedication of the pioneers of the kibbutzim. He admired the humane and ethical side of Zionism but deplored the institutions and leaders who abandoned the ideals when faced with political realities. "What's right about Zionism? Its spirit, the spirit of Judaism. What's wrong about Zionism? The institution."[62]

Agus always elevated the Diaspora over Israel, again going against the grain. Other Jewish leaders were convinced that Israel was essential to Jewish survival; Agus insisted that the reverse was true.[63] The very existence of Israel, he maintained, constituted a danger for Diaspora Judaism.[64] He argued that an American Jew should not use a political candidate's position on Israel as the principal criterion of support. He felt that by devoting its best efforts to political action on behalf of the young state, American Jewry was losing its soul. The future, Agus believed, lay in America, "a hymn to joy and hope"; here religion and morality could flow freely, without the constraints of politics.[65]

Agus was not ready to surrender any part of the Diaspora. When American Jews lobbied for the emigration of Soviet Jews during the 1970s, Agus objected. He certainly recognized the evils of the Communist regime and understood that, under the relentless Communist campaign, Judaism in Russia might well disappear. But he was prescient enough to realize that the multifaceted Soviet Union would not forever remain a monolith. He urged his listeners to pressure the Soviets to allow Judaism to flourish.[66]

Three examples from Agus' popular lectures indicate how he utilized Jewish sources idiosyncratically in service of his personal beliefs and in opposition to prevailing views. After Anwar Sadat's visit to Jerusalem in 1977, Agus gave a series of lectures titled "The Meaning of Jerusalem in Jewish History." A lecture on the Israelite monarchy praised King Solomon for establishing commercial ties with his neighbors and for giving Jerusalem an international flavor and an interfaith dimension.

Solomon's many wives and concubines, Agus suggested, brought emissaries and attachés to the capital city, giving it the flavor of a United Nations. Agus did not agree with the biblical authors who railed against the pagan shrines and Solomon's wives. Introducing both into Jerusalem was a pragmatic action, he insisted, enabling the king to keep political and religious forces in balance. More than that, Solomon's policy anticipated the prophet Isaiah, who taught, "My house is a house of prayer for all peoples."[67] There followed Agus' message for our own day: "Jewish people take literally all they have been taught about Jerusalem. This is our real problem. The problem is not to educate people in superficial things but to educate them in the deeper meaning of faith."[68]

The contemporary implication was the folly of insisting on the unity of Jerusalem, disregarding non-Jewish inhabitants of the city. "I believe that, in the future, the principles laid down by King Solomon will be the principles which will be the salvation of Jerusalem, although we cannot see it in the immediate future."[69] In another lecture in the same series, Agus criticized Jewish organizations outright for insisting that Jerusalem remain the eternal capital of Israel. If moving Israel's capital to Tel Aviv would bring peace, he would advocate it.[70]

In discussing the Byzantine period, Agus galvanized his audience with a description of the Jewish slaughter of Christians when the Jews fought alongside Persians, who conquered Jerusalem in 614 C.E. In response, Heraclius retook Jerusalem fourteen years later and massacred the Jews of Palestine. Agus accepted the Christian chroniclers here, making the point that Jews deliberately suppressed their own history.[71] Agus argued along the same lines in describing an earlier slaughter of Christians; there he blamed Nero's Jewish mistress for suggesting an attack on Christians rather than the Jews.[72] This was a not-too-subtle reminder of the dangers of power. When Jews have power, he suggested, they are capable of cruelty as vicious as that of their enemies.[73]

Equally controversial was Agus' reading of Hellenistic Judaism. As a rule, Jewish scholars portrayed Alexandrian Jewry of the first and second centuries C.E. as assimilationist and Philo's philosophy as ridden with paganism. But for Agus, Alexandrian Jewry was the very model for Diaspora Judaism. For this student of Wolfson, the Philonic synthesis preserved the integrity of the Jewish tradition and at the same time incorporated the best thinking of the classical world into Judaism.[74] What wrecked the synthesis, in Agus' opinion, was the infiltration of Jewish extremists from Palestine into the Jewish communities of

Alexandria, Cyprus, and Cyrenaica. They undermined the authority of the local Jewish leadership and incited bloody civil wars between Jews and Gentiles, effectively destroying Hellenistic Jewry and Hellenistic Judaism.[75]

We have already mentioned the fact that Agus' lay audience acquired a certain reservoir of knowledge. Nevertheless, remarkably few of his listeners disputed these revisionist views or their condemnation, stated or implied, of contemporary positions on the status of Jerusalem and the precedence of the Diaspora over Israel.

Still, Agus had many critics. In Baltimore few Orthodox rabbis would even speak to him. Most of his other rabbinic colleagues were active Zionists, puzzled by his anomalous views. No wonder Agus saw himself as a man alone, one who preferred loneliness to compromise. This was indicated in his lecture on Joseph Klausner, who had shocked the Jewish world with his book on Jesus of Nazareth and suffered for it all his life. In front of Klausner's house, Agus proudly informed his congregants, was a sign that read *Yahadut Ve-Enoshiyut*—"Judaism and Humanity."[76]

Agus clearly saw himself as a lone figure who, like Klausner, embraced humanity as well as Judaism and shunned the apologetic stance so popular among Jewish religious and lay leaders. When Israel performed an act that did not measure up to prophetic ideals, he condemned it. On occasion, he boldly blamed Jews for some of the anti-Semitism, past and present, that they encountered. Furthermore, even as Agus championed rationalism, liberalism, and universalism, he refused to accept often-repeated statements that Judaism had always cherished these values. His historical lectures illuminated the shadows as well as the bright spots of Jewish history. When fanaticism and obscurantism marred a period of Jewish life, he did not explain them away but painted them in Day-Glo colors.[77]

Agus' willingness to take on the American religious establishment indicated an independence of mind that characterized few Jews of his time. His evolution from "the Orthodox rabbi who would not shake a woman's hand" to a champion of what he and Solomon Goldman called "liberal Conservativism" proceeded fitfully and painfully. It must have been difficult for a man of his *yiḥus* and education to abandon Orthodox Judaism when his parents and most of his siblings remained pillars of Yeshiva University and Boro Park.[78] It could not have been easy to challenge Rabbi Joseph Soloveichik, his erstwhile study-mate and his father-in-law's avatar, in a court of law. (In fact, after these cases,

R. Soloveitchik refused to respond to any correspondence from R. Agus.)

Nor did intellectual integrity abandon Jacob Agus when he cast his lot with the Conservative movement. He came to Conservativism full of hope for a renewal of Judaism and discovered an organization that did not know its own mind. He found it offensive, for example, that men and women sat in separate sections of the synagogue at the Jewish Theological Seminary (JTS), when it was mixed seating above all else that distinguished Conservative from Orthodox congregations. His liberal rulings on the Law Committee of the Rabbinical Assembly did not sit well with the seminary administration. When the late Simon Greenberg, vice-chancellor of the JTS, spoke at Beth El Synagogue on the occasion of Agus' twentieth anniversary, he remarked coolly, "Even though we don't agree with Rabbi Agus, we admire him."[79] For his independence of mind, Agus paid a price; he never received an invitation to teach at the seminary, even in an adjunct capacity.[80]

To reinforce his concern for prophetic ethics, Agus entered the public arena. During the early 1950s, Senator Joseph McCarthy denounced Johns Hopkins professor Owen Lattimore as the "leading Communist agent in the United States" and the man responsible for the fall of China to Communism. The university suspended Lattimore while he was under investigation. At this time Agus invited Professor Lattimore to address his congregation and introduced him as a scholar and a patriot. As the only Baltimore rabbi to support Lattimore publicly, he became an object of criticism.[81]

"National independence and even the survival of a nation's collective identity are not absolute values. Only God is Absolute, and His image in man is the source and focus of all values."[82] This credo found public expression in Agus' open opposition to the American policy of deterrence through nuclear testing and stockpiling nuclear weapons. That this was not a mere armchair philosophy was brought home when the federal government mandated bomb shelters in large buildings. Rabbi Agus would not permit Beth El Synagogue to comply with the order. Grounds for his argument were halakhic as well as broadly ethical: he maintained that a nuclear war would destroy such a large percentage of mankind that there was no such thing as "shelter" or an "acceptable" number of casualties once it was initiated.[83]

The same sort of reasoning fueled Agus' early opposition to the Vietnam War and to the domino theory that supported American engagement in it. For this reason Agus supported peace candidates and became a principal adviser on the moral ramifications of policies and positions to Charles McMathias, a liberal Republican who was elected United States senator from Maryland for three terms.[84]

In the 1970s, Sargent Shriver organized an interfaith group that met to discuss public policy issues in the light of religious insights. For the ten years of its existence, Agus was a vocal participant in the group.[85]

After a visit with Jacob, Baila and I would comment that a session with Rabbi Agus was the closest encounter with pure mind in our combined experience. But Jacob Agus was also human and therefore not perfect. First there was his language. Early in his rabbinic career he studied with a speech teacher, who all but eliminated his foreign accent and natural lisp and taught him voice projection and good diction.[86] For a man who arrived in this country at the age of sixteen, Agus exhibited a fine command of written English, but the syntax of his native Yiddish slipped into his informal addresses. Part of the reason was that, remarkably, he seldom used notes. Yet because he relied almost exclusively on his memory, the historical data was not totally accurate. For example, in an otherwise insightful lecture on Professor Louis (Levi) Ginzberg of the Jewish Theological Seminary (an important influence on Agus' life), he incorrectly stated twice that the professor came to America with a wife.[87]

Another imperfection was a tendency to be overly critical. For example, in Agus' opinion Trude Weiss-Rosmarin, the late editor of *The Jewish Spectator,* was "pretentious."[88] Another object of his disdain was the novelist and essayist Cynthia Ozick. In response to her article in *Esquire* magazine that bore the title "The Whole World Wants the Jews Dead!" Agus released a scathing diatribe against writers who encourage self-fulfilling prophecies. His criticism of male writers was equally strong when he felt they acted as propagandists rather than expounders of truth. For example, he took issue with Martin Buber and Elie Wiesel for their exaggerated romanticization of Hasidism.

More noteworthy was Agus' attitude toward blacks. On this issue, unlike that of Israel or bomb shelters, he descended from his perch of prophetic objectivity and identified with his congregants. When the riots that followed the assassination of Martin Luther King, Jr., created grief for Jewish owners of shops and factories, Agus condemned the leaders of the riots as "outsider provocateurs."[89] Perhaps the events of 1968 awakened memories of Poland after World War I.[90] At any rate,

Agus always viewed "the mob" as the greatest threat to Jewish safety and welfare. His strong opposition to affirmative action surfaced in a letter to Vice President Hubert Humphrey, in which Agus objected to a speech by Humphrey calling for "equal results" rather than "equal opportunity."[91]

Jacob was not unaware of his shortcomings. Once he alluded to a certain "meanness" within himself. This, he explained in true Maimonidean fashion, was due to the intrusion of "matter." Every human being has a good side, the side that is fashioned by God; but then matter intrudes and causes imperfections in personality and character.[92]

In my opinion, Agus was never mean, though to outsiders he appeared somewhat wooden. His natural stiffness, however, was sometimes mitigated by light humor. In popular lectures he would establish a connection with his audience by references to his wife. Once he exclaimed, "Next to Maimonides, I love my wife best!" On another occasion he explained his tendency to criticize with the following: "Anyone who has been married for twenty-five years or more knows that a critic is not the same thing as an enemy."[93]

Agus enjoyed a certain compatibility with rabbis on the Conservative left and those whose knowledge he respected, among them Aaron Blumenthal, Seymour Siegel, Ben Zion Bokser, Morris Adler, Theodore Friedman, Robert Gordis, and David Aronson. He also worked closely with members of the Law Committee of the Rabbinical Assembly and, in the late 1950s, headed the Committee on Conservative Ideology. For a time he also chaired the Prayer Book Committee. Clearly, he had cast his lot with the Conservative movement; since he believed in operating within the Jewish fold, there was no other place for him in American Judaism. He considered the Reform movement of his day to be more shallow than Conservativism and disliked its abandonment of many rituals that enrich Jewish life.[94]

To critics who maintained that Agus was so caught up in rationalism that he lost sight of man's elemental passions and that as a universalistic philosopher he lost contact with the masses, Agus replied, "Philosophers fulfill a function, but they would abuse their role if they attempted to be 'rulers,' as in Plato. Their role is to criticize and to evaluate. In the life of a community, there is always tension between the need for collective existence, and the ideals such collectives embrace."[95]

Never resting on his laurels, Agus spent every moment of his life learning, growing, and trying to understand. He believed that every philosophy is part of an ongoing dialogue. The essence of dialogue, he insisted, is that each formulation is incomplete, that every position needs to be questioned, reevaluated, and then reformulated. Even though the vision of God is constantly before us, it is never totally grasped, and the pursuit of perfection remains an inexhaustible challenge. If we give up the quest, we risk losing the vision and turning to skepticism and despair. If, by contrast, we persist in the search, while we may never have rest, while we may never be at ease, we shall nevertheless "see all things fresh and radiant with the golden promise of tomorrow."[96]

In a letter written in the mid-1970s, Agus explained the basis of his theology: "The core of my religious philosophy is the concept of Revelation. Mine relates to a Revelation as a common religious experience—the whole-souled quest of God. The affirmative element is the fact that the quest is sustained; the negative, that it is a quest, not a possession. The image of the prophet is the common experience, made larger than life."[97] The power of that quest and the man who exemplified it have sustained me to the present day.

NOTES

1. Professor Marvin Fox, interview with the author, June 2, 1994.

2. There were four brothers and three sisters. Agus' brothers were Yitzhak (Irving), Chaim, and Pinchas (Paul); his sisters, Esther, Jenny, and another who died in childhood. The biographical information in this essay is taken largely from notes given to me by Jacob Agus' son, Robert. Future references will be cited as Robert E. Agus, "Biographical Notes."

3. My thanks to Rabbi Mark Loeb and Mr. Herbert Habel for making available to me the collection of reel-to-reel audiotapes of Rabbi Agus' lectures. These data from the Rabbi Jacob B. Agus Adult Education Library at Beth El Synagogue, Baltimore, will hereafter be cited as "Agus Library tape." See Agus Library tape "The Hafetz Hayim," January 25, 1959.

4. Lecture given at Temple University in Philadelphia: "Lecture on Maimonides and Spinoza," April 30, 1970.

5. *Neviim U-ketuvim im Perush Rashi u-Fairush Mikraay Kodesh le-Harav Meir Laibush "Malbim"* (Vilna, 1910–11).

6. David Novak, interview with the author, April 24, 1994.

7. It was Jacob's brother Irving who changed his name to Agus; the rest of the family followed his example. See Robert E. Agus, "Biographical Notes."

8. Agus Library tape "Lecture in Memory of H. A. Wolfson," December 27, 1974.

9. Ibid.

10. Agus Library tape "Jacob B. Agus—Twenty-fifth Anniversary Celebration," October 3, 1975.

11. The phrase was used in a personal conversation during one of my visits to his home.

12. Agus Library tape "Wolfson," January 27, 1974; see also "Jacob B. Agus—Twenty-fifth Anniversary Celebration," October 3, 1975.

13. Temple University classroom lectures on Maimonides, April 30, 1970, and May 7, 1970.

14. Agus Library tape *"Ḥerem,"* December 15, 1957.

15. Ibid.

16. Miriam Agus, interview with the author, July 28, 1993.

17. Robert E. Agus, "Biographical Notes."

18. Professor Marvin Fox, interview with the author, June 2, 1994.

19. These radio talks were later published in pamphlet form. A successor to Rabbi Agus in Dayton recalls that the community remembered him with affection and gratitude (Rabbi Jack Riemer, interview with the author, May 24, 1994).

20. Professor Marvin Fox, interview with the author, June 2, 1994. Dr. Fox, who first met Rabbi Agus in Chicago, acknowledges that Jacob influenced his career in Jewish scholarship. He recalls long conversations and discussions on Jewish philosophy and thought. Stationed at an army air-force base near Dayton during the war years, Dr. Fox assisted Agus in conducting services during the High Holy Days.

21. In his retirement speech at Beth El in 1980, Rabbi Agus paid tribute to his wife: "I have been blessed with a companion in life who has not only brought joy to me but every bit of achievement of which I can boast and with which my name is associated. Whatever Torah I have brought is not mine only but hers as well" (Agus Library tape "1980 Retirement").

22. Robert E. Agus, "Biographical Notes."

23. In addition, Agus published Hebrew studies on the logic of the kabbalah, such as "Le-Heker Higayon Ha-Kabbalah," *Sefer Hashanah li-Yehuday America* 8–9 (1946). Another Hebrew article analyzed Rav Kuk's contribution to the development of *devekut.* See Jacob Agus "Ish Hamistorin," *Talpiot* (Nisan 1948). In his preface to *Banner of Jerusalem* (New York, 1946), Agus thanked Heschel for reading the manuscript and making suggestions.

24. See Morris Adler, Jacob Agus, and Theodore Friedman, "A Responsum on the Sabbath," in *Tradition and Change,* ed. Mordecai Waxman (New York, 1958), 351–74. During that same period, Agus wrote an unpublished responsum, "Recording a Service on Sabbath." See *Rabbinical Assembly Law Committee Proceedings* 50 (1956): 74–76.

25. Agus Library tape "Lecture in Memory of Solomon Goldman," November 1, 1959.

26. Agus Library tape "Lecture on Henri Bergson," November 11, 1973, and personal recollections.

27. Ibid. See also Jacob Agus, *Jewish Identity in an Age of Ideologies* (New York, 1978), 232–81.

28. Temple University tape "Lecture on Maimonides and Spinoza," April 30, 1970.

29. William E. Kaufman, *Contemporary Jewish Philosophies* (New York, 1976), 231–50.

30. Author's observations from the 1960s and 1970s, when my wife, Baila, and I would visit the Agus home in Baltimore.

31. David Novak, interview with the author, April 24, 1994.

32. Miriam Agus, interview with the author, July 28, 1993.

33. Documents related to the trial were printed in the fall edition of *Conservative Judaism* (1956). The entire issue was devoted to the Cincinnati court case.

34. Agus Library tape *"Ḥerem,"* December 15, 1957.

35. Ibid. See also Baruch Litvin, *The Sanctity of the Synagogue: The Case for Mechitzah,* ed. Jeanne Litvin, rev. ed. (New York, 1987), 61, 73, 74, 314.

36. Agus Library tape *"Ḥerem,"* December 15, 1957.

37. Ibid.

38. Ibid.

39. This reading was in preparation for two of his most ambitious books: *The Evolution of Jewish Thought* (New York, 1959) and *The Meaning of Jewish History,* 2 vols (New York, 1963).

40. See Maurice Samuel, *The Professor and the Fossil* (New York, 1956).

41. Agus Library tape "Jacob B. Agus—Twenty-fifth Anniversary Celebration," October 3, 1975.

42. Miriam Agus, interview with the author, July 28, 1993.

43. A tape recording of the meeting has survived, and even after these many years, the tension and excitement of the evening are palpable. See Agus Library tape "Toynbee," December 26, 1960.

44. Letter from Herbert J. Cohen, former president of Arno Press, to author, August 23, 1993. The series was published by Arno Press (New York) in 1973.

45. Rabbi Amiel Wohl told me that when he served a Reform congregation in Baltimore in the 1960s, he attended a class in New Testament, taught by Rabbi Agus to Christian clergy, on a regular basis. The clergy were mesmerized by Agus' teaching. (See Rabbi Amiel Wohl, interview with the author, April 11, 1994.) St. Mary's is the largest school for Catholic priests in the United

States and is under the direct supervision of the Vatican. Rabbi Agus was the first Jew officially authorized by the Vatican to teach Catholic seminarians. (See Robert E. Agus, "Biographical Notes.")

46. The late Rabbi Marc Tannenbaum, for many years director of interreligious affairs for American Jewish Committee, considered Jacob Agus his mentor in ecumenical matters. He paid tribute to Jacob's work in this field in his speech at Agus' twenty-fifth anniversary celebration at Beth El. (See Agus Library tape "Jacob B. Agus—Twenty-fifth Anniversary Celebration," October 3, 1975. See also Agus conference tape "The Meanings of Shalom," March 29, 1973, which contains lectures delivered in a two-day conference held with leaders of the United Church of Christ, in a project to help them revise their textbooks in the light of an appreciation of Judaism and the Jewish heritage.

47. During the 1960s, when I occupied a pulpit in Easton, Pennsylvania, I followed Agus' example and befriended a Catholic priest and a Lutheran minister. Together we formed ProJeCt (Protestants, Jews, Catholics), an interracial, interreligious fellowship that responded to the social needs of the community. ProJeCt has continued to function to this day. In 1973, Rabbi Agus graciously accepted my invitation to address the clergy of Westchester in a full-day session. See author's tape "A Jewish Scholar Looks at the New Testament," Agus' lecture delivered during a clergy institute held at the Jewish Community Center of Harrison, New York, March 2, 1977.

48. Agus Library tape "Jacob B. Agus—Twenty-fifth Anniversary Celebration," October 3, 1975.

49. Two assistant rabbis served with Agus: Herbert Yoskowitz (1972–1975) and Mark Loeb (1975–1980). Loeb became senior rabbi when Agus became rabbi emeritus in 1980; he continues in this position. Cantor Saul Hammerman, who came to Beth El shortly after Rabbi Agus, served during the entire time of Rabbi Agus' tenure and continues to do so.

50. He died on September 26, 1986. See Pamela Nadell, *Conservative Judaism: A Biographical Dictionary* (New York, 1988), 34.

51. Temple University tape "Lecture on Maimonides and Spinoza," April 30, 1970. Cf. also Agus, *Evolution of Jewish Thought,* 311–12.

52. The ideas in this section, "Going against the Grain," reflect discussions over the years with my wife, Dr. Baila Shargel.

53. E.g., *The Apprenticeship of Duddy Kravitz, The Mad Adventures of Rabbi Jacob,* and *Oh God!*

54. David Novak told me that when he lectured at Beth El on a Sunday morning, he found the thinking of the congregation shaped by that of their rabbi. See David Novak, interview with the author, April 24, 1994.

55. Agus Library tape "The Prophet Amos," October 27, 1957.

56. Agus Library tape "Toynbee," December 26, 1960.

57. Agus Library tape, "Lecture on Solomon Goldman," November 1, 1959.

This statement indicates that Agus participated in the Zionist movement for a time.

58. Ibid.

59. Cf. Jacob Agus, "Myth, Faith, and Reality in Jewish Life," in *Studies of the Leo Baeck Institute* (New York, 1967), 179–264.

60. The conversation took place at a Camp Wohelo institute after Kaplan gave a speech on the subject "A Greater Zionism." See Agus Library tape "What's Right about Zionism?" January 10, 1960.

61. Agus Library tape "What's Right about Zionism?" January 10, 1960.

62. Ibid.

63. Cf. Jacob Agus, *The Jewish Quest* (New York, 1983), 10: "The task of Diaspora Jewry is to help Israel acquire fresh dimensions of moral and cultural greatness."

64. "That the State of Israel can affect adversely and even fatally the position of Jews in the Diaspora has been proven, again and again" (Agus, "Myth, Faith, and Reality," 246).

65. Agus Library tape "Jacob B. Agus—Twenty-fifth Anniversary Celebration," October 3, 1975.

66. Agus Library tape "Russian Jewry," November 15, 1975.

67. Isaiah 56:7.

68. Agus Library tape "The Meaning of Jerusalem—From Solomon to the Destruction of the First Temple," December 18, 1977.

69. Ibid.

70. Agus Library tape "The Meaning of Jerusalem—From Ezra to the Maccabees," December 4, 1977.

71. Agus Library tape "Separation of Judaism and Christianity," December 27, 1959.

72. Ibid.

73. Cf. Agus, *Meaning of Jewish History,* 136–37.

74. Cf. Agus, *Evolution of Jewish Thought,* 78–101.

75. Agus, *Meaning of Jewish History,* 119–38.

76. Agus Library tape "Lecture in Memory of Joseph Klausner," January 11, 1959.

77. Agus Library tape "Separation of Judaism and Christianity," December 27, 1959. Cf. also Agus, *Meaning of Jewish History,* 136–38.

78. His brother Irving was the medieval historian on the Yeshiva University faculty, and Chaim was the highly respected "doctor of Boro Park." Jacob's saintly father, Yehudah Leib, conducted a "Hevra Shas" at the Shomrei Emunah Synagogue. Agus' brother Paul and sisters Jennie Bruch and Esther Stein were also respected members of the Orthodox community of Boro Park. See Robert E. Agus, "Biographical Notes."

79. Agus Library tape "Twentieth Anniversary Celebration," June 17, 1970.

80. Agus was invited to teach for a semester at the Seminario Rabbinico in Argentina in 1965. This appointment came about through his friend Rabbi Theodore Friedman, who was the father-in-law of the late Marshall Meyer, the rabbi who pioneered the building of the Conservative movement in that country. While in Argentina, Agus played an important role in helping to revise textbooks used in Catholic schools, bringing them in line with the new ecumenical spirit. See Robert E. Agus, "Biographical Notes."

81. Robert E. Agus, "Biographical Notes."

82. Jacob Agus, *The Vision and the Way* (New York, 1966), 349.

83. Robert E. Agus, "Biographical Notes."

84. Ibid.

85. Ibid.

86. Ibid.

87. Agus Library tape "Lecture on Professor Louis Ginzberg," February 15, 1959.

88. David Novak, interview with the author, April 24, 1994.

89. Agus Library tape "Riots in Baltimore," May 5, 1968.

90. Agus' uncle, a major general in the Bolshevik army, rode into Sislowitz to rescue the Jews from the Cossacks. See Robert E. Agus, "Biographical Notes."

91. Agus Library tape "Riots in Baltimore," May 5, 1968.

92. Tape of lecture given by Jacob Agus at Temple University in Philadelphia: "Maimonides," February 19, 1970.

93. Ibid.

94. Jacob Agus, conversation with Baila Shargel.

95. Jacob Agus, letter to the author, December 20, 1976.

96. Jacob Agus, *Dialogue and Tradition* (New York, 1971), 381.

97. Jacob Agus, letter to the author, December 18, 1974.

3

JACOB B. AGUS AS A STUDENT OF MODERN JEWISH PHILOSOPHY

David Novak

AGUS AS CRITIC: HISTORICAL CONTEXT

ANYONE PRIVILEGED to have known the late Rabbi Jacob B. Agus, as was I, will certainly agree that he was a man of immense personal and intellectual integrity, and one who had the commensurate courage such integrity requires. His courage was evidenced throughout his career as a rabbi and as a Jewish thinker and writer. His intellectual integrity especially was already manifest in his first book, published in 1941 when he was an obscure thirty-year-old rabbi serving a fairly sizable congregation in Chicago. The book, *Modern Philosophies of Judaism: A Study of Recent Jewish Philosophies of Religion,* is much more than its subtitle describes.[1] It is much more than a study, something one would expect from a young man who had recently received his Ph.D. in philosophy and who still had the usually timid habits of a graduate student. Rather, it was in every sense a tour de force, for Agus did much more than "study" the leading modern Jewish thinkers with whom he dealt in his book; he boldly and cogently criticized them, and then he went on to outline what was to become his own philosophy of Judaism. I am convinced that the feat of this young rabbi-thinker can be compared only to the tour de force of another young rabbi-thinker, that of Leo Baeck, who in his 1900 book *The Essence of Judaism* confronted the view of Judaism of the leading Christian thinker of his time and place, Adolf von Harnack, and thereby presented his own philosophy of Judaism. And just as Baeck's first daring book set the tone for his future thought, so did this first book by Agus.

To better appreciate the courage of Agus' earliest work, even before we examine its intelligence and prescience of his later work, it is important to know just who Jacob B. Agus was in 1941.

Born in Poland in 1911 into a family distinguished by great piety and learning, Agus came with his family to the United States as a teenager. He soon became a student of the great Lithuanian Talmudist Rabbi Moses Soloveitchik at what was later to become Yeshiva University in New York, where he excelled in traditional rabbinic learning. Ordained as an Orthodox rabbi in his early twenties, Agus soon found himself studying philosophy and history of religions at Harvard University, where he worked with the great historian of Jewish and general philosophy Harry Austryn Wolfson, and where he was the last doctoral student of the idealist philosopher William Hocking. Already as a graduate student, however, Agus could no longer be considered an Orthodox Jew, though he served at the time as the rabbi of Orthodox synagogues in Norfolk, Virginia, and Cambridge, Massachusetts. His study of history and, especially, philosophy convinced him that Judaism required a more rationally convincing justification than could possibly be provided by Orthodox literalism and dogmatism. Even though Agus would eventually become a Conservative rabbi, and a leading one at that, he did not find in 1941—or thereafter—any non-Orthodox philosophy of Judaism that satisfied him religiously or rationally. So his integrity required that he first examine these philosophies and show how and why they were wanting. His courage and great intellect enabled him to suggest an acceptable alternative for himself and those whom he hoped to convince.

The year 1941 was an ominous one in which to be a Jew—and even more so to be a Jewish thinker—in the world. By that time it was already becoming clear that all of European Jewry was in mortal danger at the hands of the Nazis. In America, most of the Jews who had remained faithful to Judaism were doing so out of habit and sentiment, but a large number of the best and the brightest, who needed something more than the authority of the past to guide and inspire them, were convinced that Judaism was already irrelevant to the needs of the present and that it would not survive in the radical new future they envisioned. And although he knew that his book would be little noticed by the Jews of his time and place, Jacob Agus wrote it anyway, convinced that truth is more enduring and, ultimately, more attractive than popularity.

THE CRITIQUE OF JEWISH NATIONALISM

The usual alternative to Orthodoxy that was embraced by Jews of backgrounds similar to Agus' and who wanted to remain part of the Jewish people was Jewish nationalism. In the earlier part of the twentieth century, Jewish nationalism was still able to take two forms: Zionism, which advocated that the Jewish national home be in the land of Israel and that its linguistic culture be Hebrew, and what was called territorialism, which advocated that the Jewish national home be some designated sovereign area in Eastern Europe (where the greatest mass of Jews still lived) and that its linguistic culture be Yiddish. But by 1941, with the ongoing destruction of Eastern European Jewry, it was clear that Zionism was the only realistic form of Jewish nationalism left.

Zionism generally took two forms: political and cultural. Political Zionism, which was almost solely concerned with the restoration of Jewish national sovereignty in the land of Israel, had no religious point of view at all. Either its ideology became nationalism per se, as in the case of Vladimir Jabotinsky and his "revisionist" followers, or it became some form of Marxism, however diluted and adapted, as in the case of David Ben-Gurion and his followers. But cultural Zionism did at least have an interest in what could be broadly taken as the Jewish religious heritage. It was this interest that attracted the attention of Agus; for although not an anti-Zionist himself (either before or after the establishment of the State of Israel in 1948), he was convinced that the interest of cultural Zionism in the Jewish religious heritage was philosophically inadequate. Being inadequate philosophically meant, for him, that it was inadequate as a system of thought that could guide and inspire contemporary Jews engaged in a spiritual quest similar to that of Agus himself.

Agus' main critique of cultural Zionism was directed against its most influential theorist, Ahad Ha'Am (1856–1927). As in any good philosophical critique, Agus showed how Ahad Ha'Am's theory of cultural Zionism lacked proper consistency in itself and proper sufficiency in its connection to a world outside itself, the world in this case being Jewish tradition.

Ahad Ha'Am's lack of consistency is apparent in his presentation of the relation between Jewish nationalism and Jewish morality. The philosophical problem involved is no less than that of the relation of the universal and the particular.

For most modern Jewish thinkers, morality was what Immanuel Kant had insisted it could only be, namely, a system of practical maxims determined by the univeralistic criterion of the Categorical Imperative. Anything individual or particular had to be subsumed under the rule of universal morality in order to be morally justifiable. As such, Jewish nationalism, no doubt a form of particularism, would have to adapt itself to the rule of the universal in order to be morally justifiable. For this reason Jewish Kantians, first and foremost Hermann Cohen (whom Agus was probably the first Jewish thinker to examine critically in English), regarded Jewish survival to be worthwhile only on strictly religious grounds, religion being a necessary correlate of morality. For the same reason Zionism was rejected—usually quite vehemently—by the Jewish adherents of this school of thought. In their eyes, Zionism was a nationalism without a proper justification in universal morality.

Ahad Ha'Am thought he could refute this philosophical rejection of Jewish nationalism, especially Zionism, by denying that morality is universal. For him, each nation had its own "national spirit." Out of this national spirit, then, each nation produced its own morality. In his vision of Judaism, the unique morality of the Jewish nation is characterized by its devotion to the ideal of absolute justice. Ahad Ha'Am was convinced that no other nation had any such devotion to this ideal.

Agus showed quite insightfully that morality cannot be reduced to nationalism, even in the full thought of Ahad Ha'Am, for Ahad Ha'Am also accepted the ancient idea that the Jewish nation is to be "a light unto the nations," that is, the Jews have something to teach the rest of the world. It was an idea that Ahad Ha'Am accepted almost as much as did the anti-Zionist Jewish Kantians. His difference from them was one of degree rather than one of kind; for whereas they thought that Jews could best perform this enlightening function as individual citizens of modern European or American nation-states, he thought they could do it much better and with greater historical integrity collectively, as a unique nation themselves, one reestablished in their ancient homeland.[2] (On the question of actual Jewish statehood in the sense of complete political sovereignty, Ahad Ha'Am was noncommital.)

However, if the Jewish nation has something to offer the rest of the world, then it must have something in common with that world. Otherwise what it has to offer will necessarily be unintelligible. As Agus notes with characteristic directness, "Why, then, should a Jew assume a priori that the insight of his own national group is infallible? Truth knows no national boundaries whatsoever."[3] In other words, by asserting that the Jewish nation has both a national vision and a transnational message, Ahad Haʿ Am seems to imply that Jewish nationalism is not self-justifying after all. His only difference from the Jewish Kantians would seem to be that he did not place such firm faith in the European nation-states as morally the best place for Jews (and perhaps existentially as well) as they did. But for both Ahad Haʿ Am and the Kantians, a moral meaning for Jewish group survival and continuation, whether as a "faith community" or as a "national group," if pursued consistently will require a criterion that transcends the community or group itself.[4] This contradicts Ahad Haʿ Am's continual emphasis on the nonjustifiable nature of national existence, as Agus so well shows.

At this point I think it is best to see how Agus criticizes the Jewish sufficiency of Ahad Haʿ Am's view of Judaism; for Agus argues quite persuasively that nationalism requires a moral justification, based on a transcendent criterion. But morality is not enough of a criterion to maintain its transcendence independently. It requires an ontological foundation, which for Agus can only be God. And if ethics is the means whereby we know morality, religion is the means whereby we know God. Thus, if Ahad Haʿ Am's morally justified nationalism requires transcendence to be cogent, then the quest for transcendence must go all the way to the top, so to speak, in order to be sufficient. Accordingly, nationalism requires morality and morality requires religion in order to be sufficient *both* Jewishly and philosophically. As Agus puts it, "Relativistic theories of ethics require no religious foundation. But, an absolute standard of morality, the assertion of eternally valid ethical truths—what meaning can any such claim possess if we dispense with the concept of an Absolute Being, Who stands outside the flowing stream of phenomena?"[5] Because Ahad Haʿ Am was unable to do this, Agus harshly but accurately concludes that his "philosophy of Judaism is pitifully inadequate."[6]

THE CRITIQUE OF KAPLAN

In 1941, at a time when Agus was wrestling with the meaning of Orthodoxy and what Orthodox Judaism entailed, the leading non-

Orthodox Jewish thinker in America was Mordecai M. Kaplan (1881–1983). Kaplan's influence extended far beyond the Jewish Theological Seminary of America, where he indoctrinated Conservative rabbis with his ideology for over fifty years. To many of Agus' contemporaries who wanted to be modern intellectuals and remain "Jewish" Jews, Kaplan seemed able to present a coherent view of Judaism for those who could no longer believe in the literal authority of biblical revelation and rabbinic tradition. Moreover, because of his incorporation of some of the ideas of Emile Durkheim and John Dewey into his thought, Kaplan seemed to be presenting a view of Judaism that was au courant with the new thinking of the social sciences, thinking that was especially influential in America.

Yet Agus, bold as he always was, was not afraid to subject Kaplan's thought to his own rigorous philosophical critique. In the course of that critique, Kaplan came out looking even more inadequate than did Ahad Haʿ Am. The reason for this, it seems to me, is that Kaplan was philosophically more ambitious than was Ahad Haʿ Am in his constructive project, yet he was even less philosophically able.

Like Ahad Haʿ Am, whom he greatly admired, Kaplan was a nationalist. For him, the existence and continuity of the Jewish people (what he was to later call "peoplehood," a term he took great pride in having coined) needed no more justification than a biological entity needs justification to live. The inclination to live and survive was just as natural among nations as among biological entities. (Of course, Kaplan's biological analogy is problematic along Darwinian lines, for there the survival of any species is not a permanent given but must be "justified" by the capacity to adapt to the *greater* environment. But this is not a point Agus included in his critique.) Therefore, for Kaplan, anything that contributed to Jewish survival and enhanced its vitality was authentically Jewish. Since there is a wide complex of such vivifying factors, Judaism is not just a religion, not just a nation, not just a culture, but is nothing less than a "civilization." (The designation "civilization" is as problematic as the biological analogy just mentioned, and for much the same reason. Influenced by Darwinism to a large extent, theorists of civilization such as Oswald Spengler and Arnold Toynbee have argued that civilizations are not permanently given but must be "justified" by their capacity to adapt to a *greater* world—a capacity that all civilizations so far seem to have lost eventually. But again, this is not a point Agus included in his critique.)

As was the case with Ahad Ha'Am, Agus criticized the overall position of Kaplan on ethical and religious grounds. And the logical tactic was also the same, namely, to show inadequacy in terms of consistency and sufficiency.

Agus notes that Kaplan was not unaware of the danger of reducing Judaism to a mere national or "folk" religion. After all, even though Kaplan began work on his magnum opus, *Judaism as a Civilization,* long before its publication in 1934, the fact that it appeared after Hitler had already come to power in Germany, justifying his tyranny on the grounds of the primacy of "folk," could not very well go unnoticed—certainly not by a Jewish thinker considering the centrality of anti-Semitism to Nazi ideology from the very beginning. And by 1941, when Agus' critique of Kaplan came out, Nazi folk ideology was being translated into the wholesale murder of Jews who were unfortunate enough to be living within the widening Nazi net of power. Clearly, this type of folk religion was consummately immoral.

As Agus put it, quite fairly it seems, "Kaplan is not unmindful of the danger of national religions turning into consecrated chauvinisms . . . to many forms of neo-paganism."[7] That Kaplan recognized the problem (unlike some other Jewish nationalists, even after the full impact of the Holocaust) is to his credit. But how does he attempt to deal with it? The answer is that Kaplan supplies the missing universal moral factor in the assertion of the need for "personal religion," which functions as the necessary counterpoint to "folk religion"; for if folk religion is left alone, especially when it is coupled with the power of a modern nation-state, the danger of immoral nationalism is very real indeed. The suggestion is, of course, intriguing, but Agus is very quick to point out that Kaplan in no way connects the two foci of religion philosophically; indeed, "he does not inquire whether the two can logically co-exist."[8] Kaplan, as the social scientist—more particularly, the sociologist—he always took himself to be, constituted only Jewish folk religion in any thorough way. He did not really constitute personal religion at all, much less correlate it with folk religion. But without this correlation there can be no critical morality at all. At least at this stage of his thought, Kaplan simply leaves the matter at this unsatisfying impasse.

In his critique Agus sees Kaplan's problem as being more than simply ethical. It is theological. And whereas Agus could criticize Ahad Ha'Am for being so theologically agnostic, in Kaplan's case there is a theology. Kaplan is a theist. The problem, then, is not the absence of a theology but rather a theology that is inadequate. Now, there are two ways one can criticize Kaplan's theology. More traditionalist Jewish thinkers would argue that the fault lies in Kaplan's denial of revelation, a denial that became more acute with age. This argument would show that Kaplan's theology simply eliminates too much of the classical Jewish tradition to claim any real continuity with it. However, Agus is too untraditional (not just too non-Orthodox) to follow that line of argument. Even though he does not deny revelation, as does Kaplan, his view of revelation, which he developed in his later work, would hardly satisfy traditionalist requirements either. Instead, his critique of Kaplan's theology is that it is inadequate to ground any genuine ethics. In other words, Agus' critique is that of one liberal Jew vis-à-vis another liberal Jew.

Agus sees the heart of Kaplan's theological problem in his concept of God; for Kaplan saw himself as both a "naturalist" and a "functionalist." As a naturalist, he was convinced that the world of human experience, or possible human experience, is all there is. Everything is contained within its. But since God is not the object of human experience, God, like any other nonobject, can be explained only as a function of human experience. Here is where Kaplan's functionalism comes in. To maintain a connection with traditional religious vocabulary (but not with traditional religious conceptuality), Kaplan sees God's function as being salvific. That is, since human striving is within a larger natural universe, there must be something *within* this universe that enables human striving to succeed, or at least to have the possibility of success. That success is what biblical religion called salvation. So that aspect of nature which ultimately *empowers* (as we would say today) human salvation is what Kaplan designates as "God."

The question that Agus astutely asks, following his general method of liberal Jewish critique, is whether or not this concept of God is ethically sufficient, that is, whether or not it can cogently ground morality. And it should be remembered, even Kaplan is forced to admit (either by post-1933 experience or by logic) that morality is more than a matter of societal cohesiveness. But here is where Agus comes down most forcefully on Kaplan. As Agus puts it:

> The realm of ethics cannot be placed above the realm of physical events, unless God, the cosmic source of morality, is conceived as standing outside and above the sway of physical nature. We must think of God as

> the Creator of the universe and the Author of the moral law. This is quite different from the simple recognition of physicists that the universe is an "organic" unity.[9]

Agus' trenchant critique of Kaplan had important ramifications when he officially became a Conservative rabbi in the late 1940s. Before Agus' arrival, the Conservative rabbinate was basically divided into two ideological camps. On the one hand was the camp of traditionalists, centered on the great talmudic scholar Louis Ginzberg (1873–1953) and his chief disciple, the president of the Jewish Theological Seminary of America, Louis Finkelstein (1895–1991). Although these men had rather flexible theoretical views about revelation and the development of tradition, on practical grounds they reaffirmed virtually all of the authority of the tradition. Tradition for them essentially grounded its own authority. On the other hand was the camp centered on Mordecai Kaplan, which extended far beyond those who were officially to become Reconstructionists (a group that eventually separated itself from the Conservative movement in the 1960s). These men (and later, women) were convinced that without the traditional belief in revelation, which they regarded as beyond retrieval in the modern scientific world, the traditional practices of Judaism required wholesale reconstruction.

As we have already seen, Agus was dissatisfied with the theological grounding of Kaplan's Jewish liberalism for strong philosophical reasons. Ultimately, his difference from Kaplan was over the question of God. But for the most part Agus was not dissatisfied with the call for the reconstruction of Jewish religious practice, strongly demanded by Kaplan and his followers and just as strongly resisted by Ginzberg and Finkelstein and their followers. Indeed, Agus was the chief author of a controversial responsum, issued by the Law Committee of the Rabbinical Assembly (the official body of the Conservative rabbinate) in 1950, that permitted the driving of an automobile on the Sabbath if that was the only way to attend synagogue services, which was a quite radical departure from halakhic tradition (however much it was formulated in a traditional rabbinic style, using as many talmudic sources as was possible).[10] So what Agus provided for a number of "left-wing" Conservative rabbis was liberalism in practice coupled with a much more satisfying and cogent theism in theory. Indeed, if one looks at the Conservative movement today, which is left-wing by the standards of the 1940s and 1950s (the Traditionalists largely having departed in the 1980s, as did the Reconstructionists in the 1960s), it is probably closer to the outlook of Agus than to that of anyone else.

THE CRITIQUE OF HERMANN COHEN

I do not think that any Jewish scholar in America in 1941 was as capable as Jacob Agus of understanding, let alone critiquing, the thought of the most philosophically impressive of all the modern Jewish thinkers, the great German Jewish philosopher-theologian Hermann Cohen (1842–1918). For Agus, the critique of Cohen must have been a particularly daunting task, not only because of the complexity of Cohen's thought but even more because Agus' own view of Judaism seems to come closest to that of Cohen.

Both Cohen and Agus were harsh critics of Jewish nationalism (although Agus did not express anti-Zionism, as did Cohen). Both Cohen and Agus saw universal ethics as being at the core of Jewish teaching. And both Cohen and Agus saw Judaism as providing the most cogent theological grounding of ethics, thus forcefully rejecting any "naturalist" attempts to deny ethics its transcendent intentionality. Hence, if Agus could not show how his own view of Judaism was more convincing than that of Cohen, his integrity would have certainly required that he become Cohen's disciple and devote himself to the dissemination and application of Cohen's philosophy. The fact that Agus did not become a Cohenian, however, indicates that, even in 1941, Agus felt himself up to the task of challenging Cohen.

Agus' critique of Cohen consists of two main points: one philosophical, the other historical.

Agus' main philosophical point against Cohen is that no matter how much force Cohen attributes to the religious relationship with God, it always remains subordinate to the ultimate authority of ethics. For Cohen, as Agus saw quite acutely, the basic function of religion is to handle the problem of human moral guilt, to provide enough of a sense of divine forgiveness and atonement so that human beings as rational practical agents can once again be able to exercise moral autonomy. However, if this is the case, then, as Agus puts it so pointedly, "religion is well-nigh superfluous, since when it appears upon the scene of consciousness, there is no need for it." And he concludes this thought,

"If religion is to be of any significance, its roots must be shown to extend beyond the field of ethics."[11]

What Agus has shown here is that religion can be cogent only if it is first and foremost the relationship between humans and God *for its own sake,* not merely a function of ethics (in the way that it is a function of human self-fulfillment for Kaplan). Only then can religion ground ethics by placing it in the highest (Agus' favorite metaphor) ontological context.[12] But religion can do this only if it is more—but never less—than ethics, namely, by asserting that the religious relationship between humans and God is prior to and inclusive of the ethical relationship between humans themselves, rather than vice versa.

I think that Agus was able to make this type of assertion against Cohen because he was not beholden to Kant as was Cohen, however much Cohen attempted to develop and adapt Kant's own thought. The stumbling block that prevented Cohen from ascribing to religion the ultimacy it insists for itself (and that led him to "deconstruct," as we would now say, the datum of Jewish religion, with all the dangers involved in any such deconstruction) was his refusal to abandon the Kantian idea of foundational autonomy. For Kant, this meant that the only true moral obligation was what one could legislate for himself and all other rational beings in an ideal cosmic order. Agus, conversely, was not so beholden to Kantian autonomy in this foundational sense. Accordingly, despite his high regard for the role of independent human reason in the religious life, Agus would assert that the *ideals* he saw as fundamentally operative in Jewish morality (ideals as opposed to specific rules, which he regarded as essentially human applications of these ideals) were essentially God-made, not self-made, normativity. Along these lines, then, Agus was much more eclectic in his use of philosophy for theological purposes than was Cohen; hence he did not get himself into the type of philosophical conundrum that Cohen did in his unsuccessful attempt to correlate Kantian autonomy with the Jewish idea of the primacy of the convenantal relationship between man and God.

Agus' historical point against Cohen concerned the question of nationalism. Both Cohen and Agus were highly suspicious of the claims of Jewish nationalism to provide a view of Judaism and the Jewish people that would be cogent on both religious and moral grounds. However, Cohen's blind spot was that what compelled him to reject Jewish nationalism, and particularly Zionism, did not compel him with true consistency to reject German nationalism. For Cohen, the German nation-state that had been united by Bismarck when Cohen was a young academic in 1871 was the forerunner of the united humanity that he saw as the very core of the classical Jewish messianic vision. The fact that German unification into a new nation-state also brought with it the full political emancipation of the Jews made Cohen, as the lover of his people he was throughout his lifetime, that much more of a German patriot.

Now it is true that Agus, writing in 1941, had the benefit of historical hindsight that Cohen, who died in 1918, did not have. By 1941, German nationalism had turned on the Jews with a vengeance that Cohen never could have imagined. (In 1942, after being deported as a woman over eighty years of age along with thousands of other German Jews, Cohen's beloved wife, Martha, died in the Theresienstadt Concentration Camp.) Agus recognized this and was charitable in asserting in his critique of Cohen's enthrallment with nationalism that "we, today, [have been] made wiser and sadder by . . . the totalitarian organization of the state."[13] However, Agus still saw Cohen's political blind spot not just as having been historically refuted but also as the result of Cohen's faulty philosophy of history; for as Agus pointed out at the very end of his critique, Cohen went too far in attributing inherent virtue to the modern nation-state (epitomized for him by the modern *German* nation-state) precisely because, in the realm of politics, he placed too little emphasis on the independence of the individual *from* the power of the state. And Agus saw this fault as being theological, that "the cultivation of the ideal of individuality . . . can only be grounded in relation to God."[14] For Agus, then, if human value is to be able to limit and guide human power, the source of that value has to be divine, not human. Thus, in the end, Agus' dispute with Cohen centers on the issue of autonomy. Here Agus returned to an older Jewish idea of human rationality, seeing it as more responsive to an order not of its own making than constructive of its own order.[15]

THE CRITIQUE OF MARTIN BUBER

The very fault Agus found with the political philosophy of Hermann Cohen was the virtue he found in the philosophy of Martin Buber (1878–1965). As he put it when praising Buber's idea of the I–thou relationship between humans themselves and between humans and God,

"The position of Buber must be welcomed heartily. . . . Once man is regarded as solely the object of a scientific inquiry, the basis of human freedom has been undermined."[16] In this remark Agus sees Buber as a needed antidote to the determinism of the social sciences, especially that proposed by sociology and psychoanalysis (both disciplines to which Agus had a lifelong aversion).

It is important to see that in his praise of Buber, Agus is not so much countering the determinism of the natural sciences as he is countering the determinism of the social sciences. That distinction gives him a different edge than Hermann Cohen's earlier critique of determinism; for whereas Cohen could easily counter the determinism of the natural sciences (which, for him, was always epitomized by his philosophical and Jewish bête noire, Baruch Spinoza) with the Kantian idea of moral autonomy and its postulated freedom from physical causality, he was much less successful in countering ultimately totalitarian notions of the moral primacy of the state over the rights of the individual. And whereas the political power of deterministic social science was still quite minimal in Cohen's time, by Agus' time it had become the dominant intellectual force in social and political thought. Agus rightly saw how such a social science, with its rejection of the irreducible dignity of the individual human person, not only was incapable of countering the collectivist claims of totalitarian states but actually contributed to them. Thus Buber's grounding of human personhood in the relationship of the individual I with the divine Thou seemed to Agus to be capable of founding a much more cogent alternative to psychological and sociological determinism than could Cohenian idealism. (It should be remembered that *ideals* function very differently for Agus than they do for Cohen.)

However, no sooner does Agus praise Buber than he reveals Buber's blind spot; for Agus is not only searching for a truly founding relationship with God, he insists that that relationship have a strong rational component as well. Here is where Agus finds Buber to be seriously wanting. As he puts it in a note at the very end of the chapter on Buber in *Modern Philosophies of Judaism,* "The fact that Buber has no theories concerning the nature of the Deity renders his philosophy rudderless and adrift."[17] Shortly before coming to that conclusion, Agus states, "Unless the idea of God becomes a guide to the devotions of men, rather than the resultant therefrom, devotion to humanity will not prevail. . . . The idea of a God of love is capable of invigorating an ethical life, but not of replacing reason as a guide to the good life."[18] That statement needs some unpacking for us to appreciate the true intent behind it. By doing so, we can see the profoundly philosophical thrust of his critique of Buber.

It seems that the best way to appreciate what Agus is saying is to use the medieval notion of the relation of the being of God to God's attributes. For Maimonides, whom Agus always regarded as *the* Jewish thinker par excellence, God's being is affirmed but can never be comprehended inasmuch as God transcends all finite categories. Human affirmation of God's being is, in principle, the apprehension of God's ultimate omnipresence. However, the human import of that initial apprehension, which must have political ramifications (taking "political" in the classical sense of that which is coeval with authentic human existence), requires that there be some revelation of the modes of divine action that can function as exemplars for human imitation.[19] These modes of divine action are what are usually called "attributes," although I think the Hebrew term *middot* is better translated as "qualities." These *middot* seem to be what Agus means by "ideals." Since divine being transcends these qualities, attributing them to divine activity alone saves divine being from ever becoming included in finite categories. (As a contemporary French thinker nicely put it, "Un Dieu défini c'est Dieu fini.") We know and can imitate only what God wants us to know, and that is confined to what God does in the world, not what God is *in se.*

If this analysis is correct, then it seems that Agus is criticizing Buber for confusing the apprehension of divine omnipresence with the revelation of divine qualities. That is why Buber cannot really constitute a Jewish ethics. He knows only the being of God, not the content of revelation. Apprehension of divine being is the reality behind revelation (functioning similarly to Kant's *Ding an sich*), to be sure. But without the presentation of divine ideals—ideals that can be rationally comprehended and practically applied, ideals that can be the normative basis for the life of a historical community such as the Jewish people—revelation is, in essence, blind (like Kant's view of percepts without concepts).

This turns Buber and Cohen into two incomplete halves of the more complete Jewish theology Agus wants. Buber represents a position that has a relationship with God devoid of any real ethical content, whereas Cohen has ethical content devoid of a real, unmediated relationship with God. Agus, with his love of dialectical thinking, is already pushing toward a position that keeps these two poles in a creative tension. In this sense, then, one can see his own philosophical project as being most closely influenced by Buberian personalism and Cohenian rationalism.

AGUS' OWN PHILOSOPHICAL PROJECT

Jacob Agus said that "the intuition of the objective validity of ethical values . . . is the basis of my philosophy and religion."[20] We have seen how this intuition functions as the leitmotiv of his *Modern Philosophies of Judaism*. It gave him the handle whereby he was able quite effectively to critique the most important Jewish philosophies of religion of his day.

Now, Agus himself was very much aware that his argument for the universal validity of Judaism's ethical ideals left him open to the charge that he had thereby argued away any real basis for the continued separate existence of Judaism and the Jewish people. When he says, for example, "This insight has been shared by the great thinkers of humanity, in particular by the religious geniuses of Israel,"[21] we should ask him posthumously (as I asked him when he was still alive), as he asked Hermann Cohen concerning the relation between religion and ethics: Why can we not regard Judaism as having by now done its historical duty and thus move on to the constitution of a universal religion, one that is based on religious experience and ethical reason in creative dialectical tension? Is it enough to say, as Agus says at the very end of the book, "It is the duty of every group to keep alive for humanity the ideals of its peculiar heritage"?[22] Clearly, from everything he has said before, ideals are historically manifest only in "peculiar heritages"; in the full light of philosophical insight, they are essentially universal. Only the universal is eternal; the historical, being essentially temporal, is therefore contingent.

This basic question is one that troubled Agus all his life, as I can attest from our many philosophical discussions (the memory of which I cherish). Thus, some thirty years after his first book, he was still saying, "It is through the Jewish tradition that I grew up to feel the majesty and the message of God. But it is also the same tradition, that . . . kept me from surrendering to the notion that God's Will, in its fullness, is reflected within my tradition exclusively."[23] Here we see that Agus was struggling with the metaphysical problem of the relation of the particular and the universal.

Jacob Agus returned to this problem again and again. It might well be seen as a leitmotiv of his thought as a whole. The struggle became especially acute when he dealt with the traditional Jewish doctrine of the election of Israel, the idea of "the chosen people." Clearly, Agus realized how central this doctrine has been to Judaism throughout its history. Indeed, no Jewish thinker aspiring to any comprehensiveness or depth could possibly avoid its ubiquity in Judaism. Furthermore, Agus realized that election is a relational idea, that one must affirm *both* God's choice of Israel *and* Israel's choice of God. Neither side of the relation could be reduced to the other; they must function together in dialectical tension. Thus Agus wrote, some twenty-five years after his first work:

> The feeling of "chosenness" is the counterpart to the Christian concept of becoming a recipient of Grace through Baptism. . . . In Judaism, it is God who has taken the initiative, by "choosing" the Jews as His treasure-people. In his turn, the Jew feels obligated to respond with deeds of love and dedication to the Divine Call and to vindicate His choice, by enterprises which sanctify His Name.[24]

It seems from this key passage that Agus sees the Jews as rooted in the *particular* experience of being historically elected by God for a mission having *universal* significance. In this way, I think, Agus might well be thought of—philosophically, that is—as more of an Aristotelian than a Platonist; for whereas Plato assumed that the universal can be separated from the particular *through which* it manifests itself, Aristotle assumed that the universal must always be seen within the particular *in which* it manifests itself. Therefore the universal and the particular must always be taken as functioning in tandem. Thus, to use Hegelian terms, Judaism, while affirming the universal, is never subsumed *(aufgehoben)* by it. It always retains its own historical integrity. (This seems to me to be a true characterization of Agus' thought, and I am only sorry I did not think of it while he was still alive, so as to elicit his critical reaction to it.)

Nevertheless, I still cannot accept Agus' tendency to identify truth with the universal.

Now clearly, no one who uses philosophy to understand Judaism can assert that truth is exclusively Jewish. Those who make such an assertion are inevitably the most persistent opponents of anything like a "philosophy of Judaism." The acceptance of philosophical method presupposes the acceptance of the universality of reason. However, more traditional Jewish philosophers than Agus just as clearly asserted that Judaism—that is, the Torah—is the most primary manifestation of truth, and that even though truth has other locations, these other locations are ultimately subordinate to the Torah as Truth *(torat emet)* and can never be allowed to contradict it, even temporarily.[25] In essence, then, revelation is its own justification; it is answerable to no higher criterion, even though it has rational preconditions and ramifications. Without this insistence on the primacy of the Torah as Truth, one runs the risk of ultimately justifying Judaism by a universal philosophy, rather than undertaking the more modest task of simply using philosophical method to explain Judaism.

In the end, I think this was the most fundamental problem with Agus' whole approach to Judaism. However, this is a philosophical problem of the very highest order. The questions it raises cannot be addressed even to the vast majority of Jewish thinkers in any age, much less to ordinary Jewish scholars. That these questions can be addressed to Jacob Agus, both during his productive lifetime and after his lamented death, testifies that he was not only a critic of other philosophies of Judaism but that rare Jewish thinker: a philosopher of Judaism himself. For that he deserves the ultimate honor of being taken seriously by those after him who continue to philosophize about Judaism.

NOTES

1. Published by Behrman's Jewish Book House (New York, 1941).
2. A similar thought, although stemming from a very different philosophical perspective, was expressed by R. Abraham Isaac Kuk (1865–1935) in his *Orot Ha-Qodesh,* ed. D. Cohen (Jerusalem, 1971), 2:440. For Jacob Agus' great appreciation of Kuk's thought, see his *High Priest of Rebirth: The Life, Times and Thought of Abraham Isaac Kuk* (New York, 1972), originally published in 1946 as *Banner of Jerusalem.*
3. Agus, *Modern Philosophies of Judaism,* 39.
4. For Agus, then, the idea of the chosen people was one that had to be justified in terms of the end it served rather than the source from which it originated. See Jacob Agus, *The Vision and the Way* (New York, 1966), 17ff.; *The Evolution of Jewish Thought: From Biblical Times to the Opening of the Modern Era* (New York, 1973), 419–20.
5. Agus, *Modern Philosophies of Judaism,* 50.
6. Ibid., 52.

7. Ibid., 291.
8. Ibid.
9. Ibid., 304.
10. See *Proceedings of the Rabbinical Assembly* 14 (1950): 138–64. For a critique of this responsum, see David Novak, *Law and Theology in Judaism* (New York, 1974), 1:21ff. Agus once told me that although he was the main author of the responsum (the coauthors being Rabbi Morris Adler and Rabbi Theodore Friedman), he felt it should have been issued as a rabbinic enactment *(taqqanah)* rather than as a traditional *teshuvah*. He admitted to me that, along strictly traditional halakhic lines, the case for driving an automobile on the Sabbath was weak.
11. Agus, *Modern Philosophies of Judaism,* 122.
12. See ibid., 339ff.
13. Ibid., 128.
14. Ibid.
15. See David Novak, *The Image of the Non-Jew in Judaism* (New York, 1983), 400; *Jewish-Christian Dialogue* (New York, 1989), 148ff.
16. Agus, *Modern Philosophies of Judaism,* 275.
17. Ibid., 279 n. 13.
18. Ibid., 278.
19. See Maimonides, *Guide of the Perplexed,* esp. 3.54.
20. Agus, *Modern Philosophies of Judaism,* 340.
21. Ibid.., 341.
22. Ibid., 350.
23. Jacob Agus, *The Jewish Quest* (New York, 1983), 72–73.
24. Agus, *Vision and Way,* 19.
25. See David Novak, *Jewish Social Ethics* (New York, 1992), 3–4.

4

JACOB B. AGUS AS A STUDENT OF MEDIEVAL JEWISH PHILOSOPHY AND MYSTICISM

David R. Blumenthal

PURPOSE AND THRUST

IN THE PREFACE to his seminal work *The Evolution of Jewish Thought,*[1] Jacob Agus set the agenda for his entire intellectual oeuvre. It was comprised of two explicit, and one implicit, goals. Of the first goal he wrote:

> In this volume, we propose to show that Judaism in nearly every age resembled an Oriental tapestry in the plenitude of colors and shades it embraced and unified. The comparative unity of law and custom concealed the great diversity of thought and sentiment. (*Evolution,* 6)

In the same preface Agus also indicated that the epilogue of the book would raise important questions and that "some may even prefer to read the Epilogue before the other chapters" (*Evolution,* 7). There Agus repeated his position emphatically:

> As we turn back for a synpotic view of the different currents within the stream of Judaism we note first the fallacy of all monolithic renderings of this tradition. Friends and foes loved to write of Judaism as if it had a single view of life, providing one answer to all-important questions. . . . We have seen a wide variety of theological positions in the long and winding pathways of Jewish thought. How broad is the panorama thus unfolded! How rich is the spectrum of colors! (*Evolution,* 398–400)

Agus' first goal, then, was *to display the sheer variety of Jewish thought in every period,* to dispel the idea that Judaism was monolithic—in its earlier as well as its later periods.

In the same paragraphs in the epilogue to *The Evolution of Jewish Thought,* Agus unveiled the second goal in his agenda:

> How rich is the spectrum of colors ranging from the twilight moods of mysticism to the stark clarity of rationalism, from the lofty heights of universalistic idealism to the dark depths of collective "sacred egoism"! . . . In romantic and mystical Judaism, the Jewish people is elevated to the rank of a "superhumanity" which alone is capable of communing with God. . . . Even the lofty concept of the Messianic era was frequently perverted in popular literature and distorted by the proponents of this view so as to express the bitter frustration of a persecuted people rather than the noble vision of inspired prophets. . . . This caricature of the Messianic vision, however, was rarely allowed to stand unchallenged, uncorrected and untransformed by the refining genius of philosophical piety. (*Evolution,* 400, 410)

Agus' second goal, then—one that he consistently followed in *The Evolution of Jewish Thought*—was *to build a case for moralistic, universalistic, rationalistic Judaism,* whose hero image is "primarily the prophet, fighting for truth and justice, and secondarily the sage, studying and outlining the ideal patterns of the good life" (*Evolution,* 415), at the same time building a case against "the dark cobwebs of Qabbalistic mysticism" (*Evolution,* 397). Agus sounded this theme again in *The Meaning of Jewish History,*[2] where he wrote about "the polarity on the national plane between ethnicism and humanism and the polarity on the religious plane between the self-centered, closed faith of the dogmatists and the open horizons of a living faith" (*Meaning,* 458). Ultimately, "in the Diaspora, Jewish life is founded on faith—faith in the capacity of people to overcome the lingering myths of ethnic arrogance and fundamentalistic fanaticism" (*Meaning,* 482).

In this later book Agus went further and specified the historical context that framed his agenda:

> Hostility and persecution would tend to arouse the feelings of ethnic exclusiveness, causing the Jewish community to become more self-enclosed and more fanatical. On the other hand, whenever enlightenment and tolerance prevailed, the Jews would react by lowering the barriers of

> the inner ghetto-walls, deepening the liberal-humanistic currents of their own tradition and contributing to the expansion of the religious and social horizons of their contemporaries. (*Meaning,* 459)

The context of anti-Semitism and assimilation (in its positive sense), then, set the historical framework for Agus' work in intellectual history.

Recent scholarship has recognized that no history of ideas—indeed, no view of history—is devoid of an ideological stance. If Jacob Agus was clear about the two goals of his agenda and their historical context, it is up to those who read him to ask: What was his ideological stance? What was the implicit goal of Agus' agenda?

The answer seems to me to be very direct, precisely because Agus was very open about his agenda. His history of ideas was intended to accomplish two purposes: (1) to display the variety of Jewish productivity in the area of religious thought and (2) to argue for a tolerant, rationalistic, universalistic Judaism and against an obscurantist, ethnic, isolationist Judaism; and his agenda was clearly set in the historical perspective of anti-Semitism and Jewish acculturation in the modern world. The implicit, and not-so-hidden, goal here is *the justification of the liberal position within Judaism,* which accepts modern scholarship concerning the variety of expression of Judaism in all periods of its history; which positively values acculturation to the best trends of modernity, such as autonomy, democracy, universalism, and tolerance; and which honors the continuity between the modern forms of Judaism and the older elements of Jewish tradition. Agus' scholarship was openly nested in this ideology. He preached and practiced it throughout his years as a rabbi, and it informed his deepest scholarly impulses. The rest was rhetoric, and Agus' rhetoric in defense of his position was both passionate and colorful.

SCHOLARLY STANCE: PHILOSOPHY

Agus devoted two chapters in *The Evolution of Jewish Thought* to the rise and fall of medieval Jewish rationalism and two chapters to the rise of romantic Jewish thought and kabbala. In the area of Jewish philosophy, Agus' summaries are comprehensive and authoritative. His ideological commitment to the liberal position, however, made it difficult for him to see it critically—a task that I shall attempt here for three philosophers: Saadia, Maimonides, and Crescas.

Saadia

In his presentation of Saadia, Agus focused on the rational core of the thought of Saadia. He taught that according to Saadia, reason is a valid source of knowledge about the universe and about God:

> In Saadia, rabbinic Judaism acquired an unexcelled and indefatigable champion who reasserted its basic insights in clear and ringing terms. Saadia's rationalism is of particular interest because it is at once thoroughgoing and dogmatic, uncompromising in its sincere reliance upon rational thought and yet essentially uncritical and narrowly circumscribed. In his fundamental hypothesis, affirming the capacity of reason to explore the nature of the universe and to discover the meaning of God and of revelation, he ranges himself on the side of the rationalists. . . .
>
> Basically, religious truth is as demonstrable as the solution of a mathematical problem. The fear that rational reflection might lead to atheism is justified only in the case of the common untutored masses, who are steeped in myths and superstitions. The Lord revealed His Word, through His prophets, not because it was inaccessible to human reason, but on account of the slow and gradational process of human speculation. Sustained reflection cannot but lead to truth. (*Evolution,* 159–60)

On the subject of language about God, Agus taught that, according to Saadia, God can be described in certain rational language but that all other language about God is metaphor:

> Though God is unlike the material world and everything of which we have any knowledge, we may nevertheless assert that "He is one, living, all-powerful and all-wise, with no thing or action being comparable to Him."
>
> The Scriptures speak of the Deity as if He were corporeal, referring to His "right hand," His "eyes," His "face," His "feet," but such expressions are not to be taken literally. They are attempts to express the qualities and powers of the Deity in terms that are humanly comprehensible; that is, by analogy to physical objects. Since we think in physical terms, we are compelled to refer to Him in words which, in their strict sense, do not apply to Him. How else express His ineffable nature? "If we were to speak of Him in true language, we should have to forego and reject such assertions as the following—that He hears and sees, that He

> loves and wills, with the result that we should be left with nothing but His existence alone." (*Evolution,* 162)

Further, according to Saadia, such religious language may be pedagogical in its purpose:

> As a believing Jew, Saadia was certain not only of God's existence, but also of His having revealed His will through Moses. According to the Torah, some things and some actions are hateful to the Deity, while some things and some actions are pleasing to Him. But how can we speak of the one who is not subject to any qualifications as either loving or hating? Are not love and hate emotional qualities, involving changes in the nature of their subject? Saadia's reply is as follows: "The fact that we find it said that He loves or hates things is to be understood in the sense that everything commanded by Him is called 'loved' by Him and every action enjoined and prohibited by Him is called 'hated' in regard to Him." (*Evolution,* 162)

Some religious language is, however, too specific; it is the language of theophany. Saadia, according to Agus, dealt with this as follows:

> Saadia was disturbed by the fact that the prophets speak occasionally of visions of the Deity. These visions cannot be regarded merely as the vagaries of poetic fancy or as the fantasies of an excited imagination. For if it be admitted that the uncertain faculty of imagination is involved in the visions of the prophets, how can we tell where imagination stops and true vision begins? Therefore Saadia assumes that the visions seen by the prophets refer to an especially created pattern of light and glory, "superior to the angels," which God fashioned for the purpose of verifying His Word to His prophets. This mythical creation of unearthly radiance and splendor is called in Scripture "the glory of God," *Kevod Adonai,* and the sages refer to it as *Shechinah.* It is a mark of honor for a prophet to hear the divine command issuing out of this brilliant effulgence, which may or may not appear in human form. (*Evolution,* 163)

On the subject of revelation, Agus taught that, according to Saadia, the purpose of revelation is to enable people to gain reward:

> As a full-blooded optimist, Saadia boldly asserts that life is good and that the goodness of God's nature is the reason for His decision to create the

universe. But His goodness being infinite, can we assume that He designed for man[3] only the limited measure of happiness that is attainable in this world? To Saadia this assumption was unthinkable. Hence he derived the doctrine of revelation as well as creation from the belief in divine goodness. In His infinite love for His human creatures, God gave them precepts and commandments so that they might merit "final bliss and perfect happiness" in the hereafter. Was it not possible for God to award so happy a fate for man without subjecting him to a special set of ordinances? The possibility cannot be gainsaid, but would it be just or rational? As Saadia saw it, the enjoyment of a reward is doubled when it is truly deserved. . . . Revelation, therefore, is an expression of divine solicitude for human welfare. (*Evolution,* 165)

Further, Agus taught that even the commandments fall within the purview of rationalism:

> The Commandments of the Lord fall into two parts: "rational commandments," the validity of which all rational beings are compelled to recognize, and "traditional commandments," which cannot be justified altogether by the canons of reason. It is the *mitzvoth* of the latter category which were designed for the purpose of increasing the reward of the pious. . . .
>
> In addition to the many opportunities they afford for earning additional rewards in the hereafter, the *mitzvoth* fulfill an educational function here on earth. Thus, the dietary laws serve to counteract totemism, or the worship of animals. . . . One reason for animal sacrifices is to impress upon the sinner the dread consequence of sin, for the slaughtering and dismembering that is administered to the body of the animal should, but for the grace and forgiveness of God, have been done to the one who brings the sin-offering. (*Evolution,* 165–66)

Finally, Saadia's system requires a thoroughgoing and consistent system of reward and punishment:

> In order to make possible a measure of genuine freedom, it was necessary for God to arrange matters so that the wicked would not be fully punished for their sins in this world nor the righteous automatically rewarded. Else people would choose righteousness not for its own sake, but because of the rewards attendant upon it. Therefore, God ordered matters so that the wicked are frequently rewarded in this life for the few

good deeds they occasionally perform, in order that, following their death, they might go straight to hell. Similarly, the righteous may suffer on earth in punishment for those minor sins, which are virtually unavoidable, even for saints, in order to increase their heavenly reward for their patience and forbearance. "With all this, He does not forsake His servants in this world, without rewarding them for their good deeds and punishing them for their evil actions." (*Evolution,* 169)

In summary: Focusing on the rational core of Saadia's thought, Agus taught that (1) reason is a valid source of knowledge; (2) revelation is the same as reason; (3) any language in revealed texts that contradicts reason must be metaphorical or pedagogical; (4) revelation is pedagogically necessary for those not capable of reason; (5) all the commandments have a rational basis; and (6) all the traditional Jewish beliefs, such as the world to come, the existence of injustice, the resurrection, and the messiah, also have a rational basis.

Critique: Agus presented all this clearly; however, there were three important aspects of Saadia's rationalism that his exposition missed. First, Saadia distinguished clearly between *ʾiman* and *ʾiʿtiqad.* The former, connected to the Hebrew root *ʾemuna,* is used to distinguish acceptance of an idea on authority *(taqlid),* while the latter, with no parallel root in Hebrew, is used to denote acceptance of an idea on the basis of reason. For Saadia, as for all rationalists, the purpose and goal of religion were to enable people to make the transition from *ʾiman* to *ʾiʿtiqad,* that is, from "belief" to "conviction." Indeed, the title of Saadia's book, *Kitab al-ʾamanat wal-ʾi ʿtiqadat* (The Book of Beliefs and Convictions),[4] was intended to convey this.

Second, the most vexing part of Jewish rationalism is the vast number of biblical and rabbinic texts that stand in stark contrast to rationalist teaching, particularly those texts that present God anthropomorphically and anthropopathically.[5] Saadia devoted an enormous amount of energy to rereading those biblical and rabbinic texts, even to the point of setting forth the exact sequence of events at the coming of the messiah according to the texts. This exegetical effort is part of the great art of Saadia, especially in the later parts of his book, and an important component of Saadia's rationalism.

Third, Agus correctly noted that even rationalism has a fundament of religious experience as its ground; Agus called this "philosophic piety."

He developed this theme clearly when discussing Bahya Ibn Paquda (*Evolution,* 170–80) and alluded to it in discussing Maimonides (*Evolution,* 203) but missed it in discussing Saadia and the other rationalists. Perhaps this is because Agus saw Jewish rationalism as "enclaves of the life of reason" in a vast sea of "medieval dogmatism [which] imprisoned the minds of Jews and Christians within the rigid world of fanaticism" (*Meaning,* 261–62). Perhaps it was because Agus saw rationalism as the religion of the elite, always in danger of being overwhelmed by the romantic and mystical religion of the masses (*Meaning,* 280). Either way, Agus did not see rationalism as a parallel, an alternative, to mystical Judaism, although he did acknowledge that rational Judaism, too, had an experiential base. In Saadia, the classic text for this can be found at the end of the chapter on God:[6]

> Now, when a person has achieved knowledge of this lofty subject [the existence and unity of God] by means of rational speculation and the proof of the miracles and marvels, his soul accepts it as certain and it is mixed into his spirit and becomes existent in his innermost recesses. . . . Moreover, his soul has a passionate love for it, even unto complete devotion that is beyond all doubt; as Scripture expresses it, "And you shall love the Lord, your God, with all your heart."

Contemporary scholars reviewing Agus' presentation of Saadia will also note that Agus did not present much of the Islamic context of Saadia. I think this was partly due to lack of space, but it is also partly a function of the fact that, until the seminal articles of Vajda in French on that subject, very little was known of the Islamic context of Saadia.[7] In this sense Agus reflected the scholarly consensus of an earlier period.

In two areas, Agus could have drawn a critique of Saadia's rationalism without impugning his own intellectualistic commitments. First, Saadia pushed his rationalism to extremes: the compounding of arguments for creation and God's unity; the "rationalizing" of the details of such matters as the coming of the messiah, the world to come, the moment of death, and the resurrection; and the doctrine of an "impassible" God, that is, a God who cannot be moved by human compassion because God's existence does not admit change. Saadia's effort to put *all* Jewish teaching into one system was admirable—and Agus acknowledges this—but one need not assert that it is all correct to retain a commitment to rationalist Judaism.

Second, and perhaps more important, Saadia's system was very hierarchical, patriarchal, and even punitive in its theology. Saadia taught that sinners will be rigorously punished for all sins, small and large. Every Jewish catastrophe is a function of the sins of the people.[8] When sinners are forgiven it is because of God's mercy, not God's compassion. Saadia even taught the doctrine of eternal hell for sinners, although he admitted that there were probably not many of them. Erotic love and passion are out; the law is in. The opinions of others are excoriated. (Those who deny the validity of all knowledge should be starved and beaten.)[9] Despite the priority of reason, Saadia embodied, in his actions as Ga'on as well as in his philosophy, the rule of absolute authority—patriarchal, hierarchical, punitive, closed, rigid. Here Saadia was far removed from the religious sensibility of his interpreter.

Maimonides

Agus' discussion of Maimonides was fuller. He touched on almost all the key topics in Maimonides' *Guide of the Perplexed.* His comment—"It is the discovery of the self-determination of physical nature that transforms for Maimonides the basic problem of the philosophy of religion" (*Evolution,* 185)—is quite exact, for from this doctrine Maimonides' teaching on the existence of God, the nature of prophecy and revelation, the characteristics of religious language, the reasons for the commandments, and the quality of religious experience flow.

Agus begins with an exposition of Maimonides' views on the vocation of reason:

> Though Maimonides pushed the quest of reason further and more resolutely than all of his predecessors, he nevertheless was far less naively optimistic about the power of reason to comprehend the mysterious depths of being. . . . Reason is more than a series of plainly proven propositions; beyond its limited, luminous core there extends a vast and shifting penumbra, broken by occasional and sudden shafts of light. Extending toward the Infinite, reason merges into intuition or prophecy, or shades into its opposite, the dubious limbo of myth and imagination. . . .
>
> But even if the quest of reason is beclouded with uncertainties, it is still the chief vocation of man to pursue this quest, to the limit of his capacity, for he gives expression to the essential core of his being when

he engages in sustained and rational thinking. The image of God in man is not man's freedom of will, as Philo taught, but the capacity to think objectively and logically. Human reason is capable of ascending far beyond the range of utilitarian purpose, concerning itself with the essence of things. Man becomes steadily more divine, hence more human, as he liberates his mind from the concerns of the moment and contemplates the hierarchy of essences in the universe, which rise to the highest mysteries of God. Thus Maimonides accepts Aristotle's definition of man as a "rational animal" and the corollary which follows from this definition; namely, that the highest vocation of man is the contemplation of the noblest truths of existence. It is true that "human reason has doubtless a border, beyond which it cannot go. . . ." Nevertheless, it is for man to walk the pathway of reason to the utmost limit of his powers. . . .

In thus ranking the exercise of reason as the noblest task of man and the pathway to God, Maimonides did not conceive the problem of theology to be the conquest of reason by faith, but the determination of the proper domains for the functioning of each faculty. In its own sphere of operation, reason is essentially jealous, brooking no rivals in the finality of its analysis and judgment. One cannot drive bargains and patch up compromises with reason, but having determined the field extending beyond its reach, we may allow the postulates of faith to prevail in that area of indetermination. In effect, Maimonides argued for the "right to believe" in regard to matters that are not subject to rational proof or disproof. He did not set out to refute the philosophers by proving that reason is fallible in the domain of metaphysics; on the contrary, he followed reason as far as it goes and expressed the opinion current in the philosophical circles of his day when he declared, "But there is, without doubt, a limit to human reason, beyond which it cannot go. . . ." If we attempt to go beyond this limit, we must still be guided by the balance of probabilities, "believing that which poses the least number of difficulties." But in the twilight realm of doubt, when several equally tenable propositions are presented, the testimony of tradition may be allowed its due weight. (*Evolution,* 181–82, 184)

Agus then expounds Maimonides' doctrine of the existence of God:

Like Aristotle, then, Maimonides proceeded to prove the existence of God by pointing to the universality of the law of cause and effect. If all phenomena of the present moment are necessarily caused by other phenomena, which in turn are the effects of still other events, we have an endless chain of causes. It takes an infinite length of time to contain an infinite series of events; hence, the present moment and its events could not ever be reached if the past were infinite. The reality of the present means that the final cause is outside the wheel of time. In the Aristotelian system, the events of the physical universe are caused ultimately by the Active Reason,[10] which in turn is moved by higher, more ethereal spheres, with all those forces finding their ultimate source in God, the unmoved mover, Who is beyond either time or motion. Each link becomes more spiritual and less physical, more abstract and less mobile, as the chain of causation rises from earth to God. The spheres are kept in motion by the power of love, the love of God, a much subtler force than any that prevails on earth. The differences in the position and motion of the spheres are due to their respective degrees of comprehension of the Deity, but the Deity is absolutely unmoved, thinking only of Himself. (*Evolution,* 185)

Agus sets forth Maimonides' doctrine of creation as follows:

Maimonides accepted the medieval version of the Aristotelian system, going so far as to declare that "everything which Aristotle maintained concerning all that exists from the lunar sphere to the center of the earth is true, without doubt." Nevertheless, he insisted on disagreeing with his master concerning the most basic of all philosophical issues; namely, whether the world was created by God or whether it is eternal. Maimonides pointed out that Aristotle did not really prove the eternity of the universe, contenting himself with the extension of the present observable chain of causality into the timeless past. But the eternity of the creation of the universe is a question that cannot be resolved by reason alone. Either assumption takes us beyond the physical world and its dimensions of space and time to the boundary of the great unknown, where reason cannot penetrate. If we assume eternity, we face the mystery of the nontemporality of God, Who stands outside the chain of causality; if we assume creation, we assume a time when the incomprehensible act of the emergence of being out of nothingness took place. In either case we move into a transrational realm, where our rules of logic fail us. Maimonides decided in favor of creation first on the ground of the balance of probabilities, and second because the doctrine of creation "makes the Torah possible." (*Evolution,* 186–87)

On the subject of language about God in Maimonides, Agus wrote the following:

> We must stress that the principle of divine perfection was fully and unflinchingly accepted by Maimonides in spite of its extreme difficulties.
>
> Manifestly, every activity with which we are familiar involves some form of change. Hence every divine attribute must be interpreted as applying to God in a different fashion from its application to all other beings. Removing all anthropomorphic qualities from our concept of God, we must still think of Him as being "alive, wise, willing and potent," in infinite perfection. But we must not think of these divine attributes as being identical with the corresponding qualities in created objects, where they are inextricably bound up with matter. Maimonides had nothing but contempt for the pseudo philosophers who, disavowing popular anthropomorphism, imagine that they meet the demands of logic when they remove only gross corporeality from the divine being, but continue to attribute to Him the psychical qualities of personality which imply change and materiality. He insisted that the four qualities of life, wisdom, will and power apply to God, "only as homonyms, not in any other respect"; i.e., there is a correspondence but not an identity between the meanings of these earthly qualities and their divine connotations.
>
> So he wrote of the Deity as "existing but not in existence, living but not in life, knowing but not in knowledge, powerful but not with power, wise but not in wisdom . . . one but not in unity. . . ." The net meanings of these paradoxes is the negation of negatives of these qualities; to wit, God is not nonexistent, nor dead, nor ignorant, nor powerless, nor multiple. It follows that we may describe God only in negative terms, indicating what He is not. But this *via negativa,* this way of knowing God by recognizing all that He is not, must not be despised, for it is endless in extent and many-sided. As we ascend the ladder of speculation, we come to perceive more and more concepts and abstractions that cannot be applied to Him. Simple-minded people attribute all the qualities of personality to God; it takes strenuous intellectual discipline to realize that our most subtle concepts, including, of course, space and time do not apply to God Who is beyond these categories of existence. We grow in the knowledge of God as we perceive His "difference" from all things, how all the instruments of our thought fail to grasp His essence. "We understand Him in the measure in which we grasp His final incomprehensibility." (*Evolution,* 188–89)

He then laid out Maimonides' theory of revelation:

> If no common plane, hence no relationship, between the Deity and His creatures can be assumed, how does the Torah portray God as communicating verbally with Moses and other prophets? According to Maimonides, the act of speaking involved physical connotations which cannot be attributed to the Deity. While previous philosophers were content to assume a miraculous "created voice" which echoed the thoughts of God, Maimonides was consistent enough to disavow any such artificial contrivance, save as a hallucination in the imagination of the prophet. . . .
>
> The important point to bear in mind is that, according to Maimonides, the account of the Sinaitic revelation in the Book of Exodus should be read as a parable *(moshol)* and that, in general, "the inner meaning of the words of the Torah are the gems while the literal parables are no more than illustration."
>
> A prophetic vision is always accompanied by symbolic sights and sounds, the products of a feverish human imagination. The divine voice at Sinai was accordingly "not an actual voice, but a simple, rational, prophetic comprehension." We should not be surprised at the "sounds" which the people heard at Sinai, for these were simply effects of the Active Reason playing upon the imagination of the people. *(Evolution,* 190–91)

Agus followed this with an explication of Maimonides' view on prophecy:

> The prevailing concept of the universe was a combination of Aristotelianism and Neo-Platonism, postulating a continuous flow of reason and inspiration from God, through the agency of the spheres, down to the Active Reason and thence to the mind of man. The more a person disciplined and refined the powers of his imagination and reason, the better he prepared himself for the reception of this "flow" of the Active Reason. . . .
>
> Prophecy is thus compounded of both human wisdom and divine inspiration. . . .
>
> It follows that the "divine flow" derives from God, in accordance with His will, like lightning from a cloud, assuming a variety of forms and expressions as it crystallizes in prophecy; for the prophet contributes his own character and imagination to the luminous core of his inspired

> vision. Since the "divine flow" is essentially a forward thrust, aiming at the perfection of human society, it may be incorporated in a variety of inspired actions, as well as in a verbal message. Great creative achievements in almost every field of endeavor are prophetic in origin and quality, or, more correctly, "protoprophetic." (*Evolution,* 191–92)

Following Maimonides, Agus went on to describe the theory of the mitzvot and their relationship to the ideal society:

> Just as it is impossible to assign a valid purpose to every phenomenon in life, though the existence of inner purposiveness within living things is obvious, so too we can find the radiance of purpose in many portions of the Torah, though not in every verse and every detail. However, we cannot but affirm that there is a general purpose for the precepts of the Torah and that this fundamental purpose is "the improvement of the body and the soul" of men. Rationality is the noblest quality of human beings. . . .
>
> Maimonides divided the *mitzvoth* of the Torah into fourteen categories, assigning some rational motivation for each of them. In general, he declared, rituals and ceremonies are related to ideals and sentiments in several diverse ways—as practical guidance is to good intentions, as a concrete illustration is to an abstract doctrine, as a shell is to a kernel, as the body is to the soul. "For ideas without deeds which affirm and fortify them cannot continue to be effective among the people."
>
> It is impossible for great men to attain their full spiritual stature in isolation. A just and perfectly ordered society is needed as the matrix for the emergence of a small number of chosen souls who will attain the perfection of "cleaving unto the Active Reason." This select group of saintly philosophers will understand and continually contemplate the abstract conception of the Deity, outlined above. But the large masses of the people cannot be expected either to comprehend so subtle a concept or to rest content with a God idea that is so completely stripped of all elements that they associate with personality. A facade of opinion or dogmas is needed, Maimonides believed, in order to provide a foundation of ideological unity for the Jewish community. (*Evolution,* 194–95)

Agus concluded his discussion of Maimonides with the latter's doctrine of providence:

> We have seen before that the qualities of compassion and anger are attributable to the Deity only as "necessary" ideas. Does it mean then

that God is completely uninterested in the affairs of men? Is religion entirely a one-sided affair, recording man's search for God, but not the corresponding concern of God for man? To Aristotle, God is indeed completely self-enclosed, thinking perpetually only of the noblest possible object, Himself. But Maimonides operated within a Neo-Platonic modification of Aristotelianism, which assumed a continuous "flow" of divine power down through the successive spheres and by means of the Active Reason. This divine "flow" from God to man consists of a volitional phase, an element of guidance or providence, as well as the gifts of reason and prophecy. It follows that those who cleave to the Active Reason, and in the measure to which they do so, are lifted up to a realm in direct contact with the Deity, sharing in the luminosity of His reason and the serenity of His will. Like the stars and the spheres, their life is raised above the accidents of matter here on earth and drawn into an ethereal circle resplendent with the light and peace of Providence.

While most Aristotelians maintained that the Providence of God extended only to the unchanging species of mankind, not to the transient lives of individual human beings, Maimonides enlarged the domain of immediate divine Providence to include those rare souls who achieved mystic union with the Active Reason. (*Evolution,* 203)

Critique: Agus' exposition of Maimonides' philosophy is both full and accurate. However, there are three areas in this exposition that require comment. First, as in his treatment of Saadia, Agus underestimated the wrestling with biblical and rabbinic texts to make them speak in the language of philosophic Judaism.[11] Maimonides spent almost the whole first part of the *Guide* dealing with the philosophic reading of passages and terms relating to God. He also frames the types of prophecy in terms of a biblical text (Numbers 12:8), and he gives a metaphysical rereading of Ezekiel 1.

Second, while acknowledging an experiential base for Maimonides' rationalism (*Evolution,* 203: "mystic union with the Active Reason"), Agus did not develop this insight fully. Thus, while he quotes *Guide* 1.59, "We understand Him in the measure in which we grasp His final incomprehensibility," he might also have included the end of this sentence: "He [God] has dazzled us with His beauty [alt., 'His perfection'] and He is hidden from us because of the power of His brightness"—a clearly mystical (Sufi) reference.[12] Similarly, while correctly interpreting the love of God as identical to the philosophical knowledge of God, Agus omits discussion of the "worship" of God as a stage beyond knowledge-love of God.[13]

Third, Agus seems to have followed the order of the *Guide of the Perplexed* in his exposition of Maimonides' teaching. This led Agus to affirm rationalism as the guiding principle of Maimonides' oeuvre. I think, however, that Agus was right—that the "self-determination of physical nature" was probably the crucial factor in Maimonides' worldview. Hence an exposition of Maimonides' work should begin with his view of sublunar and supernal nature, pass on to his view of metaphysics, and, then turn to his theology. Using this approach, one sees the core of Maimonides' teaching in the flow of energy that emanates from God down through the heavenly spheres to the earth, particularly to humankind. The point where that energy flow first touches extradeical reality (that is, reality outside of God in Himself) is "creation"; the points where it touches the human mind are "revelation" and "prophecy"; and the point where human metaphysical meditation ("worship") touches the energy flow is "philosophical-mystical experience."[14]

Crescas

Agus' treatment of Crescas is very interesting. He discusses Crescas in the chapter in *Evolution* on the decline of rationalism and makes a strong case that Crescas represents the degeneration of the great rationalist tradition. I am not sure, however, that Agus' view constitutes the consensus of the scholars. J. Guttmann and H. A. Wolfson,[15] for example, point out that Crescas was not against philosophy or rationalism. They note it was precisely the rationality of Crecas' argument against the existence of the vacuum that was crucial—a point omitted by Agus—because this argument meant the end of medieval physics, which, in turn, was the basis of medieval neo-Aristotelian philosophy.

Medieval physics presupposed that all causation was the result of movement and that all movement was imparted from one body to another by touch. Thus the diurnal sphere moved and touched all other spheres until motion/causation reached this earth, where bodies also are set in motion by coming into contact with other bodies. There could therefore be no vacuum in medieval thought, no break in the continuity of motion, no rupture in the contiguity of bodies.[16] The argument for the existence of a vacuum, that is, a space where bodies do not touch and hence cannot communicate motion/causation, spelled the death knell for medieval neo-Aristotelian metaphysics. Crescas' arguments for this, however, were deeply rational.

Still, Agus' arguments that Crescas substituted love for thought as the focal point of Jewish religion (*Evolution,* 216–17) and that *ignorabimus* ("we don't know") is reason enough to accept the validity of prayer, amulets, and metempsychosis (*Evolution,* 225) deserve careful attention, especially since these points are not acknowledged by most other scholars.

SCHOLARLY STANCE: MYSTICISM

Agus' treatment of Jewish rationalism is, as noted, comprehensive and authoritative—partly because he was in sympathy with the concepts and goals of rationalism. His treatment of Jewish mysticism, however, is less satisfactory, probably for the same reason—he was more critical of the theoretical premises of Kabbalah than of the premises of rationalism. As he wrote, reflecting on mystical doctrines:

> As a philosophy of life, Qabbalah was a reversion to the pagan faith that Jewish monotheism set out to combat. It reasserted the doctrine of an ethnic god, who was kith and kin of one people only; it reintroduced the mystery of sex into the nature of the Divine Being; it brought back multiplicity and contradiction into the conception of God; it reaffirmed the principle of mystical inequality among men, some possessing souls attached to the noblest portions of the *Pleroma,* some belonging to the inconsequential mass of mankind; it retrogressed to the notion of religion as a ministry to the needs of God (insofar as He faces mankind), instead of being an expression of man's quest for the good life; it returned to the obscurantist notion that the course of human events was not to be understood in terms of visible phenomena and logical causes, but that, like a hieroglyphic scroll, it had to be construed in terms of esoteric myths concerning occult realities; it reverted to the dismal notion of pre-prophetic religion that the Divine Will can only be known by the authority of the ancients and the frenzy of ecstatics. And all this was motivated in large part by the aspiration to rebuild the faith and dignity of the Jew. Thus did the pathos of collective egotism stifle the heritage it set out to save.
>
> Qabbalah, let us concede, aided the Jew in his struggle for survival under adverse conditions, but it also separated him from any intellectual-

> ethical communion with the emerging society of mankind. It provided an exciting mythology, elevating every Jewish custom and every nuance of the liturgy to the rank of a world-saving enterprise. At the same time, the speculative notions and the debris of ancient philosophical systems contained within its volumes offered substitute satisfactions to the insistent quest of the intellectuals. But these services of Qabbalah were purchased at the high price of deepening the isolation of the Jew. The ritual barriers were raised higher. Even more important, the division between Jew and Gentile was now universally assumed to be one of metaphysical substance and origin. It was no longer a matter of belief that separated the Jew from "the nations," but the fact that the Jewish souls were derived from the Divine Being, while the souls of the nations were sparks from the satanic *Pleroma* of shells, the so called "other side" *(Sitro Ahro)*. (*Meaning,* 294–95)

Two questions arise: (1) How correct is Agus in his scholarly statement of the nature of kabbala? (2) Assuming he is correct, does kabbala necessarily lead to the repaganization of Jewish religion and the separation of the Jew from the blessings of modernity? The first question is scholarly; the second, ideological. The first will be dealt with here, the second in the conclusion to this chapter.

Agus began his exposition of kabbala in *The Evolution of Jewish Thought,* with a chapter entitled "The Romantic Movement"; it deals with Solomon Ibn Gabirol and Judah Halevi. Here, despite his own intellectual reservations about kabbala, Agus provides a fair and accurate presentation of Ibn Gabirol and Halevi: the Jewish faith is unique; the Jewish soul is different from, and superior to, the non-Jewish soul; the Jewish people is the "heart" of humankind and the axis of human history.

In chapter 9 of *The Evolution of Jewish Thought,* Agus expounded the teaching of the kabbala. He correctly identified the sources of kabbalistic authority to be the writings of the ancients on the one hand and lived mystical experience on the other. This he called the "personalistic philosophy" of kabbala. Finally, Agus correctly identified the projection of the Jew and the Jewish people as the "heart" of humankind and the axis of human history into the Jew and the Jewish people as the center of the cosmic drama responsible for unifying all the worlds.

Agus returned to the kabbala in chapter 14 of *The Meaning of Jewish History.* There he went into more detail about specific kabbalistic teachings, organizing his summary into three headings (290–94):[17]

1. *God:* The core of kabbalistic teaching—or more accurately, Zoharic teaching—is the doctrine of the *sefirot.* Agus seems to have understood the *sefirot* as extradeical:

> The Qabbalists agreed that God in Himself could not be the human-like Deity of popular religion. Indeed, they went far beyond the rationalists in denying that any anthropomorphic qualities could be applied to God, as He is in Himself. To the Qabbalists, God is an Infinite Sea of Being *(En Sof),* without any limits; hence, without any qualities, without desire or will of any kind. He is totally incomprehensible. But out of this Being there emanated the Ten *Sefiroth,* in the shape of Primal Man. And it is to this Secondary Deity that all the biblical adjectives apply. . . .
>
> Qabbalah aims to take account of man's existence, especially the destiny of the Jew, in terms of the categories of *life*—the rhythms of the Divine Being and the various emanations deriving from it. To the philosopher, all human history is ultimately reducible to mechanical forces and mathematical formulae. To the Qabbalist, all explanations are ultimately the narration of a series of events in the Divine *Pleroma* (the Emanation and *Sefiroth*), which stands between God and man. . . .
>
> In Himself God was the Endless *(En Sof),* a vast sea of indetermination, to which no adjective could be applied. But out of this Infinity there emerges a Divine *Pleroma,* that is at once God and not-God, and this effulgence is in continuous contact with the world. . . . The Divine *Pleroma* is the mediator between the Infinite God and the world in all its pluralistic diversity and material coarseness. (*Meaning,* 286–87, 290)

This exposition is not without controversy. The *sefirot,* as usually understood, are "intradeical," that is, they are internal to God. They are not emanated from God, separate from God, between God and created reality. They are not attributes, formal predicates of God. Rather, the *sefirot* are parts or aspects of the inner being of God; they do constitute a *pleroma,* but that *pleroma* is intradeical.

Agus then went on to summarize briefly the tension in the realm of the *sefirot* between the Master and the Shekhina and the role of the proper observance of the commandments in reuniting these two aspects of God. Agus also properly noted the sexual and erotic imagery used to describe the process of reuniting the *sefirot:*

> In the second stage, the Divine Personality was articulated in the form of a Father and a Mother, united face to face in love, or separated back to

> back in indifference, depending upon the actions of Jews on earth and on the mystical rhythms of its own life. Below this stage, six *Sefiroth* joined to form the masculine Divine ruler of the earth, "the Holy One, blessed be He," while the last *Sefira (malkhuth)* represented the feminine principle of God, the *Shechinah,* which was the spiritual counterpart of the people of Israel. The saints of Israel, by their labors here on earth, caused the *Shechinah* to ascend and join its heavenly master, "the Holy One, blessed be He," thereby producing all kinds of blessings for the world. . . . Before performing a *mitzvah,* the pietist would say, "For the sake of uniting the Holy One, blessed be He, and His *Shechinah,* through that which is secret and hidden, in the name of all Israel," a formula which certainly strains the logic and imagery of monotheism. In a farther extension of erotic imagery, the Qabbalists taught that, by means of the power of repentance, the upper couple in the *Pleroma,* the Mother and Father, were united, causing a fresh increment of Divine love and blessing to descend to earth. (*Meaning,* 291)

What needs to be stressed here, in particular, is the ultimate vulnerability of God in such a system; for according to the *Zohar,* God, Godself, needs to be "stabilized," so to speak, by the acts, prayers, and thoughts of God's loyal servants. God, in the kabbala, is not the almighty, absolutely independent God of the philosophers and popular theological reflection.

2. *Creation:* Agus pointed to the existence of a satanic *pleroma* that is parallel to the divine *pleroma,* "point for point":

> The creation of the world was not due simply to a series of emanations that proceeded from the Divine *Pleroma,* coarsening and roughening as they descended ever further from their Source. Such a theory of emanation was indeed assumed in Qabbalah from the very beginning, but in itself it could not explain the reality of evil. In all theories of emanation, evil is only the relative absence of good, whereas the later Qabbalists were obsessed with the potency and ubiquity of evil. The "outsiders" *(Hizonim)* were everywhere. Therefore, they assumed that a satanic *Pleroma* corresponded point for point with the Divine *Pleroma.* And much of their strategy in the service of God was concerned with outwitting the ubiquitous forces of evil. (*Meaning,* 291–92)

The *sitra ahra,* as seen by most scholars, coexists with the realm of the *sefirot,* is independent of the sins of humankind, and can influence the divine realm and even assume control of parts of it from time to time. However, it is not actually parallel, point for point; there are no satanic *sefirot*.

3. *Israel and Torah:* Agus correctly identified the key doctrines here—that only Jewish souls have their root in the divine *pleroma,* that the Torah is the sole expression of the divine will and the sole possession of Israel, and that the Jews thus have a special role as redeemers, not only of themselves as persons and as a people but also of the world, of the cosmos, and even of God.

> The entire worldview of Qabbalah was a desperate and elaborate vindication of the role of the Jew and the high place of Torah in the cosmic drama. . . . But the cohesion of Qabbalah consists of the aspiration to "magnify and sanctify" the role of the Jews among the nations and second, the role of the saints among the Jews. The "sacred egoism" of the Jewish people is metaphysically exalted. (*Meaning,* 292–93)

Critique: Whether kabbala is a "philosophy" is hotly debated. Gershom Scholem did not accept kabbala as a philosophy; rather, he understood it to be a system of symbols charged by mythic thinking and energized by theurgical action. For Scholem, then, kabbala constituted a revitalization of the sources of Jewish spirituality, not a flight into fantasy, and Scholem's antirationalistic, prokabbalistic polemic is well documented.[18] Georges Vajda argued that kabbala, while mystical and theurgical, also has distinct "philosophical" streams and tendencies. For him, much of kabbala was a fusion of philosophical and mystical-theurgical thought, not a flight of the one from the other. Vajda was also the first Western scholar to teach that the opposite is also true: medieval rationalism, as noted above, most often had an experiential, spiritual core that shaped and grew out of the very rationalism of philosophical thinking.[19] And Moshe Idel has argued that kabbala is mystical as well as theurgical; that is, much of it revolves around variations on the actual experience of *unio mystica.*[20]

Agus, in his turn, viewed kabbala through philosophical eyes, seeing it as a "system of thought," which, however, because it was not rooted in the "mechanistic naturalism of the Greeks" (*Meaning,* 281), among other possible sources, was not rational and hence was not a "philosophy." This led to his critique of kabbala as "fantastic flights to the upper realms," as opposed to his praise for "the austere and heroic synthesis of philosophic Judaism" (*Meaning,* 289, 284).

Agus also attributed the creation of kabbala to certain historical circumstances: "By postulating a functioning, anthropomorphic Being, the Qabbalists were able to justify the yearnings of popular religion for a Deity concrete enough to be imagined and worshiped" (*Meaning,* 286). Agus repeated this theme many times: that kabbala was created by the rabbis to sustain the depressed masses. He even titled chapter 14 of *The Meaning of Jewish History* "The Triumph of Subjectivism: Qabbalah." This view, however, is the subject of intense debate. For example, Moshe Idel has argued that kabbala developed under a momentum of its own, independent of historical circumstances. It may have proved very appealing to the men who created, studied, and practiced it in a context of oppression and exile (Christian persecution and the expulsion from Spain), but those events did not create kabbala or even generate the primary impulse for it.[21]

CONCLUSION: PHILOSOPHY AND KABBALA, INTEGRATION OR SEPARATION

As we have seen, throughout his work Agus contrasted philosophy and kabbala. This contrast flowed from his ideological commitment to the Enlightenment and expressed itself in his polemic in favor of rationalism and against what he took to be the magical, mystical (and chauvinistic) elements in kabbala. These values also influenced his scholarship—though not as much as one might expect, perhaps because, as one sees in his study of Rav Kook titled *The Banner of Jerusalem* and in his introduction to Rabbi Ben Zion Bokser's anthology on Rav Kook, Agus possessed a deeply spiritual soul that in its own way also sought immediate and intimate contact with the Divine. But are these two modes of being Jewish incompatible, or can they somehow be taken together?

It seems to me that kabbalistic thought, with all its imagistic and mythic thinking, is finally neither a "repaganization" nor a "revitalization" of Jewish spirituality; rather, kabbala is another path, another door, into the realm of the sacred and the personal that is Jewish religion. It is, as Agus wanted us to believe in the preface to *The Evolution of Jewish Thought,* one more of the varieties of Jewish religious experience—to be welcomed into the range of Jewish historical productivity and even to be adopted and adapted by those whose own inner spirituality echoes this kind of religious being-in-the-world.

Another way of looking at the juxtaposition of rationality and mysticism is to seek their common threads. Arthur Green, in his remarkable book *Seek My Face, Speak My Name,*[22] has tried to integrate mystical insight with contemporary rationalism. In this book, Green rereads twentieth-century Reconstructionism in the light of kabbala and kabbala in the light of Reconstructionism.

Yet another way to grasp the variety of Jewish spiritual experience and integrate it into one's personal life is to approach matters seriatim, that is, to be philosophical-rational at times and to be mystical-spiritual at times. The flow of life alternates in everything one does; it should alternate in religion too, even if that generates "inconsistencies." The best metaphor for this is drawn from the ancient craft of sailing. One cannot sail directly into the wind. Hence, to advance in the direction from which the wind is blowing, one must sail at forty-five degrees to one side of the wind for a while and then sail at forty-five degrees to the other side of the wind. This maneuver is called "tacking," and it is a good lesson in wise religious living.[23]

But here I venture beyond Agus' work and engage in my own creative reflections on the religious life. Therefore, let me conclude by acknowledging Agus' real contribution to the study of medieval Jewish thought in both its philosophical and kabbalistic modes. Agus' work is a dignified and learned expression of his authentic spiritual concerns—as was his life, which was devoted to the cause of reasoned religious commitment.

NOTES

1. Jacob Agus, *The Evolution of Jewish Thought; From Biblical Times to the Opening of the Modern Era* (New York, 1959).

2. Jacob Agus, *The Meaning of Jewish History* (New York, 1963), issued in two volumes but with consecutive page numbering.

3. Agus consistently used masculine-gendered language, as was customary when he wrote. Given his convictions about the equality of women, I think he would have used inclusive language today. I am not sure, however, if he would have used inclusive language for God. In any case, I have not changed his style.

4. The rendering by S. Rosenblatt of *The Book of Beliefs and Opinions* (New Haven, Conn., 1948) completely misses the point of rationalistic Judaism.

5. "Anthropomorphic" means having human form, as in "God's hand," and

"anthropopathic" means having human emotions, as in "God's love" or "God's anger." Both are unacceptable in rationalist Judaism.

6. The translation is my own. For another, see Rosenblatt, trans., *Book of Beliefs and Opinions,* 132.

7. Cf. P. Fenton, *Bibliographie de l'oeuvre de Georges Vajda* (Louvain, 1991), at the index, s.v. "Sa'adya Ga'on."

8. The evidence suggests this would be Saadia's response to the Holocaust.

9. The thirteenth theory of creation; see Rosenblatt, trans., *Book of Beliefs and Opinions,* 82–83.

10. Usually called "Active Intellect" but perhaps best designated as "Agent Intelligence." Cf. D. Blumenthal, *The Commentary of R. Hoter ben Shelomo to the Thirteen Principles of Maimonides* (Leiden, 1974), 21 n. 3.

11. One might even speak of Maimonides' *Guide of the Perplexed* as an extended philosophic midrash on traditional Jewish texts and ideas.

12. Cf. D. Blumenthal, *The Philosophic Questions and Answers of Hoter ben Shelomo* (Leiden, 1981), 145 n. 7.

13. Cf. D. Blumenthal, "Maimonides: Prayer, Worship, and Mysticism," in *Approaches to Judaism in Medieval Times,* ed. D. Blumenthal (Atlanta, 1988), 3:1–16.

14. Cf. D. Blumenthal, "Maimonides" and *Understanding Jewish Mysticism* (New York, 1982), 2:3–24.

15. Cf. J. Guttmann, *Philosophies of Judaism,* trans. D. Silverman (New York, 1964), 224–41; and H. A. Wolfson, *Crescas' Critique of Aristotle* (Cambridge, Mass., 1929).

16. Cf., e.g., Maimonides, *Guide for the Perplexed,* 172.

17. These issues are enormously complex, emotionally as well as intellectually. The following are the main works to consult in this area: G. Scholem, *Major Trends in Jewish Mysticism* (New York, 1941), chap. 6; M. Idel, *Kabbalah: New Perspectives* (New Haven, Conn., 1988), chaps. 6–8; and D. Blumenthal, *Understanding Jewish Mysticism,* part two. For the fullest exposition of the thought of the Zoharic stream of Jewish mysticism, see I. Tishby, *The Wisdom of the Zohar,* trans. D. Goldstein, 3 vols. (London, 1989).

18. Cf. D. Blumenthal, "Domesticating Mysticism: The Tension between Spirituality and Social Order," *Conservative Judaism* 43, 4 (summer 1991): 47–55.

19. Cf. Fenton, *Bibliogaphie,* at the index, s.v. "Ibn Waqqar" and "Mystique."

20. Idel, *Kabbalah,* chaps. 3–4.

21. Idel, *Kabbalah,* chaps. 1, 2, 10.

22. (N.J., 1992); reviewed in Modern Theology (April 1993), 223–25.

23. I have dealt with this seriatim approach to life in *Facing the Abusing God: A Theology of Protest* (Louisville, Ky., 1993), chap. 6.

5

JACOB B. AGUS AND JEWISH-CHRISTIAN DIALOGUE: A VIEW FROM THE CHRISTIAN SIDE

Eugene J. Fisher

PERSONAL REMARKS

JACOB AGUS began a short piece selected by Jakob Petuchowski to open his 1988 book *When Jews and Christians Meet* with a saying of a great Hasidic sage:

> My brother repeats verbatim whatever I say;
> My son tells me what I ought to say;
> My grandson tells me what I really meant.[1]

This saying, which was meant to illustrate the admission of ignorance that Agus felt was the beginning point of dialogue, also illustrates the dilemma of the commentator—especially the Christian commentator—on Agus' thought. I worked with Rabbi Agus in several dialogues and so feel myself his "brother," understanding him well enough, I trust, to synthesize his words in the field of my expertise with at least tolerable accuracy. I am also, generationally and intellectually, his heir ("son") as well as his colleague, since I began to read his writings in the field when I was doing graduate work in Hebrew studies at New York University in the late 1960s (never suspecting I would actually meet, much less engage in real dialogue with, such an exalted figure). In that sense of deep reverence, I must acknowledge the difference of our eras and the temptation, therefore, to tell the reader what Rabbi Agus "ought to have said." So I can only leave it to the selections in the companion volume to this one to correct any failures of nuance I might inadvertently perpetrate here.

In my personal library, the earliest example of Jacob Agus' lifelong involvement in Jewish-Christian relations is to be found in the 1956 volume of Monsignor John Oesterreicher's pioneering series Yearbooks of Judaeo-Christian Studies (New York, 1955–70). Titled *The Bridge* (as was each of the first four volumes, the fifth being published after a nine-year hiatus under the title *Brothers in Hope* in 1970), the Oesterreicher yearbooks both reflected the limitations and stimulated the furthering of the Jewish–Christian dialogue in the decade before the Second Vatican Council changed its nature forever.

The reference to Agus in this very early volume is in the form of an extended review of his *Guideposts in Modern Judaism* (New York, 1954) by Father Edward A. Synan, then chair of the Department of Philosophy at Seton Hall University and later professor at the Pontifical Institute of Medieval Studies at the University of Toronto. (It was in the latter capacity that Synan wrote his own, now-classic historical study *The Popes and the Jews in the Middle Ages* [New York, 1965].) After a fair-minded summary of Agus' central points, Synan the philosophy teacher worried that Agus' approach might be a bit too philosophical and not sufficiently biblical to "safeguard Jews on their journey" through contemporary America. And though he expressed both "affection" and "respect" for Agus, Synan was capable of a rejoinder to what he felt may have been an unfair criticism by Agus of Christian beliefs. Synan quotes Agus' statement that "from the Jewish viewpoint, Christianity partakes of the qualities of paganism and mythology" and proceeds to turn around rather neatly what he perceives to have been Agus' point.

I am not sure whether the two, who over the years became good friends in dialogue, ever pursued these particular issues, though I know from Jacob Agus' later writings and involvement in the dialogue that he ultimately would have more than eased Father Synan's mind on both points. In the late 1970s and early 1980s, I was fortunate to coordinate for the Kennedy Institute of Ethics a then virtually unique "trilateral dialogue" of Jews, Christians, and Muslims in which Synan and Agus both participated. The byplay between these two eminent scholars and veterans in the field was, to put it mildly, edifying as well as consistently enlightening. And for the record, in those discussions, which were intense, Jacob Agus sounded to me quite often more the rabbi citing

Torah and Talmud—and most often, indeed, the prophet, moving insightfully to the core of a given discussion to open up its meaning for us from within—than the dry philosopher Ed Synan once worried he might become.

It is in the spirit of celebrating Jacob Agus, the philosopher, rabbi, prophet, and always-willing mentor, that I offer these few reflections on some aspects of his very imposing contribution to the field of Jewish-Christian relations. That "field," it might be added, is itself a rather distinct one, being part academic (since any real understanding between our ancient traditions must rely on scholarly apparatuses to gain any objectivity) and part intensely personal (since it is in the intersubjectivity of the real people who make up our respective communities, as Agus knew so well, that any lasting progress for the future will be made). No one has ever been better suited to such a complex and delicate task than Jacob Agus.

DEBUNKING CHRISTIAN STEREOTYPES OF JEWS AND JUDAISM: AGUS ON JEAN DANIELOU AND AUGUSTIN CARDINAL BEA

In dialogue Jacob Agus spent a good deal of his effort battering down Christian stereotypes about Jews and Judaism, and also Jewish misunderstandings of Christians and Christianity. Given the context of his times and the early stages of the dialogue between our communities, his engagement in the former endeavor is perhaps more expected than the latter, which may come as a surprise to some readers even today. I start with two essays in his collection *Dialogue and Tradition* that illustrate his approach to remnants of the Christian teaching of contempt.[2] These essays reflect his thoughts and concerns from the mid- to late 1960s, at the time and just after the Second Vatican Council issued the declaration *Nostra Aetate* in 1965. The first essay is Agus' response to Father Jean Danielou's and Augustin Cardinal Bea's separate but interconnected writings on the dialogue.[3] It should be noted here that Agus' major task in this essay is a critical response, in the best sense, to two people whose work he generally admired, supported, and encouraged.

In 1967, Agus was asked to respond to the English translation of Father Jean Danielou's 1963 volume *Dialogue with Israel* (Baltimore, 1968). He did so with verve and trenchant yet ironic language (not an easy combination, I can attest!). Danielou was one of the great Catholic theologians of the time and had been an important voice opposing anti-Semitism in France and, through his writings, throughout the Catholic world for some time before that. Further, the writings of Fr. Danielou collected in *Dialogue with Israel* were all written before the Second Vatican Council and (as Agus seems to have guessed) to some extent had a positive influence on the framers of the council's declaration. So the timing and delicate irony of Agus' response need to be appreciated when one reads the exchange today.

Agus quite rightly picks up on the remnants in Danielou's writing of the ancient Christian "teaching of contempt" against Jews and Judaism, which remained despite Danielou's avowed efforts to combat just such negative attitudes. Danielou, for example, trying to argue his fellow Christians *away* from the "deicide" charge (that *the* Jews were and are collectively guilty of the death of Jesus), opened up a charge not much less defamatory. Agus states the situation concisely: "To say as Father Danielou does, 'it is sin that crucified Christ, the sin of Israel, but our own as well,' is to continue the identification of the Jew with sin. This identification is the historical substratum of mythological anti-Semitism. To fight anti-Semitism with one hand and to sow its sinister seeds with the other is to act like that general of Charles V's army who directed his cannon fire against the pope while praying that no harm might come to him" (*Dialogue and Tradition,* 119).

In point of fact, on this Agus had the better of the argument not simply from a Jewish defensive point of view but equally from the viewpoint of Catholic theology of the time. Danielou had seemingly overinterpreted a more nuanced statement found in Article 4 of the official Roman catechism, authorized by the Council of Trent in the sixteenth century. That document read:

> In this guilt are involved all those who fall frequently into sin; for as our sins consigned Christ the Lord to the death of the cross, most certainly those who wallow in sin and iniquity crucify to themselves again the Son of God, as far as in them lies, and make a mockery of him. This guilt seems more enormous in us than in the Jews, since according to the testimony of the Apostle (Paul): If they had known it, they would never have crucified the Lord of glory; while we, on the contrary, professing to know him, yet denying him by our actions, seem in some sort to lay violent hands on him (Heb. 6:6; 1 Cor. 2:8).

To give Danielou his due, most Christians in the intervening centuries had missed the nuance of the Tridentine Catechism. But this only reinforces the need for clear rejoinders such as Agus'. One does not need to reiterate all of the miscues (as we would judge them today) of the priest or all of the incisive retorts of the rabbi to see that the "dialogue" of the time still had as a major goal clearing away the detritus of the past that so heavily burdened Jews and Christians in their attempts to begin to understand one another's traditions.

Indeed, Agus himself seemed fully aware of the transitional nature of this type of exchange of sensitivities: "Perhaps I react so strongly to Father Danielou's words because a recent work I read is still fresh in my mind. It is a short volume by Augustin Cardinal Bea entitled, *The Church and the Jewish People*."[4] And why was Bea's work so important to Agus? Perhaps because Bea was the chief architect of the Second Vatican Council's declaration on the Jews, *Nostra Aetate*. Agus seemingly feared, not without reason, that limitations in Bea's understanding of Jews and Judaism, even though not embodied in the official document of the council, might have persuasive power well beyond the time frame that gave them birth. Let's look at a couple of the things that Agus objected to and see if they are, in fact, prevalent today.

In a section similar to that of Danielou cited above, just when Cardinal Bea, in Agus' words, "attacks the views of those churchmen who assert that the Jews 'must be regarded as frankly inferior to all other peoples from a religious point of view, precisely because it is a deicide people, rejected and cursed by God'," Agus notes ambiguity in Bea's approach.[5] Bea begins in a straightforward manner by arguing that "if then the formal guilt of deicide cannot be unequivocally attributed to the leaders, still less can it be imputed to members of the Jewish Diaspora, and again less to the Jews of other times."[6] The logic here, as Agus acknowledges, is unassailable and also enlightens the denunciation in *Nostra Aetate* of the collective-guilt canard against the Jewish people. So far, so good.

But Agus also believes he discerns a step or two that need still be taken for the sake of clarity. Both of the passages cited by Agus are places, it must be said, where Bea is attempting to frame New Testament language in a way that neither bowdlerizes its evident anti-Judaic polemic nor fosters modern, post-Holocaust anti-Semitism among Christians. This was not then, nor is it now, an easy task. In the context of debunking "a collective guilt arising simply from the fact of belonging to the people of Israel," Bea takes up the sermons of Saint Peter in the Acts of the Apostles and his admonition to his fellow Jews to "save yourselves from this perverse generation" (Acts 2:37–40; 3:19). Peter, Bea argues, obviously believes that any guilt for the death of Jesus must be "in the personal order" and so can only "fall upon anyone who in some way *associates* himself with the 'perverse generation' which is primarily guilty or who directly cooperated in the condemnation of Jesus, as did the Sanhedrin."[7]

Bea's reasoning in this passage with reference to Acts is thus far quite appropriate, since it reduces specifically *Jewish* "guilt" to those "who directly cooperated" at the time, excluding the vast majority of Jews even then and *all* Jews after Jesus' time from any responsibility for Jesus' death (i.e., the deicide charge). Again, this reasoning by the document's drafter is and remains helpful in discerning the intent of *Nostra Aetate*'s terse condemnation of collective guilt. It also preserves the theology of Trent that those Christians who sin knowingly also knowingly "crucify Jesus" in so doing. This theology of the personal responsibility of the Christian sinner for Jesus' death, I would argue, is necessary for Christian faith and our understanding of what is necessary for true repentance.

Where Agus believes Bea gets into difficulties is with an issue *not* explicitly taken up by the council, though *Nostra Aetate* did establish some guideposts that would prove useful in the future. Bea, extending his argument that the issue of guilt must be understood to be always one of personal "choice," continues: "Generally speaking, refusal to believe in the Gospel and in Jesus is a factor in this judgment, and so, in one way or another, is a free decision to ally oneself with the 'perverse generation,' with the powers opposed to God."[8]

Agus felt, understandably, that this phrasing clouded the issue and raised again the specter of deicide even as it argued against it; for the fact remains to this day that the vast majority of Jews do not (and doubtless will not, if the evidence of two millennia is to be taken seriously) "believe in the Gospel and in Jesus." Where Bea seems to have been going with this line of reasoning is not cited by Agus but is interesting in retrospect. The destination can be seen in Bea's conclusion to this chapter on "The Jewish People and the Passion [of Christ]": "The severity of the *judgment on Jerusalem* neither presupposes nor proves the existence of a collective guilt for the crucifixion attributable to the whole Jewish people. . . . It is further explained by the fact that it is a *type* of the universal judgment and is a divinely revealed warning to all mankind of the seriousness of that judgment."[9] While such typological understandings of Sacred Scripture are not as widely assumed today by Christian theologians as they were in Bea's time, his point was important and, for its time, appropriately stated: one cannot argue from New Testament passages—for example, Jesus' weeping over Jerusalem—that the destruction of the city or the Diaspora were God's punishment on the Jewish people for maintaining their fidelity to Torah and declining to become Christians.

This is a line of reasoning that the council itself stated in principle but did not pursue in depth. It argues for an acknowledgment by the Church of the continuing validity over the centuries of the religious bond between the people Israel and the land of Israel.[10] That is, what the ancient Romans did to Jerusalem, while it may have some religious significance for Christians as well as Jews as part of the ongoing history of the people Israel, was *not* God's punishment on the Jews for "rejecting" Jesus. This clarification in turn would allow the Church to develop a positive theological assessment of both the Diaspora and the rebirth of a Jewish state in the land of Israel in our own time. Such an assessment was made explicit by the Holy See twenty years after the council:

> The history of Israel did not end in 70 AD. It continued, especially in a numerous Diaspora which allowed Israel to carry to the whole world a witness—often heroic—of its fidelity to the one God . . . while preserving the memory of the land of their forefathers at the heart of their hope. Christians are invited to understand this religious attachment which finds its roots in Biblical tradition. . . . The existence of the state of Israel and its political options should be envisaged not in a perspective which is in itself religious but in their reference to the common principles of international law.[11]

Agus' critique of Bea goes on to note yet another equivocal reference in the cardinal's book. Bea refers to Romans 11:28–29: "In respect to the gospel, they are enemies [Bea has 'odious'] on your account, but in respect to election, they are beloved because of the patriarchs. For the gifts and call of God are irrevocable." Interestingly, *Nostra Aetate,* while referencing Romans 11:28–29 in its text, actually cites only the latter, positive portion of the Pauline statement to bolster its argument that "the Jews remain most dear to God," that is, in full, salvific covenant with God. I believe this to be another point that was implicit in *Nostra Aetate* itself and made increasingly explicit in the later documents of Pope John Paul II and the Holy See's Commission for Religious Relations with the Jews.[12] Agus, not having the example before him of the more recent papal addresses[13] and subsequent official teaching documents of the Holy See, understandably wondered where Bea might be heading when the cardinal stated that the latter part of Romans 11:28–29 "does not contradict the immediately preceding one. . . . This last passage simply stresses that while God still loves the people for the sake of their fathers, he holds them as 'odious' because he detests their attitude toward the Gospel."[14]

While Bea, in a note to this passage and in subsequent sections of his book, neutralizes the more obvious negative connotations of his framing of the issue in this sentence, based upon history, Agus argues, Christians cannot be too sensitive in their use of language about Jews. Even biblically based language can give support to anti-Jewish or anti-Judaic stereotypes if not carefully couched. Agus states, "I submit that this characterization of Jews loyal to Judaism either as 'odious' or as 'guilty of deicide' even while they are 'dear to God' is a vestigial remnant of medievalism that is incompatible with the emergent liberalism of the Church and its moral-rational integrity. . . . The residual elements of 'deicide' and 'rejection' may be exceedingly minute in the total view of Cardinal Bea or Father Danielou, but as long as Father Danielou retains that hate-soaked rhetoric, he provides a verbal screen behind which pathological and mythological anti-Semites may continue to operate" (*Dialogue and Tradition,* 127–28). If they were here today, I believe Cardinal Bea and Father Danielou would agree.

DEBUNKING JEWISH MISUNDERSTANDINGS OF CHRISTIANS AND CHRISTIANITY: AGUS ON LEO BAECK

While Agus could take on even the friends of Catholic-Jewish dialogue in the Church for their use of negative or ambiguous language about Jews and Judaism, he was equally capable of reminding his fellow Jewish scholars of their need to attend more carefully to what they said about Christianity and Christians. In an essay in *Dialogue and Tradition* aptly titled "Mutually Challenging, Not Mutually Contradictory," for example, he introduced an analysis of the views on Christianity of Leo Baeck (whom Agus refers to as "the saintly rabbi of Berlin and Bergen Belsen") by stating:

> As Christians were wont to glorify their faith by using a caricature of Judaism for their foil, so Jewish scholars were tempted to do likewise. They identified the many-sided historic heritage of Judaism with their own modernist "enlightened" faith, and then they proceeded to contrast it with a primitive or medieval version of Christianity. (*Dialogue and Tradition,* 57)

That Agus' essentially constructive critiques of positions taken by fellow Jewish scholars toward Christianity remain as pertinent and probing today as when they were written is amply illustrated not only by the fact that Leo Baeck's and Martin Buber's works (which Agus also criticized; cf. 19, below) remain widely available in print but also by the fact that they were two of a list of five Jewish thinkers on Christianity recently selected for a major anthology, *Jewish Perspectives on Christianity.*[15] Perhaps one reason for my deep admiration of Agus' ability to critique so honestly the Jewish representatives he did (and *when* he did) comes from the fact that my own first publication in the field was an article in 1973 titled "Typical Jewish Misunderstandings of Christianity," which reflected my experiences as one of the very few Christians at the time in New York University's Institute of Hebrew Studies.[16] I was not familiar with Agus' writings on Baeck and Buber at the time but am fascinated by how close many of his points were to my own. I say this to emphasize that for the period in which he wrote so much of his large output—that is, at the very beginnings of what I would call serious dialogue between the Catholic Church and the Jewish people as two communities of faith—Agus had a remarkably good "ear" for understanding what we Christians were really trying to say. It was and remains a rare gift to find someone so thoroughly imbued with his own tradition and yet so able not only to comprehend but to empathize with another tradition—especially in view of the tragic history between the two.

Agus begins his brief but incisive critique of Baeck's analysis of the "contrast" between Judaism and Christianity with a description of Baeck's distinction between what the latter felt were "two kinds of religion—the classical and the romantic."[17] For Baeck, romantic religion indulged in the "sentimental," the "phantastical," and "exultant emotionalism." This, of course, was Christian religion, whose "dynamic core" was to be found in "the Dionysiac orgies of the pre-Socratic Greek world" in which "laws are suspended by miraculous action . . . shrouded in mystery and turned into sacraments." Christianity for Baeck, and especially "Pauline faith," was "genuinely romantic," "founded . . . on passivity," a "mystery religion . . . without any real access to . . . culture." The small stirrings of "social consciousness" that one could, after diligent search, find in the Christian world from time to time were "merely the exceptions which prove the rule; for they have grown on the Old Testament soil of Calvinism and Baptism." All of this is contrasted by Baeck to the reasonableness and "classicism" of Judaism.

In Baeck's defense, Agus notes the impossible context in which Baeck was forced to work by the Christian world, which he understandably lampooned in his writings. "It was," Agus states, "the sad fate of Dr. Leo Baeck to endure the incredible horrors of the Nazi frenzy, and as a sensitive scholar, he was aware of the deep roots of Nazism in the romantic movement of the nineteenth century. We can therefore understand why he was so bitterly sensitive to the sickly stigmata of German, especially Lutheran, romanticism."

Without for a moment denying the dangers inherent in the elements of "romanticism" (as Baeck defined it) within Christianity, Agus sets the issue in a wider and, I believe, healthier perspective for us today: "In general, Baeck's way of contrasting Judaism and Christianity breaks down because it does not take into account the many variations within the two faiths." That is, Baeck has indulged in stereotyping—understandable within his time, but stereotyping nonetheless. Agus goes on to point out that Judaism "as a historical faith contained romantic, mystical and mythical strands as well as those of classical wisdom. Had it been conceived in the wisdom of moderation and classical balance, Judaism would not have produced the saintly martyrs that assured its survival." Both traditions, Agus argues persuasively, flourished precisely by being able to "synthesize" Hellenistic logic and biblical fervor. And both, he concludes aptly for us today, "are perpetually in danger of succumbing to the disease of fossilization": a "frozen creed" for Christians and a "rigid legalism" for Jews.

One passage of Agus' on Paul—whom Baeck, like so many Jewish scholars, wanted to scapegoat as the sole source of all that went wrong with Christianity and Christians over the centuries—deserves to be cited here at some length, since I would wager that most of the Jewish readers of this volume to some extent still share Baeck's polemical attitude toward Paul and so may profit from Agus' perpetually fresh look at the evidence. Likewise, many of the Christian readers will benefit equally from the freshness of Agus' insights into the "apostle to the gentiles":

> The romantic-mystical faith of Paul can be understood only when it is viewed within the perspective of the feverish expectancy of his time. Paul gave his life to save as many Jews and Gentiles as possible before the final curtain of Judgment Day was lowered. . . . He admonished his converts to abide by the noblest ethical teachings of Judaism. His hymn on love or charity was a magnificent expression of a "great rule of the Torah" *(Torat Kohanim, Kedoshim 19)*. . . . When he spoke of the impossibility of fulfilling the Law, he cited as an example the prohibition of "coveting," a prohibition that belonged to "duties of the heart," which were infinite in scope. To the truly pious, the Law was unfulfillable, precisely because it contained this infinite dimension of interior feeling. . . . In Judaism too the saints thought they were sinners and the sinners thought they were saints. I cannot agree that Paul was unconcerned with ethics and with people. (*Dialogue and Tradition,* 59–60; cf. 66ff.)

As we shall see, Agus does provide "contrasts" between the relative emphases Judaism and Christianity will put on various spiritual truths, but he does this within a theory of dynamic tension in which each "side" has something to learn from and something to teach to the other—not quantitatively a quid pro quo, of course, but "mutually challenging" nonetheless.

AGUS' VISION OF JEWISH-CHRISTIAN DIALOGUE

Agus appears to have had great respect for and affinity with the writings of Martin Buber, whose views on ethics Agus anthologized in *The Vision and the Way*[18] and whom he cited approvingly on a wide variety of topics over the years. But although he understood Buber's notion of dialogue, Agus had his own vision. By dialogue, he did not mean the intersubjective encounter of Buber's "I and Thou" (though Agus did not eschew the value of such encounters). Rather, Agus defined dialogue primarily as "a truth-seeking effort" carried out between communities of people in an "attempt to understand and to appropriate the truths of others as well as to exhibit the truth of one's own heritage." He was fully aware that such an endeavor must result "at any one time in partial, relative truths," not the real but humanly unattainable "absolute truth" of philosophy.

In contrast to the either-or, zero-sum approach to Judaism and Christianity adopted by Martin Buber in his *Two Types of Faith*—in which, in a neat reversal of Baeck's approach, the Christian "faith" of *pistis* is described as dry, academic, and pessimistic, as opposed to the dynamic, relational, and existential *emunah* of Judaism[19]—Agus' approach to the two traditions stressed their mutually challenging aspects. His was an attempt to bring out the best in both.

Agus' first major essay in a volume dedicated to interreligious dialogue is not itself dialogical but rather a straightforward essay on Jewish history and thought. Titled "The Concept of Israel," it was designed to explain Judaism to Christians at a symposium of scholars of the two traditions held in January 1965 at Saint Vincent's Abbey in Latrobe, Pennsylvania. The participants at this pioneering theological exchange were significant. On the Jewish side were Solomon Grayzel, Solomon Freehof, Samuel Sandmel, Robert Gordis, Marc Tanenbaum, Gerard Sloyan, and Arthur Gilbert. On the Catholic side were the Catholic bishop of Greensburg, Pennsylvania, where the monastery was located (its then abbot, Rembert Weakland, O.S.B., is now archbishop of Milwaukee and chairs the Ecumenical Committee of the National Conference of Catholic Bishops); Bishop (later Cardinal) John J. Wright; John Sheerin, C.S.P.; Aidan Kavanagh, O.S.B.; Roland Murphy, O. Carm.; John Cronin, S.S.; and Gerard Sloyan, who would also be a member of the Kennedy Institute "trialogue" a decade and a half later.[20] I mention the occasion and the participants because this was one of the earliest in-depth theological dialogues in the spirit of the Second Vatican Council, having taken place just before the issuance of *Nostra Aetate,* and to my knowledge, it was the very first to be published after the Council (the imprimatur was given by Bishop William G. Connare on January 17, 1966). There is, then, a historical aspect to the symposium and to Jacob Agus' inclusion in it, worth mentioning in a volume such as the present one.

Agus, it should be noted, also presented one of six Jewish papers delivered in January 1972 in New York City at the first National Colloquium on Greek Orthodox–Jewish Relations. Organized by the American Jewish Committee, the Jewish delegation included Marc

Tanenbaum, Zvi Ankor, Seymour Siegel, Salo Baron, and Eric Werner. The Greek Orthodox contingent included Archbishop Iakovos, Bishop Maximos, D. J. Constantelos, Stanley Harakis, Theodore Stylianopoulos, D. J. Geanakoplos, and George Bebis.[21]

In attempting to understand Agus' approach to dialogue, it must be made clear that he did not enter into it with any naïveté about Christian history or past misdeeds. His essay "New Grounds for Jewish-Christian Understanding" (*Dialogue and Tradition,* 66–93) opens with an evocation of "the melancholy records of history": "The Hitlerian interlude shocked many people into the belief that the dragon-seeds of mythological anti-Semitism are deeply imbedded in the mass-mind of Christian people" (66). Yet he argues just as passionately that only theological dialogue provides a realistic opportunity to surface and combat such mythological views of the other. In the context of a discussion of chosenness and messianism in the two traditions, Agus comments that "considered as myths, Judaism and Christianity contradicted each other—the one operating on the assumption that the other had been tragically and woefully misled and perverted. . . . Only one group could be right, absolutely so. . . . As dynamic faiths, moved by the quest for truth and reality, Judaism and Christianity can regard each other as allies in the battle against nihilism and the quasi-religions of our day" (88). "The opposite of these complementary concepts of *vocation* and *Messianism* is the couplet of religious *indifferentism* and *pseudo-Messianism*" (92). That, I would argue, is as bold a conclusion today as it was twenty years ago.

THE NECESSITY OF THEOLOGICAL DIALOGUE: AGUS' RESPONSE TO JOSEPH SOLOVEITCHIK

In the opening essay of *Dialogue and Tradition,* "The Case for the Dialogue" (11–17), Agus makes reference to "one objection in principle" that had "been raised to the dialogue movement" (11). This was the objection to "theological" dialogue issued by Rabbi Joseph Soloveitchik in an article published in the Orthodox journal *Tradition* in the year before *Nostra Aetate* was promulgated by the Second Vatican Council.[22] The context of Soloveitchik's objection therefore was more that of the medieval disputation than an awareness of the nature and possibilities of theological dialogue as we have known it now for a generation since the council.

Without mentioning Rabbi Soloveitchik by name, Agus takes his views seriously but responds tellingly. The Soloveitchik article had argued that while it would be permissible for Jews to cooperate with Christians on social action of mutual concern, purely "religious" or theological dialogue was precluded. What prevented such dialogue for Soloveitchik was not the dictates of halachah but the nature of the exchange. Religious dialogue was, simply put, impossible and therefore not to be attempted. It was impossible, Soloveitchik argued, because religion is an entirely subjective and personal phenomenon, "what the individual does with his isolation" (*Dialogue and Tradition,* 11). This isolated nature of religion, Soloveitchik argued, is true communally as well as individually. Every religion has its own pattern of rhetoric, values, symbols, and nuances stemming from its own history and nature. These are, by definition, incommensurable and incommunicable to people outside the particular faith community. But any real dialogue requires a common realm of discourse. Thus dialogue is impossible between different religious communities.

Agus responds to this argument first by acknowledging what is valid in it. "This insight is true and precious," he states, "but one-sided." What is true is that the inner dimension of faith "can only be experienced; it can neither be weighed nor measured" and thus cannot be compared with another such experience. But this "inner experience" does not, for Agus, preclude the fact that "religion does possess an objective or universal phase, which is essential to its nature as a meaningful philosophy of life."

Agus goes on to argue that the Jewish religion itself "has always undertaken to appeal to the intellect as well as to the private promptings of the soul. . . . Its very character as a faith derived from its emphasis on reason and ethics; hence its condemnation of magic and its repudiation of the comforting myths that appealed so powerfully to man's feelings and phantasies." Agus gives as an example the communicability of the scholastic philosophy of the high Middle Ages: "As one reads the medieval works of Jewish philosophy, one can easily translate the same arguments into their equivalent formulations in Christian or in Moslem thought."

Agus is precisely correct on this point, as I discovered while studying Jewish philosophers such as Bahya ibn Pakuda with rabbis at New York University in the late 1960s. I had previously studied scholastic philosophy and theology in a Catholic seminary, and in my work at

New York University, I was at times able to grasp the thrust of arguments such as Pakuda's more easily than my classmates, simply because of my exposure to the larger philosophical school of which he, no less than the Christian scholars I had studied, was a part.

Agus then—and again rightly, in my opinion—goes after the supposed distinction made by Soloveitchik between Jewish philosophy and theology:

> It is said that philosophy may be discussed, but not theology. What then is Jewish theology? Is it the priestly component of the tradition as distinct from the prophetic and philosophical ones? . . . The peculiar reasoning of the Halachah? . . . Personally, I consider that "Jewish Theology" consists of the various *taamai hamitzvot* ("reasons for the Commandments"), for it is in this area that general philosophy and the historical faith converge. Should a rabbi, then, refrain from discussing the various reasons for, let us say, the dietary laws? I see no reason why he should.

Agus does note that he would expect "all Orthodox rabbis" to concur in the judgment that Christians are not to be placed in the category of "worshippers of stars," whom the Talmud would not permit to be instructed in the precepts of Torah.[23] He asks whether the Catholic Church seeks to "promote the dialogue movement as an instrument of conversion" and answers in the negative. Even though he feels that the Church may well still "desire the conversion of Jews," he concludes quite properly that for the Church "the dialogue movement is a good in itself, valid within the human context." Here again is where Agus' direct involvement in the dialogue over the years gives him such a great edge over even someone of the stature of Rabbi Soloveitchik, who simply did not have the advantage of the three decades of dialogue that we enjoy today on which to base a judgment.

The issue of "theological" dialogue between Catholics and Jews is still very much debated within the Jewish community. As a Catholic, it is not my business to become involved in the debate in any formal way, although my own practice of and dedication to dialogue is, I trust, apparent to all. I shall leave the last word on this topic to Jacob Agus, with only the explanatory note that the "accidental . . . accumulated encrustations of history" that he mentions as needing to be separated from the "genuine message" of religion would seem to refer to the Christian teaching of contempt against Jews and Judaism. Agus quite rightly understood that to counter misinformation about Jewish beliefs and practices, better information needs to be given to Christians by Jews:

> The attempt has been made to delimit the area of dialogues by drawing the line of demarcation between social problems and concerns, on the one hand, and principles of belief, on the other. But the purpose of dialogue is to achieve a larger measure of understanding. To understand one another we have to refer to first principles, which are matters of faith; furthermore, there is a history to every problem, and historic attitudes to live down as well as historic affirmations to live up to. Hence, there is the need of revealing criteria, whereby the essential is separated from the accidental, and the genuine message of religion is distinguished from the accumulated encrustations of history. As a matter of fact, differences in regard to contemporary issues constitute the greatest source of interreligious friction today. It is therefore impossible to set arbitrary limits to the scope of the dialogue, nor is it necessary, since the discussants generally choose their topics by unanimous consent. (17)[24]

DIALOGUE AS THE SEARCH FOR COMPLEMENTARITY

Jacob Agus maintained his methodological refusal to dichotomize Judaism and Christianity with admirable consistency over the years, using terms such as *dialectics* to indicate the dynamic quality of the relationship. For example, he concluded his 1966 book on Jewish ethics, *The Vision and the Way,* with a brief section on "comparison of Jewish and Christian ethics." Noting the extreme difficulties of such an enterprise, given the great antiquity and consequent internal plurality of views of each tradition on a given issue, he risks the generalization that

> the differences in the nuance of each (ethical) ideal within the two traditions are fruitful and enriching for both. If love in the Christian tradition evokes the images of self-giving and self-denial, and if in Judaism it evokes primarily devotion to the building of the community, the two traditions gain in depth as they welcome each other's insights. In the infinite quest for perfection, people can only follow one pathway at a time, but by imaginative empathy they can feel the zest and grandeur of their confreres climbing by other paths toward the same broad summit. (*Vision and Way,* 360)

In the process of applying his methodology of approaching the two traditions, which he generally did, as we have seen, within the context of actual dialogues (thus exposing his work to Jewish and Christian respondents at the same time—an exposure that, I can attest, greatly aids one in achieving both nuance and balance), Agus came up with scores of penetrating insights into the relationship, many of which have still to be adequately explored today. For the companion anthology volume to this one, I have selected two of Agus' works on the New Testament and so will not go into those here. A couple of examples from *The Jewish Quest* will have to suffice for many that could be chosen. They will also suffice, I believe, for a conclusion to the present study of Agus' vision of dialogue:

> We have to transcend the rhetoric which foisted upon us mountains of misunderstanding. It is said that for Christians, the world is already redeemed, while for Jews it is unredeemed. This is a specious juxtaposition. We might say with equal justification that for Christians, the world is in a "fallen" and corrupt state, while for Jews, the world is "very good." Actually, the tension in Judaism between an unfinished universe and a radiant vision of redemption was retained in the Christian philosophy of history, as presented in Augustine's *City of God*. . . . To be sure, Judaism and Christianity project different categories for the judgment of the course of history, but the categories are mutually supplementary at times, mutually challenging at times, and the variations within both faiths are so vast as to render meaningless the ancient controversies about the "fulfillment" of Scripture verses. (*Jewish Quest,* 140)

> Christians turn in hope to the second Advent and Jews to the coming of the Messiah. Both are joined in the certainty that there can be no salvation for any nation or faith save in the salvation of all mankind. Both can accept each other as partners in the task of preparing the way for His Kingdom. The task is so great that the contributions of all historic groups are indispensable. (*Jewish Quest,* 58)

NOTES

1. Jacob B. Agus, "Between Faith and Skepticism," in Jakob J. Petuchowksi, ed., *When Jews and Christians Meet* (Albany, 1988), 3–7. Agus notes that this essay synthesizes a longer essay from his *The Jewish Quest: Essays on Basic Concepts of Jewish Theology* (New York, 1983), 43–61.

2. Jacob B. Agus, *Dialogue and Tradition: The Challenges of Contemporary Judeo-Christian Thought* (London, 1971).

3. Ibid., 114–29.

4. Agus refers to Augustin Bea, *The Church and the Jewish People* (New York, 1966), in *Dialogue and Tradition,* 126.

5. Cf. Bea, *Church,* 68.

6. Ibid., 70.

7. Ibid., 78.

8. Ibid., 85.

9. Ibid., 88.

10. "Although the Church is the new people of God, the Jews should not be presented as rejected or accursed by God as if this followed from Sacred Scripture" (*Nostra Aetate,* no. 4). This provides an authoritative hermeneutical guide today for Catholic scholars approaching such texts as Luke 19:44, which was cited specifically by the council and thereby given this binding interpretation. The text of Luke reads: "As he drew near, he saw the city [of Jerusalem] and wept over it, saying: if this day you only knew what makes for peace—but now it is hidden from your eyes. For the days are coming upon you when your enemies will raise a palisade against you; they will encircle you and hem you in on all sides. They will smash you to the ground and your children within you, and they will not leave one stone upon another within you because you did not recognize the time of your visitation" (Luke 19:41–44). This "lament," which is found only in Luke, is redolent of prophetic utterances (e.g., Jer. 14:17; 15:5; Isa. 6:9–10; 29:3), which is the basis for Bea's comment that the "gravity" of the "judgment of Jerusalem" is "explained by the fact that it is the culmination of a whole history of opposition and disobedience to God and of crimes committed against his messengers" (this last presumably in reference to the sermons of Peter and Stephen in Acts). Again, the very force of the hermeneutic of *Nostra Aetate* with regard to Luke 19 would today be seen as necessarily precluding Bea's own "explanation" by removing the category "judgment on Jerusalem" as a viable theological utterance. Obviously, if there is no "collective guilt" for the Jews to be punished for, then there is no "judgment" leading to punishment.

The significance of the conciliar statement and its clarification twenty years later by the Holy See (see note 11, below) cannot be overstated. Dating back to the fulminations of Saint John Chrysostom (actually, before; he just said it more strongly and effectively than anyone else), precisely this text of Luke's and others that could be associated with it had been used by Christians as key elements of their anti-Judaic polemic (the "teaching of contempt," as we could call it today). Arguing backward in a sort of counterclockwise circle, the church fathers and their medieval successors opined that because the city of Jerusalem was destroyed and the Jews dispersed, God must have wanted to punish them.

And what better cause for divine punishment could there be than the fact that the people Israel had missed its "visitation" by God's own son? The council's definitive and unequivocal removal of this ancient polemic from Church teaching, of course, simultaneously removed any shred of *theological* hesitancy the Church might have for recognizing the legitimacy of the people Israel's covenantal bond with the land of Israel. It is therefore highly significant that when Pope John Paul II visited the Great Synagogue of Rome in 1986 (the first bishop of Rome to do so in the history of the papacy since Saint Peter, who was quite possibly a regular), the selected reading was from Genesis 17, including the verse on the giving of the land to the Jewish people "as a permanent possession."

11. Holy See's Commission for Religious Relations with the Jews, *Notes on the Correct Way to Present Jews and Judaism in the Preaching and Catechesis of the Roman Catholic Church* (June 24, 1985), no. 26. The two works cited in note 12, below, contain this text, as well as *Nostra Aetate* and other relevant major Church documents.

12. For an analysis of the process of drawing out the text of *Nostra Aetate* with ever greater explicitness and clarity, to resolve the concerns expressed by Rabbi Agus and others in the dialogue, see Eugene Fisher, "The Evolution of a Tradition from *Nostra Aetate* to the 'Notes,'" in *Fifteen Years of Catholic-Jewish Dialogue, 1970–1985,* International Catholic-Jewish Liaison Committee Papers and Documents (Vatican City, 1988), 239–54. A more popular and extended discussion of this and similar issues of the development of Church doctrine on Jews and Judaism since Vatican II can be found in Eugene Fisher and Leon Klenicki, *In Our Time: The Flowering of Jewish-Catholic Dialogue* (Mahwah, N.J., 1990), 3–26.

13. Cf. Eugene Fisher and Leon Klenicki, eds., *John Paul II on Jews and Judaism, 1979–1986* (Washington, D.C., 1987), for a collection of papal texts and commentary on them.

14. Bea, *Church,* 94.

15. Fritz A. Rothschild, ed., *Jewish Perspectives on Christianity: Leo Baeck, Martin Buber, Franz Rosenzweig, Will Herberg, Abraham Heschel* (New York, 1990). The editor likewise understood the need for critical response, since he chose five Christian scholars (J. Louis Martyn, Ekkehard Stegemann, Bernhard Casper, Bernhard Anderson, and John Merkle, respectively) to "introduce" the selections from the works of the five Jewish thinkers. For a compilation of more contemporary Jewish perspectives on Jewish-Christian relations, see Leon Klenicki, ed., *Toward a Theological Encounter: Jewish Understandings of Christianity* (Mahwah, N.J., 1991). Klenicki includes essays by Norman Solomon, Elliot N. Dorff, Walter Jacob, David Novak, Michael Wyschogrod, S. Daniel Breslauer, and David G. Dalin. The figures in the Rothschild collection, of course, are among the most prominently cited in the Klenicki volume, so there is a healthy

continuity and exchange of views between the generations represented in the two works.

16. Eugene J. Fisher, "Typical Jewish Misunderstandings of Christianity," *Judaism* (spring 1973): 21–32.

17. Agus deals especially with Leo Baeck's *Judaism and Christianity* (Philadelphia, 1958), 190–215. I cite here from Agus, *Dialogue and Tradition,* 57–62. Both references are short enough to find citations easily, so I will not give page-by-page notes from these two selections.

18. Jacob Agus, *The Vision and the Way: An Interpretation of Jewish Ethics* (New York, 1966), 300–320.

19. Martin Buber, *Two Types of Faith* (New York, 1961). The collection *Martin Buber: A Centenary Volume,* edited by Haim Gordon and Jochanan Bloch, contains helpful analyses of Buber's comparative approach to Judaism and Christianity by Maurice Friedman (367–84), Lorenz Wachinger (437–56), and Michael Wyschogrod (457–72). Wyschogrod's essay is especially helpful on Buber and Saint Paul. A very strong Christian critique of Buber's dichotomized version of Jewish versus Christian faiths was given by John M. Oesterreicher in his Buber Centennial Lecture at Tantur, Israel, titled "The Unfinished Dialogue: Martin Buber and the Christian Way." Agus' "complementary, not contradictory" approach to Jewish-Christian relations likewise distinguished his position from the absoluteness of Buber's dichotomy between the two religions. In "Between Faith and Skepticism," Agus stated tersely, "Nor do we accept Martin Buber's distinction between the Greek type of piety, or *pistis,* and the Hebraic expression of trust, *emunah.* It is in history that contexts arise, and their meanings change imperceptibly" (5).

20. Philip Scharper, ed., *Torah and Gospel: Jewish and Catholic Theology in Dialogue* (New York, 1966).

21. "Greek Orthodox Jewish Consultation," *Greek Orthodox Theological Review* 22, 1 (spring 1977), special issue.

22. Joseph Soloveitchik, "Confrontation," *Tradition: The Journal of Orthodox Jewish Thought* 6, 2 (spring–summer 1964): 10–24. The philosophical study in religious anthropology begun in the 1964 piece was carried further in Soloveitchik's "The Lonely Man of Faith," *Tradition* 7, 2 (summer 1965): 5–67; but that piece, profound as it was, is not pertinent to the substance of the present discussion. (In 1992 it was republished in a separate volume by Doubleday.)

The 1964 Soloveitchik dictum still prevails as the ruling rubric for participation in the dialogue by the Synagogue Council of America, which includes Orthodox bodies, and therefore for the International Jewish Committee for Interreligious Consultation (IJCIC), which, as an umbrella group, must work on the basis of consensus. Interestingly, when the eminent Orthodox scholar Joseph H. Lookstein wrote an article ten years later for *Tradition,* based on his experience as chair of the IJCIC delegation to the International Catholic-

Jewish Liaison Committee meeting in Rome in January 1975, he wrote a glowing report of the consultation and of an intensely theological statement on Catholic–Jewish relations issued that year by the Holy See—without once referring to Rabbi Soloveitchik's dictum. The meeting dealt with matters of liturgy and Church doctrine (such as the relationship between the Scriptures). Referring to the Vatican document *Guidelines and Suggestions for Implementing* Nostra Aetate (December 1, 1974), Lookstein concluded that the religious document represented "a giant step forward in Catholic-Jewish relations" and "should be accepted as such," noting that "dialogue must continue with increasing 'give' by the Catholics and with decreasing fear by Jews" (Joseph Lookstein, "The Vatican and the Jews 1975," *Tradition* 15, 1–2 [spring–summer 1975]: 5–24). Frankly, it must be said from the Catholic side that such progress would have been impossible save for the successful accomplishment of theological dialogue in the intervening years. Ironically, this intense interreligious dialogue was, on the Jewish side, organized mainly by Jewish communal agencies such as the American Jewish Committee and the Anti-Defamation League of B'nai B'rith rather than the religious groupings, although there was also the active participation of Reform and Conservative Jewish individuals and groups.

23. Agus refers here to *Hagigah* 13a, *Sanhedrin* 59a, *Abodah Zara, Tosafot* 2a, *Baba Kama* 38a. For a general discussion, see Jacob Katz, *Exclusiveness and Tolerance* (New York, 1961), 34.

24. For two major exchanges that were designed to observe the Soloveitchik rubric but which, I believe, more aptly document the points made by Rabbi Agus in this paragraph, see the two volumes of papers, both published by the University of Notre Dame Press and edited by Eugene Fisher and Daniel Polish, *The Formation of Social Policy in the Catholic and Jewish Traditions* (1980) and *Liturgical Foundations of Social Policy in the Catholic and Jewish Traditions* (1983).

6

JACOB AGUS' IDEOLOGY OF AMERICAN JUDAISM: AMERICAN JEWS OR JEWISH AMERICANS?

Milton R. Konvitz

WRITING ABOUT THE WORK of David Neumark, Jacob Agus said that although Neumark's contributions to the study of Jewish philosophy are invaluable, he never became an independent philosopher.[1] One can say of Agus himself that his contributions to the study of Jewish philosophy are invaluable and that he became an independent philosopher. Very few scholars were as deeply immersed in the study and interpretation of Jewish philosophy, from Philo to Franz Rosenzweig and Martin Buber, as was Jacob Agus, but at the same time he kept his own counsel, nurtured his own thoughts, and, being a pragmatist, brought his own philosophy to bear on the problems that agitate American Jewry. He was always the scholar and teacher; he initiated no movement and did not seek to make disciples, and on some important issues he courageously took a radical, unpopular stand. But his thoughts on practical questions always had a philosophic base; they were not spontaneous, emotional reactions but the results of deep soul-searching, deep study, deep thought. To understand and appreciate his views on American Jewry—his ideology of American Judaism—it is essential to place these views against the background of his philosophic thought, where they have their roots. "All the decisions that we make out of the depths of our being," Agus wrote, "involve some reference to a philosophy of life, a grasp of the ultimate."[2]

Agus identified himself as belonging to the rationalist school of Jewish thought, at the head of which stands the great Maimonides. He believed not only that God revealed Himself in the Torah but that He reveals Himself continuously "through the twin lights of conscience and intelligence," that the written documents of revelation need to be interpreted by the mind and conscience, that the mind and conscience make the written word a living word, and that the primacy of this concept of the living word (not necessarily the written word) is the "central insight of Judaism."[3]

But Agus was no absolutist. We may have, he wrote, a glimpse of the absolute, but he quickly added that "we can never possess the absolute."[4] And so it is that the rationalist must to a degree find accommodation for other approaches, including the romantic view of Judaism (such as that of Yehudah Halevi), the mystic approach of the Kabballah, and the legalistic approach. Agus liked to quote the saying of the sages that there are fifty gates of wisdom.[5] The rational mind is only one of the gates. Furthermore, any line of thought or argument must take into account the fact that it is not free from tensions, for the principle of polarity is ever operative. Thus ethnocentrism is countered by humanism; particularism is countered by universalism; emphasis on nationalism triggers an emphasis on religion; tradition at times must give way to creation.[6]

Agus took the principle of polarity from the philosopher Morris Raphael Cohen. This principle, Agus wrote,

> as formulated by Cohen, states that "opposites, such as immediacy and mediation, unity and plurality, the fixed and the flux, substance and function, ideal and real, actual and possible . . ." all enter into the pattern of our understanding. . . . If only one polar concept is insisted upon as the one true principle, knowledge is reduced to absurdity.[7]

"Dynamic polarization," wrote Agus, "is the mark of a living faith."[8] Reference to the principle of polarization can be found in almost each of Agus' writings, for he firmly believed that "in nearly every human situation requiring an act of decision, a polarity of principles applies."[9] "Tension," he wrote, "is of the essence of living faith; there is hardly any phase of it that is not a reflection of a polarity."[10]

In his research, in his search for answers, Agus tread softly and humbly, ever hoping to hear, "after the fire, a still small voice"; for he believed that

> at the base of human thought, lies the feeling of humble reverence. . . . There can be no cocksureness in matters of religion. . . . Often the restless agnostic comes nearer to genuine piety than the professional religionist. For piety is, at bottom, a seeking and a quest.[11]

Agus opposed theories of society that were derived from Darwinism and an emphasis on "biologism" and the struggle for existence; from the Marxist theory of the class struggle; or from a Freudian psychologism. All such theories, he held, dehumanize, degrade the human being and the human mind. Instead, Agus projected a "spirit-centered" conception of the human being and society. By this conception he meant "the unity of all values as they are unfolded in the course of man's quest for reality, a quest that alternates between the depths of subjectivity and the furthest reaches of objective reason. . . . The reality and validity of human values, esthetic, ethical, and religious, is the basic axiom, though the content and nature of any one value may be periodically re-examined. This axiom may also be called an assertion of faith, but it is that residual minimum of faith that our human nature invariably contains as it confronts the mystery of existence."[12]

Another central belief held by Agus was the centrality of ethics. Ethical values are the foundation on which philosophy and religion must be based. In accord with the principle of polarity, it must be expected that other values will compete with ethics for recognition and even dominance, but as we shall see, Agus seems to accord to ethical values the final word. Agus wrote that the "intuition" of the "objective validity" of ethical values "is the basis of my philosopy and religion." He wrote, "In moments of intense fervor, we feel that rightness and wrongness are eternally fixed in the scheme of things; that it is not our own personal dictates and impulses that are the source of ethical feeling; that the things we call 'good' and 'bad' are . . . designated by the Eternal One, Who stands outside of us and yet dwells with us."[13]

Finally, it remains to be mentioned that Agus was a staunch pluralist, especially as concerns religion. "Once we admit that many ways lead to God," he wrote, "we no longer feel called upon to prove that only our faith, whatever it be, is true."[14] He did not feel that he needed to argue on behalf of a pluralistic position, for by now, he was persuaded, "the pluralistic articulation of the religious impulse is taken for granted."[15] Agus maintained that there must be an openness to experiences, intuitions, thoughts, approaches, from whatever source they may come.

Even within one's own historical tradition, a variety exists of views from which one may learn and benefit, and no one tradition has a monopoly on all fifty gates of wisdom.[16]

These, I think, are the basic organizing principles or thoughts that Agus arrived at from his study of both Jewish and non-Jewish sources. As a student of William Ernest Hocking at Harvard, Agus was an avid student of comparative religion. "And what should they know of England who only England know?" Rudyard Kipling asked. Agus applied this thought to religion. We become fully aware of the meaning of our heritage, he wrote, "only as we learn to understand with sympathy the religion of our neighbor."[17]

This radical openness of mind and spirit Agus manifested in all his writings as he applied it to all problems and challenges. Typical of this approach and commitment is the way he considered the idea of chosenness, the belief in the principle of Israel as the Chosen People. This was a subject on which he wrote extensively; it crops up in almost all of his works. In Agus' mind the concept of chosenness was inextricably tied to the idea of covenant, that the people of Israel were the Chosen People with whom God made a special covenant. Both ideas, Agus maintained, unfortunately lend themselves to the perversion of ethnocentrism. Agus tried to salvage these conceptions from the distortions to which they were exposed over the centuries.

Agus noted that the problem of a chosen people is not peculiar to Judaism, for every religious tradition and the impetus of nationalism tend toward the assertion of chosenness, a belief in its supreme value. Every religion and every nation in some way claims to be "a light unto all the nations."[18] In the Jewish tradition, however, the concept has manifested a polar tension between ethnocentrism and a recognition of the wrongness or evil of exclusive claims to virtue or holiness. Between "the lofty heights of universalist idealism" and "the dark depths of collective 'sacred egoism'," Agus never hesitated to choose the former.[19]

In every possible context Agus chose to remind his readers and students that the ancient rabbis maintained God had made a covenant with the sons of Noah, to whom He had revealed seven laws of morality known as the Noahchide Laws, or the Seven Laws of the Sons of Noah,[20] which constituted a universal revelation of morality and religion, a body of natural law and the essence of a natural religion. The rabbis also maintained that true prophets had risen among non-Jews, so that it is possible there is more than one body of revealed laws. There were prophets in Israel who believed that God could conclude Torah-like covenants with other peoples, such as Egypt and Assyria.[21] Agus quotes the following illuminating passage from Albo's *Sefer Ha-Ikkarim,* the fifteenth-century classic:

> And there is no doubt that the other nations attained human happiness through the Noachian law, since it is divine; though they could not reach the same degree of happiness as that attained by Israel through the Torah. The Rabbis say, "The pious men of the other nations have a share in the world to come."
>
> This shows that there may be two divine laws existing at the same time among different nations, and that each one leads those who live by it to attain human happiness.[22]

In a "personal confession" of faith published in 1981, Agus wrote that it was through the Jewish tradition that he grew up to feel the majesty and the message of God—a God who transcended nature and history. But the emphasis in Judaism on God's transcendence kept him from surrendering to the notion that God's will, in all its fullness, is reflected exclusively in his own tradition. Although he could live within the confines of his own tradition, he believed that "divine revelation in all its dimensions is universal and all-human."[23]

Agus was, of course, thoroughly familiar with the uncomfortable fact that another stream of teaching in Judaism made an ethnocentric claim on the concept of chosenness and the concept of covenant, but he believed there was ample warrant for the universalistic, open-ended line of interpretation, and so he concluded his personal confession by stating that he took the phrase "Chosen People" in Judaism to mean that the ideal Israel was to be and act as an *example* to others, individuals and nations, and not that Israel was an *exception;* that, in the words of Isaiah, Israel was meant to be "a covenanted people, a light to the nations."[24]

The moral law is the essential message of the biblical prophets; linking that message with the Noahchide laws makes ethical monotheism a religion open to non-Jews no less than to the Jewish people. Judaism therefore shares ethical monotheism with other monotheistic religions. The prophetic message and the Seven Laws of the Sons of Noah, by their very nature, give an openness to Judaism. Agus quotes with approval the following statement from the Talmud, tractate *Megil-*

lah: "Anyone who denies idolatry is called a Jew."[25] And Agus cites Maimonides as authority for the proposition that both Christianity and Islam are divine agencies that help prepare the way for the Messiah.[26]

Judaism, Agus contended, "is the central, all-pervasive and all-absorbing element of the civilization of the Jewish people."[27] By Judaism he meant the religion in its various, pluralistic expressions. But what of Jewish nationhood? Agus wrote repeatedly on this subject, which troubled him no end; but the conclusion he reached was not to deny nationhood entirely but to give it a minor role. "I believe," he wrote, "that the motive of nationalism [among Jews] is productive of good only when it is kept in the background, as subordinate to the universal ideals of ethics and religion."[28] The Jewish people have survived because of their religion; "the survival of the Jewish nationality was an effect rather than a cause."[29] Agus spoke of nationalism as a myth, "characterized by the assumption of a dark and mysterious 'national soul', which is apprehended in intuition."[30] It is probably impossible to free ourselves completely from this myth, but it is most important, argued Agus, that we surmount the myth of nationality or ethnicity by emulating the prophetic example to deflate the myth as promptly as it arises;[31] for the prophet is the foe "of self-glorifying ethnicism, of self-sanctifying dogmatism, of human arrogance in all its subtle variations."[32]

The principles, concepts, and beliefs we have thus far discussed—notably the concepts of covenant, chosenness, the centrality of religion, the subordinate role of nationality, the primacy of ethical values, pluralism—Agus brought to bear on the status and future of Jews in the United States. It is not possible to tell from his extensive writings whether his thoughts on religion and Judaism, on nationalism and ethics, came first, and he then applied them to the American Jewish scene, or whether he derived his general conceptions from what he thought about American Jewry. In all likelihood these thoughts were intertwined, for he was a student of rabbinics and of philosophy, a rabbi and a teacher-scholar, throughout his adult years. At the same time that he was a congregational rabbi he was also a college professor; he wrote his treatises and books at the same time that he thought about his sermons.

As Agus looked on the American Jewish scene, he saw that secularism and Zionism—both a Zionism that was secularist and a Zionism that was, in his words, "dressed up in dubious religious garb"[33]—were inherently nationalistic. But, he held, "as an independent motive, sheer nationalism—especially as 'normalized' since the establishment of the State of Israel—can only lead either in the direction of headlong assimilation or toward the status of a racist minority."[34] The military victories of Israel have given an emotional boost to Jewish pride and may have worked to remove an inferiority obsession, but this could only stimulate the drive to assimilation. The important truth is, said Agus, "that the national impulse, as such, is not capable of functioning in America as a goal of Jewish living." Jewish nationalism, however, when subordinated to higher considerations, "may continue to be a powerful creative force, serving the ends of Jewish religion, as it did in the past, by bringing to the aid of piety additional motivation, and by supplying foci of sentimental loyalty within the Jewish community."[35] But Agus repeatedly stressed the belief, to which he firmly adhered, that the nationalist ideal, if elevated to the status of a supreme goal or value, can only lead American Jews into a dead end, "since it cannot offer a worthy *raison d'être* for American Jewish life."[36] When made into a supreme goal, Jewish nationalism would have the tragic end of relegating Jewry to the status of a self-segregating, racist minority that would reject the goal of assimilation, although assimilation is "the natural end of other immigrant nationalists in America."

The relegation of American Jewry into a nationality or an ethnic entity would mean to Christians that Jews persist in being a nation within a nation, a foreign element, an enclave "unabsorbed and alien." In such a case, it is reasonable to expect American gentiles to ask why the Jews remain here; why do they not go to their national homeland, the State of Israel?[37]

It was Agus' firm belief that there was no future for a variety of ethnicisms in American life; "for the ineluctable fact is," he wrote, "that the *natural* tendency for all national groups is to dissolve and disappear within the American melting pot." Here and there, one may still see colonies of European nations continuing in the "isolation of self-imposed ghettos," but they are the exception to "the mighty expanse of America's mainstream life. The bland assumption that Jewry is a national entity does not protect American Israel against the absorptive effects of the melting pot."[38]

The stereotype of the Jew as an unassimilable element will be strengthened in the mind of the non-Jew if the latter takes seriously the classic Zionist claim that the Jewish homeland is intended to gather in all the Jews of the diaspora. This can be avoided only

> if it is made sun-clear that the intention in establishing the homeland was not at all the evacuation of American Jewry . . . , but the founding of a haven of refuge for the persecuted Jews in other lands, and the creation of a cultural-religious center for World Jewry. In that case the emergence of a new type of "productive" and fighting Jew will help to banish the time-worn Jewish stereotype from the minds of Christians, and . . . aid the American Jew to accept his Jewish origin with pride and his religious heritage with ease and naturalness, as all other Americans accept their origin and religions. To this end the theses of Herzlian Zionism must be repudiated insofar as American Jewry is concerned. . . .
>
> We are led, irresistibly, then, to emphasize the religious purpose of Jewish group survival in this country.[39]

Agus quoted with approval the statement by Robert Gordis that "a secularist who is a Zionist must, if he is logically consistent, become a *Sholel Hagolah,* a negator of a Jewish future in the Diaspora."[40]

Accordingly, in American Jewish life the movement must be "from ethnicism to Judaism." Ethnic feelings and loyalties must be directed into religious channels,[41] and the synagogue must become the center of Jewish life. But if this is to happen, the Jewish religion must be viewed as not a static body of dogmas "but the upward surge of the human personality in all its fullness," and the "synagogue-center" must "embrace under its wings every cultural and uplifting interest of the Jewish community" and include in its program social, recreational, and all kinds of cultural activities. Its message should be "Nothing that is Jewish or human is alien to me."[42]

Agus of course recognized the fact that large numbers of Jews are not affiliated with synagogues or temples. Many such are spiritually sensitive persons, "whose entire being is profoundly stirred by Jewish associations and problems." How, he asked rhetorically, can they be termed "marginal" without a perversion of Jewish values? In addition, there are, he recognized, "masses of indifferent materialists" who are, in one way or another, included in the Jewish organizational complex but who are unmoved by any kind of appeal to spiritual values. What does one do about them? Agus answered by saying:

> The moral task before us, then, is to transmute deep ethnic consciousness into reawakened dedication to the ideals and values of the Jewish spirit. We must chart a path from the sense of being part of an embattled camp to the sense of being a partner of the Lord in the creation of a world patterned after His Word.[43]

As it appears, Agus saw a distinction between Jews who are spiritually sensitive and Jews who are both spiritually sensitive and religious. If the synagogue would stress the ethical and spiritual ideals and values of Judaism, a bridge could be established between the nonreligious but spiritually sensitive Jews and the religious community:

> By cleaving to the spiritual interpretation of Jewish experience we provide a means for the non-religious among us to progress in the realm of the spirit through their Jewish identification. To be sure, we have not shown how the gulf in many men's minds between adherence to spiritual values and the convictions of religion may be bridged. There is in fact a plus of conviction in religious faith, with regard to the roots in eternity of spiritual values, which cannot be obtained by the cultivation of a humanist attitude alone. Spiritually minded people will still find congregational life the best means of continuing their own spiritual progress, through self-identification with Jewish experience in the religious interpretation . . . and by promoting its values in the social grouping of which they are a part.[44]

As Agus surveyed the Jewish scene in the United States and in Israel, the two main centers of Jews after the Holocaust, he saw that "in Israel the Jews are becoming a secular nationality, with the ancient faith as a subordinate reality, while in America, the Jews are becoming a religious denomination, with an ethnic underside."[45] This may mean that the Jewish people are falling apart into separate peoples. The tragic separation can be avoided by many factors, chief among them if the Jewish tradition will continue as a living appeal to the members of the Jewish family:

> So long as that tradition is cultivated and made part of the lives of successive generations, the family will be a living reality. Every son and daughter need only be concerned with his own relation to the spiritual treasure of the family—does he [or she] cherish it and live by its light?

> The unity of a widely scattered family is the product of the loyalty of its members to their common tradition.[46]

Since the Jewish tradition is the Jewish religion, with only an underside of ethnicity, in the final analysis only a spiritual-ethical-universalistic Judaism can keep the Jewish people together as a single family, in both Israel and the diaspora.

Agus naturally viewed the situation as a very worrisome one, and he moved from pessimism to optimism and back again. He was fully aware of the secularization and assimilation forces in America and of the deep gulf between the religious community in Israel and the majority of its population. Yet he saw merit in the conception of the late Solomon Rawidowitz that Israel and America may constitute two centers of Judaism. With this thought in mind, Agus wrote:

> It is as impossible for the Jews of Israel to think of themselves completely in secular terms, ignoring the burden of the all-Jewish tragedy and the import of ancestral faith, as it is for American Jewry to proclaim itself to be just another religious denomination. Inescapably, the past is reclaimed by every living generation, though in varying interpretations.

The conclusion he drew is that it is the burden of the Jewish intellectuals in both Israel and America to pattern the diverse elements of the Jewish tradition in such a way that the result will be a synthesis "that is meaningful and elevating for the people of a particular time and place."[47]

For American Jews, Agus saw in Christianity a wholesome challenge—a call to Jews to break down "the self-exalting impetus of ethnicism and to caution against the externalization of religion and its hardening into a series of lifeless rituals." And for American Christians, Agus saw Judaism as a challenge to them to make the world "more prophetic, more communal minded, more rational and ethical, more concerned with the 'works' of love."[48]

American Jews need have no fear of contact with the Christian community. Judaism, Agus believed, attained its highest intellectual levels when it was in contact with foreign civilizations. "In history, as in nature, productivity springs from the intermingling of cultures and influences. Isolationism in thought is as sterile as it is inane and futile in politics."[49]

But what of anti-Semitism? Agus believed that "the battle of anti-defamation is waning into insignificance, primarily for lack of antisemites to combat." Of course, one cannot be absolutely certain that anti-Semitism will never again be aroused, but there are certain objective factors working against this ugly possibility: the anti-Semitic ideology fostered by Nazism has been thoroughly discredited, and the creation of the State of Israel robs that ideology of the stereotype of the "wandering Jew"—the Jew is now normalized, no longer the mysterious alien. And so, once again, Agus draws the conclusion:

> In relative freedom from the virulent sting of antisemitism, we may expect the pattern of Jewish loyalties to shift ever more decisively from the pole of ethnicism to the one of a personal faith.[50]

American Jews and Christians cannot be indifferent to one another; they must be in a dialogue relationship. Jews and Christians can come together as religious humanists and discover how the respective traditions can be harmonized "with that universal, growing truth in which all of us share."[51] The dialogue will not end in a syncretism but in a new openness;[52] for we must remember the words of Micah: "For all the peoples walk every one in the name of his god, and we will walk in the name of the Lord our God for ever and ever."[53] Such a relationship will be an expression and reaffirmation of American religious pluralism.[54]

Agus disparaged the idea of a secular Jewish culture for American Jews. Immigrant Jews needed a Jewish culture before they became acculturated to the American civilization. That was a temporary phenomenon, satisfying a nostalgic longing for the past. "Insofar as secular 'Jewish culture' attempts to supply the same values as American culture, it is superfluous. . . . Hence, to saddle a secular 'Jewish culture' upon the American Jew is just as gratuitous as to lumber him with an additional national allegiance."[55] Agus was quite emphatic on this point: "The only healthy function of the Jewish heritage in the American Jew is to supply the element of religion. American life is culturally monolithic but religiously pluralistic." Judaism as a religion changes the image of the Jew from being simply a "non-Aryan" to a "son [or daughter] of the living God."

The image of the Jew as thus perceived can find ample expression in scholarship, literature, music, and art, which can constitute a distinctive religious culture "as distinguished from the phony secular 'Jewish culture.' " The latter is both superfluous and inferior. "And it is preposterous to speak of the works of every writer, painter and musician who happens to have been born a Jew, but is devoid of Judaism, as constituting 'Jewish culture.' "[56]

But it would be a grave mistake to conclude from the above passages that Agus believed the Jews in America constituted just another religious minority. The Jews, he contended, are a special kind of minority, not just a religious minority or just an ethnic minority. "Ours is more than a creed, more than a so-called 'way of life', more than even the ethnic-cultural ties of a people. *We are the living bearers of a tradition that both supplements and corrects the onesidedness of the Christian tradition.*"[57] Jews in America can be a "creative minority." Repudiating only those who negate the value of the American diaspora and those who are "Zion-centered," American Jews can place their emphasis on "autonomy, on creativeness," and cherish and foster "whatever cultural and spiritual values are generated by every individual interpretation, every aspiration, within the community." While conscious of its own distinguishing attributes, this creative minority will sense "its underlying and essential unity with the general population," and it will not feel itself isolated, for its history and tradition "constitute a vital part of the realm of ideas and experience upon which American civilization is based. Thus we are part of Christian culture, though apart from it," for the "Judeo-Christian tradition" forms "the spiritual substratum of Western civilization."[58]

Furthermore, as a creative minority the Jewish community can expand the cultural horizons of all Americans by developing the truths that are implicit in its peculiar status and thus unfold fresh insights for the guidance of all Americans. Finally, as a creative minority the Jewish community is value-centered and oriented toward the future, toward "the sunlight of spiritual growth." All this can be accomplished "through the impetus of our specific religio-cultural tradition in continuous interaction with the Christian tradition."[59]

This line of argument, by its inherent forceful logic, led Agus to the conclusion that the Jews in America are on the way to becoming "Jewish Americans." What was adjectival becomes substantive and what was substantive becomes adjectival, so that *American Jews* will become *Jewish Americans*:

> If to be at home is not only to be in the possession of "rights" but also to be part of the people to whose service the political machinery of the state is dedicated, then the Jew can be here utterly at home, thinking of himself as an American of the Jewish faith, as "normal" in the civil sense of the term as any other citizen of the great country.

Agus was, of course, fully aware that not every Jew would embrace the change from the genus "Jew living in America" to that of "Jewish American." "The Jewishly ignorant and the embittered, the eager opportunists and the dust-dry rationalists, the rootless intellectuals and the witless hangers-on will be likely to desert our ranks in a steady procession." In contrast, however, Jews will find ways to express themselves in positive acts of identification, for being a Jew will no longer mean falling into a category automatically with or without one's will. Because the American pattern is that of a nation that unifies multiple faiths—*e pluribus unum*—"Jewish loyalty will derive accessions of strength from both the pervasive atmosphere of American culture and the momentum of the Jewish tradition":

> Standing at the threshold of the fourth century of Jewish life in America, we can foresee the progressive "normalization" of Jewish feeling: hence, the shrinking of the ethnic strands of loyalty, the forging of ever stronger bonds of fraternity with the American people, and the steady growth of the ideal and religious components of Judaism.[60]

In September 1789, during the French Revolution, deputies in France's Constituent Assembly were alarmed by the report from Alsace that peasants had attacked Jews. Count Stanislas de Clermont-Tonnerre demanded the assembly act to extend protection to the Jews, and several months later, when the debate about the Jewish question was resumed, he stated that the rights of the Jews had been implicitly recognized by the Declaration of the Rights of Man, which states that no person shall be persecuted for his or her religion. In the course of his speech Clermont-Tonnerre declared, "Jews should be denied everything as a nation, but granted everything as individuals."[61] Seventeen years later, when Napoleon Bonaparte considered the situation of the forty thousand Jews who lived in France, he saw that they constituted a "nation within a nation," and he instituted measures that would change their condition, that would confer civil rights on them as individuals but abolish their "national" character.[62]

Despite these measures and other developments, we know from the recent tragic history that Jews in France and in Germany were hated and looked on as an element that could never be assimilated. This was due to the fact, noted Agus, that Germans and Frenchmen considered themselves as constituting nations by a blood relationship; that they were, in some sense, natural "races," nations by birth:

> The romantic reactionary circles in Europe [in the time of the French Revolution and in the Napoleonic period] tended generally to demand the ultimate disappearance of the Jewish group as the condition for emancipation. Doubtless, too, they echoed in this the unexpressed feelings of the masses who, for the most part, were able to think of brotherhood only in biological terms as blood-kinship.[63]

This emphasis on the biological basis of nationalism made it impossible for Jews to become an integral part of any European nation-state.[64]

The situation in America, Agus contended, is quite different. Although the possibility of an intensified anti-Semitism cannot be altogether ruled out, there are good reasons to believe that what happened in Europe will not happen here:

> The indubitable fact, enshrined in the memory of the American nation, of its having arisen out of a mixture of races and nationalities, interposes a supreme obstacle to the emergence here of a romantic blood-based brand of nationalism, with its corollary of racist antisemitism. America is the one great state where the emergence of the nation did not precede the formation of the state. The American nation came into being, in fact, as a massive protest against the voice of blood by the voice of reason and morality.[65]

This is a persuasive line of argument. Certainly, America is different from the European nations where today, almost throughout the continent, nationalities make unsettling demands of self-determination, demands for nationalisms based on birth and blood. But in the United States today we also hear shrieking voices that demand racial and ethnic self-determination, a search for "roots," a clamor for "multiculturalism" that is mostly a euphemism for racialism and ethnicism, a demand for cultural pluralism but without the orchestration of the pluralism into a national unity—for a *pluribus* but not for *e pluribus unum.*[66] The American ideal was an *orchestrated* pluralism of cultures and not a segregation of ethnic, national, or religious groupings. We see the present-day demands and their tendency, and the picture is far from reassuring; for in many instances we see public and private educational systems and institutions capitulating to the strident voices and compulsive demands.[67] The character of American demography is undergoing radical changes, and what these changes will do to the American ethos is impossible to say. It may well be—this one may hazard—that in the resulting maelstrom, the only safety net for American Jewry will be the claim of being a religious minority.

And the demography of American Jewry is also undergoing radical and deeply disturbing changes. The National Jewish Population Survey, sponsored by the Council of Jewish Federations, showed a core of 5.5 million Jews defined by birth or religion, based on the screening of more than 125,000 randomly selected households across the United States, with a follow-up survey of those who met the screening criteria. An additional 625,000 persons identified themselves as Jews by ethnic background or preference while identifying themselves as practicing a religion other than Judaism. In addition, some 700,000 children were identified as Jews by parentage or ethnic background but were practicing a religion other than Judaism. Then there was a category comprising some 1.4 million who had been born non-Jews and were now part of a household with at least one Jewish member.[68]

Another survey, released in 1991 and commissioned by the Graduate School of the City University of New York, which polled 113,000 households throughout the continental United States, found that 12 percent identified themselves as Christian and another 22 percent said they had no religion or were identified as belonging to a non-Christian faith. This means that one-third of American Jews are no longer Jews by religion. The findings in both surveys show that American Jews are rapidly assimilating by conversion, by intermarriage, or by shedding all religious belief.

Agus was aware of the problem and the challenge that it presents. His response was rational rather than emotional. What he wrote on this deeply disturbing subject needs to be quoted at length:

> Only liberal Jews can bring to an intermarried couple a message of self-acceptance based on genuine feelings of mutual reverence. From the liberal standpoint, the core of faith is the same in all forms of enlightened religion. Hence, devotees of different religions need not confront each other with the implacable choice of *either* one religion or the other. They can view their own faith and that of their marriage partner in the spirit of "mine and thine."
>
> To the Jewish member of the marriage, liberal Judaism can bring an interpretation that represents the Jew as an integral member of Western society and Judaism as a creative element in Western civilization. The Jew could learn to accept his heritage as one of the most important sources of enlightened religion and modern culture. The non-Jewish partner could simultaneously learn to accept the Jewish memories and loyalties of the Jewish partner as positive aids to the creation of an atmosphere of religious dedication in their home. Similarly, the Jewish partner could learn to recognize the essence of his liberal faith in the religious heritage of his non-Jewish partner. The children could learn to acquire a *positive* attitude to *both* religious traditions of their parents. When they reach adulthood, they will choose to identify themselves with one or the other religious community. Whatever their choice, they will possess a warm appreciation of the Jewish faith. On their pilgrimage through life, they will be sustained by a sense of wholehearted identification with *both* religious traditions of their parents. Perhaps, too, they will recognize themselves to be peculiarly suited for the role of overcoming the multiple barriers of hate and prejudice that still plague our society.
>
> At the present time [1971], this vast marginal group of possibly half a million people is totally neglected by the Jewish community. Here is a task of vast proportions for liberal Judaism to undertake.[69]

One may reasonably question whether this is a realistic view of the situation. Agus, I think, described an ideal intermarried couple maintaining an ideal home, where there is a maximum of love, understanding, and tender consideration. There probably are some families that approximate perfection, but such are a small minority. The ideal picture, however, is a tribute to Jacob Agus' equably maintained liberal spirit and reasoned consideration and to the fact that he invariably had the courage to say what he thought, without resorting to circumlocutions, indirections, or obliquities. It may be said of him that he was a

Jewish American, for he felt himself to be fully and comfortably at home in America, where he could be, and was, fully and happily a Jew. And it may be said of him that he was, indeed, an American Jew, for the Jew defined the substance of the man, while his Americanism was only adjectival; that although he was an assimilated American, he was in no sense an assimilated Jew. The principle of polarity that played so large role in his thinking can be readily applied to Agus himself, for he was a hyphenated American and a hyphenated Jew and so was never free of tension. He was both attached and detached, both rooted and transient, both a priest and a prophet; a man at home and a man who is a stranger; someone who saw the possible as he looked at the actual and saw always the ineluctable tension between the actual and the possible.[70]

> Whatever drove or lured or guided him,—
> A vision answering a faith unshaken . . .[71]

NOTES

1. Jacob B. Agus, *Modern Philosophies of Judaism* (New York, 1941), 388; hereafter, referred to as *Modern Philosophies.* Cf. *Encyclopedia Judaica* (Jerusalem, 1971), 12:1014.
2. Jacob B. Agus, *Dialogue and Tradition* (New York, 1971), ix; hereafter referred to as *Dialogue.*
3. Jacob B. Agus, *The Evolution of Jewish Thought* (New York, 1959), 410–11; hereafter referred to as *Evolution.*
4. *Dialogue,* ix, 30–31, 65, 357.
5. Jacob B. Agus, *The Jewish Quest* (New York, 1988), 12; *Rosh Hashonah* 21b.
6. Jacob B. Agus, *Meaning of Jewish History,* 2 vols. (New York, 1963), 2:458, 462, 473, 477; hereafter referred to as *Meaning.*
7. Jacob B. Agus, *Guideposts in Modern Judaism* (New York, 1954); 236–37; hereafter referred to as *Guideposts.*
8. *Meaning,* 477.
9. *Dialogue,* ix.
10. Ibid, 432.
11. *Guideposts,* 347
12. *Dialogue,* 376.
13. *Guideposts,* 340–41.
14. *Dialogue,* 36.
15. *Quest,* 12.

16. *Dialogue,* 92.
17. Ibid., 508
18. *Evolution,* 420.
19. Ibid., 400.
20. *Dialogue,* 540. See *Avodah Zara* 64b; *Sanhedrin* 56a; Maimonides, *Melhakim* 8:10.
21. Isa. 19:24; cf. Micah 4.
22. *Dialogue,* 472. The passage from Joseph Albo (*Sefer Ha-Ikkarim*) is from the translation by Isaac Husik (Philadelphia, 1946), vol. 1, chap. 25, 198. See also Jacob B. Agus, "The Covenant Concept," *Journal of Ecumenical Studies* 18 (spring 1981): 226.
23. Agus, "Covenant Concept," 229.
24. Ibid., 230. Cf. Milton R. Konvitz, "Many Are Called and Many Are Chosen," *Judaism* 4 (winter 1955): 58.
25. *Quest,* 116; *Megillah* 13a.
26. *Quest,* 56; *Hilchot Melakim* 11, uncensored version. See also 193n. 9. See I. Twersky, ed., *Maimonides Reader* (New York, 1972), 226–27.
27. *Modern Philosophies,* 350.
28. Ibid., 357.
29. *Guideposts* 326–27.
30. *Dialogue,* 373.
31. Ibid., 378.
32. Ibid., 381.
33. *Guideposts,* 178.
34. Ibid.
35. Ibid.
36. Ibid., 179.
37. Ibid., 186.
38. Ibid., 145.
39. Ibid., 186–87.
40. Ibid., 196.
41. Ibid., 414.
42. Ibid., 17.
43. Ibid., 197–98.
44. Ibid., 201.
45. *Meaning,* 2:483.
46. Ibid., 484.
47. Ibid., 462.
48. *Evolution,* 415.
49. *Guideposts,* 303–4.
50. *Dialogue,* 14.
51. Ibid., 27.

52. *Quest,* 121.
53. *Dialogue,* 28; Mic. 4:5.
54. *Dialogue,* 28.
55. *Guideposts,* 159–60.
56. Ibid., 162.
57. Ibid., 208–9.
58. Ibid., 213–15.
59. Ibid., 215.
60. *Dialogue,* 578–80, 587, 588.
61. *Encyclopedia Judaica* 5: 605–6. See *Dialogue,* 22, 57ff.; *Guideposts,* 164.
62. *Encyclopedia Judaica* 7:23. See *Dialogue,* 582.
63. *Guideposts,* 164.
64. Ibid., 166.
65. Ibid., 168.
66. See Milton Konvitz, ed., The *Legacy of H. M. Kallen* (Rutherford, N.J., 1987).
67. See Dinesh D'Souza, "The New Segregation," *American Scholar* (winter 1991): 17; also Dinesh D'Souza, *Illiberal Education* (New York, 1991). See also Edward Alexander, "Multiculturalism: The Jewish Question," *Forward* (August 16, 1991).
68. *American Jewish Yearbook 1991,* Philadelphia, Jewish Publication Society of America p. 206.
69. *Dialogue,* 566.
70. Cf. Milton Konvitz, "Of Exile and Double Consciousness," *Encounter* (October 1980): 82–83.
71. Edwin Arlington Robinson, "The Man against the Sky," in *The man against the Sky* (New York, 1916).

7
THE CONCEPT OF GOD IN THE THEOLOGY OF JACOB B. AGUS

William E. Kaufman

IN HIS INTRODUCTION to the *Daily Prayer Book of Beth El Congregation,* Rabbi Jacob Agus, spiritual leader of Beth El, wrote of prayer as "the integration of personality," describing worship as a process in which "all that is fragmentary in us is unified."[1] Dr. Agus maintained that a basic theme animating his religious philosophy was his belief in the unity of the human mind.[2] What did he mean by this principle?

First, he intended it to negate any kind of compartmentalization of the human mind, such as faith versus reason, the irrational as opposed to the rational, and the like. Rather than compartmentalization, Agus stressed *wholeness.* Differentiating true from false prophets, Agus claimed that the former articulated the negative-objective aspects of the faith as well as its affirmative-subjective character. The true prophets thus brought their *whole* personality to the religious experience. Agus continued:

> That *wholeness* must be regarded as the essence and hallmark of authentic holiness is self-evident. "Complete ye shall be with the Lord thy God" (the word *tamim* means complete) (Deuteronomy 18:13). The quality of wholeness introduces a dynamic element into the very heart of religious experience. For man's objective universe changes in keeping with the growth of his knowledge. Philosophy, in the Socratic sense, is an attempt to render the whole of knowledge intelligible, relating man's ethical and esthetic values to his intellectual categories. Philosophy is, therefore, an

> essential expression of religion, as is the fervor of ethics and the calm joy of esthetics.
>
> The union of faith and philosophy, exemplified in the thought of Maimonides, I consider to be the classical current in Judaism. My own thought is simply a modern development of the same basic approach.[3]

Thus, by the unity of the human mind Agus meant, first, the union of faith and philosophy. Of all contemporary Jewish philosophers, Agus is the most emphatic on the *necessity* of philosophy as the completion of faith.[4] Faith points beyond itself to an objective realm of ultimate truth and knowledge, of which it is the task of philosophy to clarify and render intelligible.

Second, "the unity of the human mind" signified for Agus a methodological principle negating the notion that any people, *including the Jewish people,* are mystically or metaphysically set apart from other peoples. The notion of the chosen people Agus considered to be a "metamyth," by which he meant "the myth of Jewish metaphysical difference."[5] This myth consists of "the complex of fantasies about the peculiarity of Jewish existence—being blessed and cursed, set apart and made different from all the nations of the earth."[6] Agus opposed this myth, maintaining that all humans share the same potential for logical thought. He asserts:

> As an axiom or dogma, Jewish uniqueness need only be analyzed into its separate components for its mystical aura to be dispelled and refuted. All analytical writing, in fact all logical thought, is based on the assumption of one mind, one way of logical thinking; the same pathways to error are open to all the children of men.[7]

Of all contemporary Jewish thinkers, Agus most emphatically emphasizes *essence* rather than existence. His concern is with the universal rather than the particular. Diametrically opposed to Jewish existentialism, Agus places the accent on a philosophy unifying faith and reason.

Having delineated Agus' methodology, epitomized in his dictum "the unity of the human mind," we note his use of this method and other philosophical avenues as we examine his concept of God.

GOD AS THE ABSOLUTE SELF

The first points to notice concerning Agus' concept of God are the God-ideas he rejects. He adamantly repudiates the religious naturalism of Mordecai M. Kaplan. Agus clearly had Kaplan in mind when he wrote, "Conceptions of God as a 'power' or as a 'process' are altogether worthless for religion. The concept of 'power' is derived from the science of physics, where it is employed to designate a potential force. Clearly, then, this term cannot be applied to God, since He must be an actual Being."[8]

Why *must* God be an actual Being? Agus' argument is that metaphysics should start with the highest concept available, that of personality. Moreover, the term *personality* is the most inclusive in our vocabulary, including the elements of matter, spirit, mind, and will in a unity in which they are all fused. By referring to God as personality, we are expressing the idea that all the multiple and diverse phenomena of existence are reconciled and explained through His nature.[9]

But Agus is not proposing an anthropomorphic supernaturalism. Rather, he is striving to develop a conception of God outside of, but not in opposition to, natural elements. He states, "The concept of God that I assume is neither naturalist nor supernaturalist. It is not the personification of the forces of nature, or a force standing over, against and beyond nature. Its starting point is not force, but the human spirit."[10]

By "spirit," Agus means "a realm of relations in respect of meaning."[11] The human spirit is thus epitomized in the capacity of the human being to communicate symbolically. Through symbols we relate and connect disparate things, endowing them with meaning. And "meaning," for Agus, is "the relation of any one event to a class, and that class, in its turn, to a more inclusive whole, reaching up to the ultimate Being that is God. In this way, spirit is the polar opposite of a mechanical universe. While the latter is ideally understood through the interaction of the smallest conceivable particles, the former imposes the reign of meaning through the operation of the whole upon each of its component parts."[12]

Agus here develops a metaphysics of holism, wherein "wholes" in nature impose their patterns on their constituent parts. The central feature of the philosophy of holism is an alleged whole-making tendency running through nature, with the wholes becoming more homogeneous, more complex, higher from the standpoint of value.[13]

The analogy that Agus is striving to develop is that of the individual self of the human being to the notion of God as the Absolute Self. The self as a whole is more than the sum of its parts, and it teleologically directs the parts. Similarly, God as the Absolute Self of the universe is reflected in the wholeness of the universe being more than the sum of its parts and teleologically directing the parts. Let us follow closely Agus' reasoning.

The first point Agus emphasizes is a defense of metaphysics. He criticizes the scientific imperialists—those who maintain the omnicompetence of science to solve all problems and who stress the pointlessness of metaphysical speculation. To these proponents of "scientism" who hold that "any attempt to go beyond the catalogued and classified body of proven knowledge is futile" and who see the world merely as "a maddening whirl of atoms and electrons, particles and waves,"[14] Agus has two replies. First, he maintains that, by our very nature, we cannot leave the "unknown" alone, for "it comprises the essence of our being, the very ground of our existence, and the meaning of our strivings."[15] Second, he contends that scientific materialism—the view that atoms, electrons, particles, and waves are ultimate—represents "the failure to realize the logical insufficiency of the concepts of physics for the understanding of the essential 'stuff' of the universe."[16] To be sure, Agus acknowledges that his quest is not for the type of clear and certain knowledge that we have in mathematics and physics. Rather, what he seeks is "proximate" knowledge of the realm that supervenes knowledge, grounds for faith, the direction of the curves leading from the known to the unknown. Bearing in mind Agus's critique of scientism, his defense of the tragic earnestness of the metaphysical quest, and his realization that he is not dealing with hard facts but rather grounds for faith that would justify a religious interpretation of the universe, let us now explore how Agus develops his argument for God as the Absolute Self.

Agus' fundamental hypothesis is, as we have noted, the analogy of the human self and the Divine or Absolute Self. He states emphatically, "The quest for God and for our own innermost self is one and the same, for if the riddle of selfhood is solved, all is given."[17]

Agus acknowledges that neither the self nor the whole of the universe can be an object of knowledge in the strict sense of the term, for there is no way we can gain a distance from them and thereby attain objective knowledge of them.[18] Yet, Agus continues, we are aware of the self as a unity, and since the universe is governed by identical laws of cause and effect, we realize that the concept of the whole is not merely a verbal generalization. Moreover, Agus holds to an epistemological realism, maintaining that "there must be a point by point correspondence between ultimate reality and the concepts to which the path of reason ultimately leads."[19] Thus, Agus repudiates the Kantian critique of reason; instead, he seeks to apply principles of "reason in operation"[20] to the twin unknowns—the self and the whole.

The rule of reason that Agus utilizes for his quest is the principle of polarity, formulated by the philosopher Morris Cohen in his *Reason and Nature.* According to this principle, "opposites, such as immediacy and mediation, unity and plurality, the fixed and the flux, substance and function, ideal and real, actual and possible, etc., like the north (positive) and south (negative) poles of a magnet, all involve each other when applied to any significant entity."[21]

Agus' argument, in general, is this: Just as the human personality, as a chunk of reality, is understandable only in terms of the polar concepts of purposiveness and mechanism, may it not be, then, that "God and the mechanical universe imply each other, even as the one and the many, space and time, the point and the field?"[22]

For the details of his argument, Agus puts the accent on the "field" and "point" polar relationship in the physical universe. He defines this relationship as follows: The "field" is the pattern of infinite relations to which every "point" in space is subject. (Agus here is clearly indebted to Alfred North Whitehead.) Agus states, "Things are not spatial entities alone, but 'events', in Whitehead's terminology, units of space-time, reflecting the tension and rhythm of the polar relationship."[23]

Whitehead's basic metaphysical unit is variously called an event, a prehensive unification, an actual entity, an actual occasion, an occasion of experience. He conceives of nature as a complex of prehensive unifications. A prehension (literally, a grasping) is an appropriation of the many into the arising unity of experience, or unity of feeling, or unity of enjoyment, or prehensive unification. (The many become one and are increased by one.) The important point is that a prehensive unification or actual entity is a realized perspectival harmonization of the world. The unity of a prehensive unification is the unity that results from the immanence of the whole in each part and of each part in every other part. Each actual entity is the totality of nature in microscopic perspective; each perspective is therefore essentially linked with every other perspective. Agus clearly has this kind of Whiteheadian framework in mind when he writes, "Nothing exists that is wholly self-enclosed, but things are real insofar as they partake of the two opposites—particularity reaching down to a point in space, and responsiveness to the total field of relations."[24]

Ultimately, reality as Agus sees it consists of tensions and rhythms. Agus thus arrives at a conception of the universe in which all parts exist in a state of tension—tension between the tendency to particularization and responsiveness to the total system of which it is a part. There are, for Agus, two dimensions of this process: the horizontal plane of space-time and the vertical plane of individuation and freedom.

The human personality represents the highest observable field of individuation and freedom. We may notice, Agus' argument proceeds, a rising scale of being, from the electromagnetic field of force that is space to the human personality, which is a self-maintaining field. Now, assuming an infinite tendency in the rising scale of being, it is logical, according to Agus, to posit "an Infinite Personality, representing the ultimate pole of being, on the vertical coordinate of freedom."[25] This Infinite Personality is "the Absolute Personality representing the highest measure of the field building capacity," a pole of being over against the mechanistic universe. The conclusion of the argument is that "God and the physical universe are two polar concepts of thought, and since logical thought is in correspondence with reality, we are justified in concluding that the space-time continuum, as it exists in itself, and the Deity, as the projection into the infinite of the field-making capacity, are the two poles of being."[26]

It is important to ask: Precisely in what sense is Agus justified in this conclusion? On strictly philosophical grounds, there is a problem. Agus places a great deal of weight on Morris Cohen's principle of polarity. But Cohen maintained that this principle helps us to understand only entities within nature. He did not believe that this principle could be applied to the totality of existence, because for him, the whole is not an object of knowledge.

Agus notes that Cohen refused to draw this inference to the whole. Agus, however, states that "once we grant that it is not knowledge in the technical sense, that we seek but grounds for faith, such an application becomes logically incontrovertible."[27]

Agus here is basing himself on the Judaic rabbinic view of man as created "in the image of God" as a co-creator. God is revealed in the human spirit at its best. Thus the basis of Agus' argument is that the human self is created in the divine image. Agus contends that "the whole, in a qualitative sense, is given to us in our consciousness of our own personality."[28] Logically, this assumption is based on an extrapolation from the self to the "whole" of things. It is important in this context to clarify the concept of extrapolation.

To extrapolate is to project by inference into an unexplored situation from observation in an explored field, on the assumption of continuity or correspondence; as meteorologists extrapolate local weather conditions from reports of distant stations. Agus contends that nature exhibits a procession from physical fields of force to the human being as a field builder in the world of freedom. Extrapolating from this progression, Agus posits the notion of God as the Field Builder of all fields, the Absolute Self, the most integral whole.

It is important to query the analogy from a physical field of force to man as a field builder in the world of freedom and, finally, to God as the Field Builder of all fields. In physics the term *field* designates a region of space traversed by lines of force, as of a magnet or electric current (magnetic force). In human affairs a field represents a sphere of activity or opportunity. But what empirical meaning can be given to the notion that man is "a field builder in the world of freedom"? Finally, the leap from a physical field of force to God as the Field Builder of all fields is so tenuous as to become virtually devoid of empirical content.

Agus is not alone among theologians who begin with scientific notions and stretch them to their breaking point in an alleged application to God. Mordecai M. Kaplan notoriously uses the scientific concept of process, widening it to virtual amorphousness in application to God. John A. T. Robinson, bishop of Woolwich and author of the best-selling *Honest to God,* delivered a series of academic lectures at Stanford University that eventually were published in book form as *Exploration into God.* In a chapter titled "The Divine Field," Robinson maintains that one can talk of " 'the divine field' as a physicist might talk of a magnetic field."[29] Utilizing the seductive analogy of a "field," Robinson goes on to argue that there is no aspect of nature or history "that is not *ultimately* to be seen in terms of spirit, freedom, love."[30]

In his book *The Return to Cosmology: Postmodern Science and the Theology of Nature,*[31] Stephen Toulmin explains that mythology is not merely a thing of the past, exemplified by the personification or anthropomorphic thinking that created Atlas, Ceres, Wotan, and Poseidon. Toulmin holds that in contrast to the ancient myths, the myths of the twentieth century are not so much anthropomorphic as mechanomorphic. When we think of the universe as a machine, and when we remove words like *force, energy,* or *field* from their clearly defined scientific contexts and apply them to the universe as a whole, we are thinking not scientifically but mythically. Toulmin writes, "What gives the term a meaning for science is the part it plays in these (scientific) explanations. One can think of such a term as a piece in a jig-saw puzzle; and, like such a piece, it loses most of its significance as soon as we try to make anything of it out of context."[32] Agus' use of the physical concept of field to buttress his theology is thus an example of what Toulmin calls "scientific mythology."[33]

Agus is on stronger ground when he argues on the basis of the Judaic rabbinic conception of the human being as created in the image of God. To be sure, from a purely philosophical view, there are objections to the notion of God as the Absolute Self. The major objection was emphatically stated by the skeptic David Hume—namely, the inference from the human mind or self as the best we know to Mind or Self as the ultimate reality is an instance of the fallacy of composition, an illicit movement from part to whole. In Hume's words: "But can a conclusion, with any propriety, be transferred from part to whole? . . . What particular privilege has this little agitation of the brain which we call *thought,* that we must thus make it the model of the whole universe? Our partiality in our own favor does indeed present it on all occasions, but sound philosophy ought carefully to guard against so natural an illusion."[34]

But Agus' notion of God as the Absolute Self is enriched by its firm basis in the Hebrew Bible and the rabbinic world of the Midrash and Aggadah. Just as Agus' faith is clarified by reason, so his rationalism is rooted squarely in the Judaic rabbinic faith.

GOD AND THE HOLOCAUST

For Agus, the Holocaust is a personal loss and an acute theological challenge.[35] One may infer his approach to the problem of evil from the way he treats the theological issues raised by the Holocaust in his essay "God and the Catastrophe."[36]

The problem of evil has traditionally been posed in these terms: If

God is perfectly good, He would wish to abolish all evil. If God is omnipotent, He must be able to abolish all evil. But evil exists. Therefore it appears that God cannot be both omnipotent and perfectly good.

Formally, an additional premise to the effect that an omnipotent, perfectly good being eliminates evil to the extent to which it is logically possible is needed to render the set of premises *logically* contradictory. Nevertheless, the *evidential* problem of evil, that is, the apparent profusion of gratuitous evil, constitutes inductive, empirical evidence against the probability of a Deity both omnipotent and perfectly good.

Another way of articulating the problem of evil occurs in the play *J.B.,* a contemporary interpretation of the biblical book of Job, by Archibald MacLeish:

> If God is God He is not good,
> If God is good He is not God;
> Take the even, take the odd.[37]

Let us now explore how Agus deals with this perennial problem.

The first alternative is to retain both traditional attributes and simply acknowledge that God has His reasons, which we finite mortals cannot understand. Agus expresses it in these words, that "though God is both all-powerful and all-good, His ways are mysterious; we cannot fathom them."[38]

This alternative, according to Agus, reflects the religious phase of human nature. The death of the six million is one of the mysteries of Divine Providence. Agus emphasizes, however, that we must not think of the Holocaust in terms of an alleged peculiar destiny of the Jewish people. Agus holds that the Jews are chosen as an example, not as an exception. We must not pretend to know the will of God—to interpret the Holocaust, for example, as punishment for sin or the Lord "hiding His face." Agus is adamantly opposed to what he calls the meta-myth—the idea of Jewish supernatural destiny, the "chosen people" concept.

Thus, for Agus, the acknowledgment that finite man is incapable of understanding the infinite mind of God is a response appropriate to the *religious* side of man's nature, as long as we leave it a mystery and do not attribute more to the will of God than we are justified in knowing.

The second alternative Agus mentions is that God is omnipotent but not good, that is, beyond good and evil. In this Agus identifies with the way of Baruch Spinoza, who thinks of God as the totality of all forces in the universe. This worldview corresponds to our quest for objective knowledge. But, Agus notes, it offers scant comfort to those who contemplate the martyrdom of the six million.

The third alternative declares that God is all-good but His power is limited. Agus sees this theological option as reflecting our quest for the good.

Each of these three alternatives indicates for Agus that "the concept of God is a projection or an extrapolation of an inquiry that begins with man and—however far it advances—cannot reach its goal."[39] Agus thus correctly observes that the reality of God is asymptotic to our human concepts of God. Faith is thus required to unify the quests for truth and goodness.

What, then, is the conception of God that emerges from Agus' discussion?

Agus states that his concept of God is neither naturalist nor supernaturalist.[40] It is not naturalist: it is not the personification of the forces of nature. And it is not supernaturalist: it is not a force standing over, against, and beyond nature. Rather, the starting point for Agus' conception of God is the human spirit. Extrapolating from the human spirit, Agus arrives at a conception of God as the "Universal Mind or Spirit," the "Infinite Mind," that to which "the ascending ladder of wholes in the universe"[41] points; the "Infinite Being," "the goal of all our self-transcending quests," the "one goal of the three infinite progressions of reason, of ethics, and of esthetics," "true being, love and harmony."[42]

Elsewhere Agus states, "I accept [Charles] Hartshorne's assertion that God is dipolar—immanent and transcendent, abstract and concrete, being and becoming."[43] Indeed, this dipolarity is adumbrated in the Torah: God as *Adonai* and *Elohim*.

But there is a problem here. In his essay "God and the Catastrophe," Agus criticizes the notion of "the God who becomes" on these grounds: "If God himself evolves, where are the standards of right and wrong, good and evil, the holy and the profane?"[44] Agus here seems to imply that once we admit a "becoming" aspect of God, we have removed the possibility that God can be the ultimate ground of ethics. In fact, an entire chapter of Hartshorne's *Man's Vision of God and the Logic of Theism* is titled "God and Righteousness."[45] In this chapter Hartshorne takes note of the ambiguity of the term *perfection* as applied to God: He states, "Perhaps a being may be conceived as perfect in one sense and capable of increase of value in another."[46] Hartshorne correctly observes that the biblical sense of the unchanging nature of God refers to the divine constancy, His "unalterableness of character, not of value in the full sense of aesthetic enjoyment."[47] It is precisely the classical Thomistic concept of God's immutability coupled with His foresight of absolute details that "would entirely eliminate temporal passage, and with it choices, actuality, or purpose, in any intelligible senses. The ethical dimension would thus be banished altogether."[48]

But Hartshorne's philosophical process theology fails to encompass all aspects of the issue. Agus is more successful here. Agus notes that the religious side of man's nature merely accepts the problem as an ultimate mystery; the quest for knowledge leads to the idea of God as the Spinozistic totality of *all* the forces in the universe, as omnipotent but not good (beyond good and evil); and our ethical impulse gives rise to the notion of God as limited in power but perfectly good. Seeing that the tools of philosophy alone cannot resolve these conflicting values, Agus wisely invokes faith and mysticism to unify our quests for truth and goodness into an ultimately mysterious divine unity: "one in their ultimate essence. This is our faith, for God is the ultimate source and final purpose of both quests."[49]

This is not to say that Hartshorne's dipolar theism removes all mystery. Rather, Hartshorne places the mystery in the concrete actuality of God. For Hartshorne, all we can grasp is the abstract essence of God, not His concrete actuality. It is important to note precisely how he arrives at this distinction.

Hartshorne's dipolar theism essentially is the concept of God as the union of supreme being and supreme becoming. He criticizes classical theism for its monopolar prejudice, that is, the practice of putting God on only one side, or one pole, of a pair of metaphysical contraries. Thus, according to classical theism, the Deity is absolute, creator, infinite, and necessary, while the world is relative, created, finite, and contingent. Hartshorne holds that this view is too simple. He maintains that God is both absolute and relative, creator and created, infinite and finite, necessary and contingent—in short, the union of supreme being and supreme becoming, being in the process of becoming. He refers to this double predication as the principle of dual transcendence; that is, it takes both sides of metaphysical contraries to characterize God. Hence, Hartshorne envisages the Deity as dipolar: God has an absolute aspect and a relative aspect, a necessary pole and a contingent pole, and so forth.

Hartshorne's dipolar theism seems vulnerable to the charge of self-contradiction and inconsistency. He attempts to avoid inconsistency by distinguishing various aspects of the predication of divine attributes. For example, he holds that God is not necessary and contingent in the same respect. Although the divine existence is necessary (God must be the ultimate source of explanation), the particular manner in which His existence is actualized is contingent. Thus, Hartshorne distinguishes divine existence from divine actuality: the fact that God exists is necessary and can be grasped by reason, but that God exists with just the knowledge, feeling, and value He has is contingent on the state of the universe at a particular time. And Hartshorne locates the mystery in God's concrete actuality—namely, *how,* or *the manner in which,* God knows, feels, and values the world.

But Hartshorne's dipolar theism has difficulties of its own.[50] Agus has the advantage of his profound knowledge of rabbinic Judaism and Kabbalah. Moreover, his rich philosophical background renders him among the most rationalistic of contemporary Jewish thinkers.[51] It is to Agus' great credit that he reckons with philosophy, unlike several other contemporary Jewish thinkers. And there can be no question but that Agus has advanced the contemporary Jewish philosophical discussion of the concept of God.

TOWARD A DIALECTICAL THEISM

I see Agus, in the development of his concept of God, working toward a dialectical theism in the sense defined by the theologian John Macquarrie. Macquarrie holds that there is a dialectic built into the very idea of God: "Whatever we say about him, it seems we are bound to correct it by saying something of opposite tendency. This may be traceable to the double meaning that is always present in the word 'God'—highest value, from the point of view of the religious consciousness, highest reality, from the point of view of the intellect."[52]

This was precisely the kind of view Agus was moving to in his essay "God and the Catastrophe." We recall that there he said the view of God as omnipotent and all-good responds to our *religious* stance; the concept of God as limited but all-good respects our *ethical* orientation, our quest for the good; and the view of God as omnipotent but morally indifferent reflects our quest for objective *knowledge.* Agus states in that context, "The pursuits of logic, of ethics, and of religion pull us in seemingly divergent directions, disturbing our 'peace', for it is man's fate to live in tension and ultimate uncertainty."[53] From a logical point of view, all three positions are in tension with one another, disturbing our peace. Thus, Agus posits an act of faith wherein these "lines of inquiry converge in our souls."

We are reminded of fifteenth-century philosopher Nicholas of Cusa's doctrine of the coincidence of opposites *(coincidentia oppositorum).* The idea of God here is the mysterious metaphysical unity of the clash of contraries. Thus, Agus writes:

> My view is that God alone is Eternal Being as well as the holistic process in the various levels of creation. . . . We reject the notion of metaphysical dualism. God is the source of darkness as of light, of death as of life. But, it is light and life that express His purpose and will. As the Kabbalists put it, there is His will *(raava),* reflected in the laws governing all experience, and then there is "the Will of wills", *(raava diraavin)* expressed in the bursts of love and compassion that illumine our lives.[54]

For Agus, it is faith in God's unity, with mystical kabbalistic overtones of *yihudim* (unifications), that "tips the scale. Faith is itself a 'holistic' phenomenon, when it is the response of the soul to the divine thrust toward perfection, toward greater, more perfect wholes."[55]

Agus' concept of God is thus of an all-inclusive spiritual whole (Eternal Being) as well as the holistic process (Becoming) in the various levels of creation. God is "the spiritual pole of Being, descending into the structure of the lowliest particle of matter and ascending to inscrutable heights of field-building,"[56] manifested in our human quest for holiness, for integration of the self, making it part of the greater wholes and subtle unities that lead to God.

The theology of Jacob B. Agus is an inspiring, aesthetic crescendo of wholes working toward the mysterious unity and whole of the divine nature, where opposites, contraries, and tensions are resolved in a harmony transcending human understanding. In our finite, limited, human viewpoint, we are forced to live with a tension of world-pictures of the Infinite, in ultimate uncertainty. Agus' faith is that in the Absolute, Infinite Being of God, these tensions are resolved in a harmony and peace that surpasses our understanding.

This is Agus' faith. Hartshorne's decision "to trust reason to the end"[57] is not without its difficulties. Agus seeks a sensible middle ground between a too-hasty retreat to faith and a total rationalism. This is also expressed in the notion of "an intellectual imperative"[58] to take reason as far as we can, to stretch our cognitive powers as far as possible before resorting to the language of fideism.

Agus was in the process of developing a dialectical philosophical and mystical theology. His theology exhibits penetrating philosophical insights and adumbrations.

Jacob Agus' concept of God is rich, illuminating, and inspiring. He reckons with philosophy far more than several other contemporary Jewish philosophers. His philosophical and rabbinic theological erudition is manifested in his quest to articulate a tenable concept of God. He has given us much to ponder in the ongoing dialogue between philosophy and Jewish belief.

Jacob Agus has contributed immensely to advancing the "conversation" of contemporary Jewish philosophical theology. Utilizing his insights, we continue to work at the difficult task of articulating a concept of God consistent with Jewish tradition and at the same time responsive to contemporary philosophical and cosmological concerns, as we move toward the twenty-first century.

NOTES

1. *Daily Prayer Book of Beth El Congregation,* with an introduction by Rabbi Jacob B. Agus, edited by Rabbi Jacob B. Agus and the Religious Service Committee of Beth El Congregation; published by Beth El Congregation, Baltimore, Maryland. From the introduction, vi.

2. Dr. Agus stressed this theme continually in private conversation with me.

3. Jacob B. Agus, "My Basic Beliefs," in *Varieties of Jewish Belief,* ed. Ira Eisenstein (New York, 1966), 5.

4. On this point, see William E. Kaufman, *Contemporary Jewish Philosophies* (Lanham, Md., 1985), 232ff.

5. Agus, "My Basic Beliefs," 12.

6. Ibid., 11.

7. Jacob B. Agus, *The Meaning of Jewish History* (New York, 1963), 1:32.

8. Jacob B. Agus, *Modern Philosophies of Judaism* (New York, 1941), 346.

9. See ibid., 343.

10. Jacob B. Agus, *Dialogue and Tradition* (New York, 1971), 251.

11. Ibid., 252.

12. Ibid.

13. See Jacob B. Agus, *Guideposts in Modern Judaism* (New York, 1954), 247.

14. Ibid., 232.
15. Ibid., 233.
16. Ibid., 234.
17. Ibid., 233.
18. Ibid., 234.
19. Ibid., 235.
20. Ibid., 236.
21. Ibid., 236, 237; based on Morris Cohen, *Reason and Nature* (Glencoe, Ill., 1953), 165.
22. Ibid., 239.
23. Ibid., 243.
24. Ibid.
25. Ibid., 248.
26. Ibid.
27. Ibid., 238.
28. Agus, *Guideposts,* 239.
29. John A. T. Robinson, *Exploration into God* (Stanford, Calif., 1967), 97.
30. Ibid., 102.
31. (Berkeley, Calif., 1982).
32. Ibid., 27.
33. See ibid., 21–85.
34. David Hume, *Dialogues Concerning Natural Religion,* in *Classics of Western Philosophy,* ed. Steven M. Cahn (Indianapolis, 1977), 798.
35. Jacob B. Agus, "God and the Catastrophe," in *Dialogue and Tradition* (New York, 1971), 260.
36. Ibid., 259–71.
37. Archibald MacLeish, *J.B.* (Boston, 1956), 11.
38. Agus, *Dialogue and Tradition,* 261.
39. Ibid., 268.
40. Agus, "Response to the 'God is Dead' Movement," in *Dialogue and Tradition,* 251.
41. Ibid., 253.
42. Ibid., 255.
43. Jacob B. Agus, "Holism and the Jewish Religion," in *The Jewish Quest* (New York, 1983), 38.
44. Agus, *Dialogue and Tradition,* 267.
45. Charles Hartshorne, *Man's Vision of God and the Logic of Theism* (Hamden, Conn., 1964), 142ff.
46. Ibid., 158.
47. Ibid., 159.
48. Ibid.
49. Agus, *Dialogue and Tradition,* 271.

50. For an account of the virtues and difficulties of Hartshorne's dipolar theism, see William E. Kaufman, *The Case for God* (St. Louis, 1991), chap. 6.

51. Cf. William E. Kaufman, *Contemporary Jewish Philosophies,* 2d ed. (Lanham, Md. 1985), 231–50.

52. John Macquarrie, *In Search of Deity: An Essay in Dialectical Theism* (New York, 1985), 27.

53. Agus, "God and the Catastrophe," 268.

54. Agus, *Jewish Quest,* 40.

55. Ibid., 41.

56. Agus, *Guideposts,* 255.

57. Charles Hartshorne, *The Logic of Perfection* (La Salle, Ill., 1962), viii.

58. Kaufman, *Contemporary Jewish Philosophies,* 19.

8

JACOB B. AGUS ON THE MEANING OF JEWISH HISTORY AND EXPERIENCE

Neil Gillman

THE READER who approaches the voluminous writings of Jacob Agus for the first time cannot but be struck by the sheer range of his concerns and the scope of his knowledge. There is hardly a single philosophical, theological, moral, social, or political issue that escapes his exacting and critical gaze. There is barely a single major statement bearing on his agenda, Jewish or otherwise, from biblical and Hellenistic times through to the modern age, that he does not use to elucidate his own perspective.

Yet throughout this material a principal issue, constantly at the center of his attention, is the question of what it means to be a Jew. The immediate focus of that question is on our own time: what does it mean to be a Jew in the light of what Agus considers to be the great transformation of Jewish life in the modern era, that is, in light of the momentous possibilities relative to human autonomy now available to Jews, as to all modern men and women? And what does it mean to maintain Judaism and the Jewish people in the contemporary age of nation-states and radical nationalism? Then again, and necessarily related, what does it mean to be a Jew after the Holocaust, the creation of the State of Israel, and the flowering of American Jewry? In taking up these fundamental questions, Agus insists that we can never hope to deal with them satisfactorily without understanding the Jewish past. For this reason he devoted himself to the study and analysis of the turning points in Jewish history and the history of Jewish thought, hoping thereby to discern the essential dynamics of the Jewish historical experience.

Finally, since Agus was engaged in the issues on which he wrote and saw himself in the traditional mode of the classical rabbi, he was concerned with what history has to teach us. If this is what the past teaches us, this is what we must do today in order to achieve our ultimate goals in the future.

In studying these issues, Agus' preferred methodological device is to view the Jewish experience as evolving around and between a set of polarities. These polarities are, of course, Agus' own constructs. They are the spectacles or organizing structures through which he seeks to make sense of his data. They are the source of whatever meaning the data convey. Though Agus usually describes the particular Jewish readings of the given issue under analysis as existing in a dynamic tension between these polarities, he is rarely reticent in suggesting which of the two polarities he finds most useful and healthy.

These polarities appear first (structurally, not chronologically) in his theology. Agus understands revelation, for example, as a "divine pulsation [that] consists of a rhythmic thrust and retreat. In its forward movement, the divine word is articulated in a new vision of freedom," the message of the first of the Ten Commandments. Then, "the outgoing flow of the tide of spirit is followed by an ebb which is expressed in the second commandment—namely, submission to the One God." Here the polarities are freedom and submission.[1]

Again, Agus understands living faith as "a response that is itself paradoxical, because it is composed of both a feeling of *possession* and a conviction of *privation.* I feel that I am embraced within a supreme design, embraced and transcendent at one and the same time, in the basic rhythm of exaltation and worthlessness."[2] Here the polarities are possession and privation. And later in the same statement: "The prophets were intensely possessed of the objective dimension as well as the subjective ardor of a living faith." They were "seized by the spirit of God," yet they scrutinized their faith "in the light of objective morality."[3] Agus insists that though God is revealed in "the infinite outreach of man's quest for understanding," yet, at the same time, "the awareness of negation, knowing that we do not know," is integral to the experience.[4]

The objective–subjective version of the polar structure is omnipresent in Agus' writings on religion and nationalism, though in each case, these fairly neutral terms are given much more substantive formulations.

"Essentially, religion is a wave-like movement, a polar tension between the abiding reality without and the ultimate self within." Either humankind understands the world in terms of images of the self, or it understands itself in terms of the outside world. These two orientations become philosophical alternatives. The universe is interpreted "as the work of an infinite Self," or man may see his own being "in terms of what he conceives to be the components of the external world." Either the cosmos is viewed as "macroanthropos" or humanity is viewed as a "microcosmos."[5]

The objective perspective correlates with humans as intellectual beings, as rational, critical, analytic: the subjective, with humans as feeling beings, where fear, anxiety, love, or hope is deepened and intensified. In the former, man sees himself and his group dispassionately, from the outside. In the latter, he reevaluates rationality, surrenders to God, and tends to extol all that is associated with his group. The former impulse leads to positivism, the latter to existentialism.[6]

At this stage Agus notes that religion is a "dynamic phenomenon," that "it necessarily contains both orientations of heart and mind."[7] We return to that claim in greater detail below.

When Agus turns to nationalism, the same tension returns. "Nationalism is . . . a compromise between the two orientations of the soul," between a subjective mood that sanctifies the clan, the tribe, the nation, and an objective mood that breaks through the barriers to embrace humanity as a whole. Thus "within the domain of nationalism . . . , a perpetual tug of war ensues between objective ideals and sheer, blood-based ethnicism." Agus ties this tension to his earlier distinction between intellect and feeling, for it is "the dawning of objective intelligence" that overcomes the "subjectivity of tribalism."[8]

Finally, in his most comprehensive statement on the polarities, Agus uses the distinction between the "classical" and the "romantic." The chief traits of classicism are "the qualities of wholeness, balance, and reasonableness. It glories in a dispassionate evaluation of all opinions, and it shuns all forms of extremism. It values truth above all other virtues, objective truth that does not vanish like a dream in sober daylight."[9] In contrast, romanticism exalts the mystical, the irrational, the subjective, submission to God, and, in certain forms, an exclusivist ethnicity.

Agus acknowledges his debt to Leo Baeck for this distinction between classical and romantic religion, but he disagrees with Baeck's identification of Christianity as the paradigm of the romantic religion and Judaism as the paradigm of the classical. Though, like Baeck, "my own philosophy is definitely classical," Agus acknowledges that Judaism contains "romantic-mystical currents as well as a rationalist-humanist stream."[10]

But Agus then lists the "rare moments" when Jewish classicism has prevailed: in classical prophecy, Hillel, Philo, Rabbi Judah the Patriarch, Saadia, Maimonides, Mendelssohn, Krochmal, and Baeck. However, even the prophets "lapsed into atavistic sentiments when they fell from their own highest standards and extolled the sacred mystery of divine election."[11] As exemplars of the romantic stream in Judaism, Agus cites Halevi, the Zohar, and, more generally, "the dark seclusion of kabbalistic mythology in the long centuries of persecution and despair." In our own day, "the eruption of Jewish romanticism" is viewed as a reaction to the Holocaust and the creation of the State of Israel. Agus also deplores the wild excesses of the romantic temper at large in our general culture, "the gut reaction, the exhibitionist wilderness of the spirit, or anomie, the fervent exaggerations, and the general myopia that is induced by mass-enthusiasm," and he argues that the reaction to this temper is still in its initial stages.[12]

The "tug-of-war" between these two impulses was felt by Agus within his own life. He was born into a distinguished rabbinic family and raised in a traditional shtetl environment. In Europe, Palestine, and America he studied in major yeshivot, and he went on to receive a Ph.D. at Harvard University. It was not until the age of twenty-five that he began his serious secular studies. And it was not until he was at Harvard that he intimately interacted with non-Jews and non-Jewish scholarship. In that context he began to reexamine the teachings and perspective of the Orthodox tradition in which he had been raised. He tried to maintain a balance between the active, rational, objective, and universal and the passive, nonrational, emotional, subjective, and ethnic, and he recognized the polar oppositions this entailed.

Agus' critique of the romantic temper in all of its guises emerges most clearly in his critique of what he calls the "meta-myth" of "Jewish exceptionalism." In all of his writings in his wide-ranging corpus, from his concise overview in *The Condition of Jewish Belief* to his two-volume

The Meaning of Jewish History, this is one of the most important themes, accorded a great deal of space, energy, and passion. It reoccurs as a refrain in multiple and varied contexts and is a key to many of his programmatic suggestions.

In one of his discussions of the issue, Agus recognizes that this meta-myth is not identical with the doctrine of the chosen people. The latter can be interpreted "in historical and rational terms" as a fact of history, for the Jewish people did bring monotheism into the world. But that was at God's initiative, and apart from this historical datum, Israel does not have to be intrinsically different from any other people.[13]

In this analysis, Agus acknowledges that every religious community feels itself to be chosen. But it makes all the difference in the world if the group is chosen because of its innate qualities or as a condition of its service to the highest ideals of humanity.[14] In a distinction that appears frequently in his work, he notes the difference between being chosen as example and being chosen as exception.[15] When the doctrine of Israel's chosenness becomes a statement about Jewish "uniqueness" or "exceptionalism," we have bought into the meta-myth that Agus views as the single most problematic theme in Jewish history.

The substance of the meta-myth is the notion that "the Jewish people are mysteriously and metaphysically different from the rest of humanity."[16] Both of the qualifying terms, *mysteriously* and *metaphysically,* are crucial to Agus. The mysterious quality of the difference makes the claim a matter of dogma and faith rather than of inquiry and examination; it shuts the gates to rationality and research.[17] Its metaphysical quality makes Jewish uniqueness deeply embedded in the very nature of things, unexpungeable, a matter of unalterable fate and destiny.

Agus explores different versions of the uniqueness doctrine: as the key to God's redemptive plan for humanity, as the "suffering servant" of humanity, as the eternal challenge to the culture of the age, as a peculiar impulse buried in the Jewish racial heritage, as the cause of Judaism's unparalleled ability to preserve a strong national feeling, as the Jewish will to live, as the key to Jewish survival. In these contexts the attack on Jewish exceptionalism becomes conflated with a more generalized attack on the doctrine of chosenness itself, which, in what Agus calls some future ecumenical "Jerusalem Council," should be radically reinterpreted.[18]

In Agus' view, the major flaw in the doctrine of Jewish exceptionalism is that it can be—and indeed, has been—stood on its head. The plus becomes a minus, and the myth then becomes the motive/power for the impulse to brand the Jew as pariah among the nations. This is the obverse side of the meta-myth. Jewish exceptionalism, then, is the underlying, "metaphysical" cause not only of anti-Semitism—that would be a singularly mild result of the myth—but, even more, of the deliberate and conscious attempt to rid the world of the Jewish people. And this metaphysical impulse is again also "mysterious," for "about the Jew, the wildest charges were believable. After all, they were an enigmatic mystery, akin to that of Incarnation: only unlike the latter, they incarnated, in the Christian view, God's Love turned into Wrath."[19]

The meta-myth of Jewish uniqueness is the ultimate product of the romantic temper in Judaism, that side of Jewish self-expression that emphasizes Jewish subjectivity, ethnicity, tribalism, irrationality, emotionalism, and imagination. It is also an illusion that we best rid ourselves of. "Have not some of us turned ourselves into a myth, uprooted from humanity and endowed with a unique, mysterious sanctity? Have we allowed the momentum of this historic myth to seduce us to the worship of 'blood and soil'? Have we joined in the chorus of the Israeli chant of despair, 'the whole world is against us'? Has the messianic mood, in all its millennial depth, distorted our perception of reality, like a psychedelic drug? Have we lost the capacity to glory in the imageless Absolute, the source of ideals of rationality and humanism?"[20] To Agus, these questions are not merely rhetorical devices. Taken together, these impulses identify a programmatic thrust that holds a seductive allure for contemporary Jewry, and which Agus feels is simply disastrous.

In contrast, and in keeping with his own classical, universalist temper, Agus proposes that "the feeling of being covenanted should be generalized: every person should find a vocation and dedicate himself to it. So, too, the pride of belonging to a historic people should be universalized. All men should take pride in the noble achievements of their respective peoples."[21]

This proposal lies at the heart of Agus' intense interest in the future of the ecumenical movement, his hopes for the United Nations, and his faith in America. He is convinced that the kind of blood nationalism that flourished in Europe and expressed itself in virulent anti-Semitism will never sink roots in America. America arose out of a mixture of races and nationalities; in America, the nation emerged after the state, not before it; America stands for the voice of reason and morality and as a protest against ethnicity and tribalism; America is humanist in character and stresses the rights of the individual.[22]

It is not surprising, then, that Agus has a complex understanding of Zionism and its many differing manifestations. From one perspective, the creation of the State of Israel is "the most remarkable event of Jewish history," its creation being a result both of the classical religious ideals of Judaism and of European nationalism.[23] Thus, while critical of certain forms of Zionist ideology, Agus approved of what has been described as the "spiritual Zionism" of such thinkers as Ahad Ha-Am and Rav Kook. However, other forms of Zionism represented, as Agus understood them, the menace of the meta-myth. That is, in its various guises, Zionism revealed the inherent tension within Jewish nationalism. In its Western European form, as espoused by Theodor Herzl and Max Simon Nordau, it was a rebellion against the notion of Jewish alienation. These men sought to "overcome the 'abnormality' of the Jewish status, so that the Jewish individual and the Jewish group would be liberated from the 'peculiarities' of Jewish life and destiny." In this form Zionism was a deliberate challenge to the meta-myth. Alternatively, when Zionism was espoused by such thinkers as Leon Pinsker, it emerged as a deliberate flaunting of the meta-myth. Here Zionism became "an invigoration of ethnic zealotry, a reassertion of ancient loyalties, leading to the emergence of an inner world of hypnotic certainty, in defiance of any objective evaluation and considerations."[24]

Thus there is an inherent tension within the Zionist impulse, which became embedded in Israeli culture as well. On one side there is the cultural or spiritual Zionism of an Ahad Ha-Am and of Judah Magnes' *Ihud* group; on the other, the rabid zealotry of the ultranationalists.[25]

What, then, is the meaning of Jewish history? Agus, who devoted a two-volume book to that inquiry, summarizes his conclusions in the following paragraph, quoted in its entirety:

> It [Jewish history] is a demonstration of the high potential of freedom in human affairs and a record of the melancholy consequences of the failure to utilize its opportunities. As society moves to ever larger associations, it encounters the tension between the ideal vision of nationalism and the narrow sentiments of ethnocentrism. As it advances toward the Divine, it confronts the tension between religion as a dynamic quest for reality

> and religion as a finished and fixed body of dead certainties. The Jews contributed mightily to the ideals of prophetic nationalism and of monotheistic faith. But they suffered most grievously wherever the balance of nationalism and religion in their own tradition and in the mentality of their neighbors shifted toward the poles of racism and fundamentalism. Insofar as Jews were frequent victims of external forces, their destiny reflected the recurrent breakdown of free thought and genuine religion in the countries where they lived. Freedom is the quality of a culture, not merely a social arrangement; it consists in the extent to which rational and ethical ideals restrain the passions of people and neutralize the momentum of popular myths.[26]

This paragraph is redolent with Agus' preferred categories of interpretation and also with his personal judgments—the dynamic as opposed to the fixed, nationalism in its ideal form as opposed to "narrow ethnocentrism," "free thought and genuine religion" as opposed to "racism and fundamentalism," "rational and ethical ideals" as opposed to "popular myths."

Agus is convinced that the dynamic processes he perceives at the heart of Jewish history apply equally well to all civilizations. Hence, Jews were vulnerable to these dynamics as they worked themselves out in various host cultures; but within the Jewish community itself, the dynamic was intensified and doubled because of Judaism's unique coalescence of religion and nationhood. "In Judaism, the unity of ethnic awareness and religious loyalty is fundamental and of a peculiar intimacy.

Accordingly we may expect to find the usual tensions of ethnicism and faith magnified and intensified. . . . Instead of the usual monolithic picture, depicting either nobility of soul or meanness of spirit, we shall expect to find both extremes of the universal tensions of the human spirit. In Jewish experience, we see exemplified the basic tensions of humanity—only more so."[27]

In another context Agus describes "a quadripolar field of consciousness" where "all four poles of consciousness in religion and nationalism were dynamically represented and tempered with the 'strange fire' of being set apart."[28] In theory, each of the four poles of Jewish consciousness "could achieve dominance within the soul of the Jew, drawing the other foci of loyalty into its service. What is 'shell' for one philosophy is 'kernel' to the other, with the protean character of our sacred tradition providing the inner field of tension and the outer facade of unity."[29]

Agus is concerned with setting his own philosophy of Jewish history within the broader context of similar attempts to provide "integral" approaches to the inquiry. An integral approach proposes to account for the overall direction of the curve of Jewish history. It is opposed to those "derivative" approaches that try to understand the curvature of the line at specific points in Jewish history. These derivative approaches focus on specific issues such as the emerging schism between Judaism and Christianity, the fact of anti-Semitism, and how and why Judaism has survived in the face of multiple challenges. These issues, Agus contends, can be understood only in the light of a much broader integral approach to the material as a whole. Agus identifies four such approaches: the idealistic, the nationalist, the economic, and the synthetic.[30]

In brief, the idealistic approach, as exhibited in the work of such representatives of classical Reform Judaism as Samuel Hirsch, Solomon Formstecher, Solomon Steinheim, Abraham Geiger, Hermann Cohen, and Leo Baeck, tries to isolate the pure essence of Judaism in the idea of ethical monotheism and traces the gradual evolution of this idea from its earliest manifestations in the Bible through the modern emphasis on Israel's "mission" to the world. This mission is to exemplify pure monotheism and extend its influence throughout the world. To Agus, the weakness of the idealistic approach is its excessive abstractness and its arbitrary singling out of one idea as sufficient to capture the complex history of a vital people.[31]

The nationalist approach, as exemplified in the work of Nachman Krochmal, Ahad Ha-Am, and Simon Dubnow, views the Jewish people as another nation or "ethnic group," gifted with a unique "spiritual insight." The major failing of all nationalist explanations of Jewish history is that they invariably fall into the trap of Agus' meta-myth of Jewish uniqueness. Nor can this approach deal adequately with the major turning points of Jewish history.[32]

The economic approach of the Marxist school of history explains Jewish history in terms of the interplay of economic factors. Agus dismisses this approach as a "curiosity" and as symptomatic of a "sickly age" but acknowledge its influence in certain forms of Zionist socialist thought, as in the work of A. D. Gordon.[33]

With the synthetic approach of thinkers such as Heinrich Graetz, Salo Baron, and Yehezkel Kaufmann, Agus comes closer to his own thinking. What makes an approach "synthetic" is its attempt to avoid oversimplifications or monolithic interpretations that reduce the play of forces to one central impulse. A synthetic approach captures the complexity of impulses that affect Jewish destiny, though historians of this school may disagree on the interpretation of how these forces function. For Graetz, Judaism is a blend of political and religious ideals; for Baron, a working out of the tension between nature and history; for Kaufmann, a unique blend of "a perfectly universalistic religion with an intensely nationalistic ethnic group."[34]

It is against this background that Agus presents his own version of a synthetic approach to understanding Jewish history, one that avoids the "fragmentary" quality of the other approaches and that is founded on the "quadripolar" tension among the polarities of "self-transcendence" and "dogmatism" in religion and "spiritualization" and "nihilistic chauvinism" in nationalism. For Agus, the advantage of this approach lies in its accepting the inevitable tension and interaction that characterize the historical experience of a vital, living community.[35]

In these contexts Agus typically acknowledges the inevitable power of the polarities of self-assertion and self-transcendence. "In both domains (religion and nationalism) the tension cannot be broken since the ideal ceases to exist as a massive human drive when it is severed from its corresponding instinctive gratification."[36] The dynamics of Jewish history can then be understood in terms of the varieties of nuance and emphasis given to each of the four poles in their interaction with one another. And what is unique about the Jewish experience is the way the two sets of polarities reinforce each other in response to events outside the Jewish world and to currents within the Jewish soul. This alone, Agus contends, can capture the multifaceted nature of Jewish historical experience.

Finally, it is the convergence of the pole of self-assertion in the realm of nationalism and proud dogmatism in the religious realm that accounts for the emergence of the meta-myth of Jewish chosenness or uniqueness, and for its obverse, anti-Semitism.

Agus concludes by applying this analysis to the three major centers of Jewish life: the Soviet Union, America, and Israel.

In the Soviet Union—and one should remember that Agus wrote these words decades before the massive emigration of Russian Jewry and the breakup of the USSR—nationalism is proscribed and religion discouraged. Hence, Agus forecasts the gradual dissolution of all that is distinctively Jewish in the lives of Soviet Jews. In response to this situation Agus encouraged the support and expansion of Jewish cultural and religious activity, to the extent possible, within the Soviet Union.

In America, Jewishness is primarily defined in religious terms, while in Israel, in national terms; though in neither will the other current be completely ignored. However, in each this bifurcation is colored by the polarities within each ideal. Here Agus is clear. Only the spiritual brand of nationalism will enable Israeli Jews to deal with their Arab population, and similarly, in America, only the pole of religious universalism will enable the Jew to participate fully in the richness of an open American setting. It is Agus' dream that with the achievement of these ideals, the meta-myth will fade; the ideal phases of both nationalism and religion will predominate, and the Jewish community will make its rightful contribution to a universal human spirit.[37]

Agus, then, clearly rejects the notion of a single, dominating center for world Jewry in favor of a bipolar model, with Israel and the Diaspora communities providing different centers for a vigorous Jewish life in the modern age. He repeatedly attacks the deniers (or negators) of the Diaspora as reflecting a narrowly chauvinistic reading of Jewish history. These deniers may be right in noting the element of danger that inheres in Diaspora existence, but they are totally wrong in assuming that the danger is either natural or inevitable. The peril facing Diaspora Judaism "is no more natural than the instincts of collective pride, collective envy, and the perverse sentiments of national mythologies. . . . It is no more inevitable than a mass-psychosis."[38]

Instead, Agus views American Jewry as potentially a "creative minority" in American life. Such a creative minority, first, senses its essential unity with the general population; second, "it evolves new values for the general community of which it is a part out of the peculiar circumstances which set it apart"; third, it is value-centered and oriented to the future.[39] Programmatically, this means that Jewish leaders should not preach fear about the impact of the American setting on Judaism; Diaspora Judaism should never be portrayed as unworthy or shameful; and finally, we must never permit the cultivation of a sense of alienation from America.[40]

The ultimate significance of Judaism for the larger context of Western civilization lies precisely in serving as a challenge for dealing with the universal and perennial tensions that confront every community. These tensions are threefold: between the belief in the one true faith and the claim that all faiths are equally true for each community of worshipers; between the inner and outer expressions of the faith, that is, between the "service of the heart" on the one hand and an overemphasis on sacramental ritual on the other; and between the view that a community's "chosenness" rests in its intrinsic welfare, as opposed to its devotion to eternal ideals. In its attempt to deal with these three central tensions, Judaism can legitimately hope to become a "light unto the nations."[41]

There is, then, a strong eschatological impulse within Agus' reading of Jewish history. In one of his later papers,[42] Agus contends that in modernity, the messianic vision among Jews became fragmented with the pent-up messianic fervor being channeled into one of the many possible dimensions of that classical vision. Thus, in the middle of the seventeenth century, Spinoza's thought embodied a rational impulse, Shabbatai Zevi's a mystical one. A century later, those same two impulses became embodied in the messianism of Moses Mendelssohn on the one hand and Hasidism on the other. Still later, the rationalist/universal impulse was manifest in political liberalism or socialist utopianism, whereas the mystical vision was incarnated in Zionism.

Can we hope for a progressive convergence of this fragmented vision? Agus is cautiously optimistic. Characteristically, this optimism rests in Agus' hope that the more humanist/rational/universalist, or the classical polarity in Jewish life and thought, will emerge victorious over the more chauvinist/mystical/dogmatic, or the romantic impulse, both in America and in Israel.[43]

In particular Agus is optimistic about the future of American Jewry. He thus concludes his discussion of the evolution of Jewish history with this judgment:

> It is altogether possible for the American Jew to achieve that fullness of integration with the "people of the land" that was denied to the Jews of Central Europe. . . . The Jew can be here utterly at home, as "normal" in the civil sense of the term as any other citizen of the great country. This consummation, so ardently desired by the Jews of Western Europe for a century and a half, is here embraced in the cherished tradition of the country and in its basic social structure.[44]

Apart from the issue of Agus' evaluation of the American temper, which would be strongly disputed in some sections of American Jewry, his conclusion that American Jews should try to found their Jewish identity on religion alone and that this identity would be strong enough to withstand the even more corrosive challenges of assimilation and its correlate, intermarriage, is, some would argue, challenged by recent demographic studies.[45]

This judgment, however, should be placed in the broader context of Agus' career. He was never simply the dispassionate scholar, though he was certainly that. One has to be reminded that throughout his career Agus was also a congregational rabbi, forced by his calling, week after week, to preach and teach Judaism, to apply the lessons of the tradition to contemporary events, to face real Jews who brought their total life experience into his office, searching for guidance on how to live as Jews in a difficult and complex age. Programmatic issues are never far from the center of his concern. He constantly addresses the leadership of the American and Israeli communities—rabbis and educators, leaders of federations, and Israeli governments. Dispassionate scholars may well have the luxury of indulging in detached, objective judgments. But Agus was acutely aware of his responsibility to serve as an advocate for specific courses of action in the face of complex challenges. Still, the question remains: Were Agus serving as a rabbi today, in the light of the recent concerns about assimilation and the sharp rise in intermarriage, would his programmatic suggestions be modified?

However, it must be conceded that this same critically engaged perspective accounts for Agus' strikingly candid and courageous critique of popular Zionist rhetoric, with its emphasis on *aliyah* as the exemplary expression of Jewish nationalist identity. There is no question but that long before this critique came to be part of mainstream American Jewish culture, Agus perceived that, by and large, American Jews were rooted in America and that American Jewish institutions would—and indeed, should—devote their main energies to creating conditions for a vital and articulate American Jewry, however much they advocated the Zionist cause, contributed to Israel, and used their political clout to support the policies of the State of Israel and its governments. We today accept much of that reality, but on this issue Agus was well ahead of the rest of the community. He trod the fine line between American Council for Judaism–type rejection of Zionism, on the one hand, and the uncritical acceptance of classical Zionist rhetoric—which most of his contemporaries espoused, at least in public—on the other.

However we feel about Agus' specific judgments and advocacies, then, we must be grateful for the candor, the forthrightness, and, above all, the concern that illuminate every page of his writing. In a striking comment toward the end of *The Meaning of Jewish History* (in the context of a concluding statement on the dangers of romantic Zionism), Agus pleads that "the voices of self-criticism" in American Jewry be attended to. He bemoans the fact that rabbis, traditionally the independent thinkers within the community, are now more dependent on their congregations and more vulnerable to the fears of offending national organizations. That there is no device for promoting self-criticism among American Jews is the "gravest danger to Jewish life."[46]

This model of the independent scholar-rabbi, confirmed by the testimony of his many students (who to this day speak with admiration of their experience in the Agus home on a Shabbat afternoon, spending hours poring over the classical texts of our tradition), may well be his most precious legacy to us all.

NOTES

Guide to Abbreviations

CJB *The Condition of Jewish Belief: A Symposium Compiled by the Editors of* Commentary *Magazine* (London: Collier-Macmillan, 1966).

DAT Jacob Agus, *Dialogue and Tradition: The Challenges of Contemporary Judeo-Christian Thought* (London, New York, and Toronto: Abelard-Schuman, 1971).

EJT Jacob Agus, *The Evolution of Jewish Thought: From Biblical Times to the Opening of the Modern Era* (London and New York: Abelard-Schuman, 1959).

GMJ Jacob Agus, *Guideposts in Modern Judaism: An Analysis of Current Trends in Jewish Thought* (New York: Bloch Publishing Company, 1954).

MJH Jacob Agus, *The Meaning of Jewish History,* 2 vols. (London, New York, and Toronto: Abelard-Schuman, 1963). Henceforth 1MJH and 2MJH.

MPJ Jacob Agus, *Modern Philosophies of Judaism: A Study of Recent Jewish Philosophies of Religion* (New York: Behrman's Jewish Book House, 1941).

TFH Jacob Agus, "A Theological Foundation for the Halakha," *Judaism* 29, 1 (winter 1980): 57–63.

TJQ Jacob Agus, *The Jewish Quest: Essays on Basic Concepts of Jewish Theology* (New York: Ktav, 1983):

VJB *Varieties of Jewish Belief,* ed. Ira Eisenstein (New York: Reconstructionist Press, 1966).

1. CJB, 9–10. This statement is an excellent, concise introduction to Agus' theology. For more extended discussions of these issues, see the essays collected in sections 2 and 3 of GMJ (on God, revelation, and law) and in TJQ. On the polarities of revelation, see particularly the essay "The 'Yes' and 'No' of Revelation" in TJQ, 77–86. For a critical evaluation of this material, see William Kaufman, *Contemporary Jewish Philosophies* (Lanham, Md, 1985), 231–48.

2. VJB, 3. On Agus' conception of God, see GMJ, Chaps. 4 and 5.

3. VJB, 4. On prophecy, see also "The Prophet in Modern Hebrew Literature" in DAT, 385–426, and 353ff.; and EJT, chaps. 1 and 13.

4. TFH, 58.

5. 1MJH, 12–13.

6. Ibid., 13–14.

7. Ibid., 14. On the place of religion in Agus' thought, see also the concise summaries in CJB, TFH, and VJB, and also TJQ, 35–38; DAT, 35–42; and MPJ, 336–51.

8. 1MJH, 24–27. On the role of nationalism in Agus' thought, see also the epilogue to 2MJH; part 1 ("Introduction") to MPJ (particularly 21–53); and the essays collected in part 1 of DAT. See also the trenchant critique of MJH by Ben Halpern in *Midstream* 10, 2 (June 1964): 96–101.

9. TJQ, 9. This volume, along with DAT and part 2 of GMJ, consists of essays originally published earlier and elsewhere. This reference, taken from the essay "Jewish Self-Definition: Classicism and Romanticism: Our Basic Alternatives," dating from 1972, is a concise summary of the mainstream of Agus' thinking on all of the issues covered in this paper.

10. TJQ, 18.

11. Ibid., 19.

12. Ibid., 21. The classic–romantic version of the polarities in the essay "Jewish Self-Definition," in DAT, 11–22, is arguably Agus' most illuminating summary of how the polarities function throughout the Jewish experience.

13. TJQ, 23ff. This essay, "Exceptionalism as Meta-Myth" (1979), is an excellent summary statement of Agus' thinking on the meta-myth of Jewish exclusiveness. See also, *inter alia,* "The Concept of Israel," in DAT, 450–500; GMJ, 181–87; and CJB, 14–15.

14. DAT, 222–23.

15. TJQ, 23; CJB, 13. On the doctrine of the chosen people, see also 1MJH, chaps. 1–3; GMJ, 172ff.; DAT, 222ff.; EJT, 419ff.; and the epilogue in 2MJH.

16. TJQ, 23.

17. 1MJH, 1–3.

18. CJB, 12–13.

19. TJQ, 24. On anti-Semitism, see also, *inter alia,* CJB, 15; TJQ 4–6; 1MJH, 35–39; GMJ, 181ff.; and DAT, 228ff.; and, more extensively, in 2MJH, chap. 16.

20. TJQ, 32.

21. CJB, 13.

22. GMJ, 168–69. On the future of Judaism in America, see TJQ, 7ff.; and, more extensively, GMJ, chaps. 2 and 3; and 2MJH, 475ff. On the ecumenical movement, see the essays collected in part 1 of DAT.

23. 1MJH, 44–45. See also the contrast between "rationalistic Zionists" and "romantic Zionists" in EJT, 397–98.

24. DAT, 234–35. This paper dates from 1956–1957. This positive evaluation of Herzlian Zionism is echoed in a later (1966) paper in the same collection, where Herzl is identified with a "humanist approach" to Zionism (DAT, 486), and in a third reference (dating from 1959) in the same collection, where Herzlian Zionism is part of a "rebellion against the 'uniqueness' of the Jewish status." For a contrary evaluation of Herzlian Zionism, see GMJ, 184–85 (published in 1954, though the original publication date of this particular paper is not noted), where Herzl is portrayed as advocating total assimilation and the liquidation of the Diaspora, hence as " 'Exhibit A' of the meta-myth—to wit, that the gulf between Jew and Gentile is absolute and unbridgeable." In contrast in this context, Pinsker and the other Eastern European Zionists hoped to "explode" the meta-myth by "demonstrating the sameness in quality and aspiration of Jewish and non-Jewish loyalties." In the same spirit, see the reference in 2MJH, 475, where "the works of Herzl and Pinsker" are condemned as denying the worth and the future of Diaspora Judaism. The former interpretation seems to be much more in line with the broader thrust of Agus' thought. It is difficult to conceive of Agus evaluating the work of Pinsker in a positive light.

25. On Zionism, see GMJ, 184ff.; EJT, 397ff.; DAT, 234f.; and, more extensively, in 2MJH, chap. 16.

26. 2MJH, 484–85.

27. 1MJH, 31. On the interplay of nationalism and religion in Judaism, see also MPJ, 21ff., 328ff.; the epilogue in 2MJH; DAT, 220ff.; and GMJ, 163–68.

28. DAT, 225.

29. Ibid., 227.

30. Ibid., 176–78.

31. Ibid., 178–86. Part 1 ("Introduction") to MPJ includes extensive discussions of the thought of Geiger, Steinheim, Hirsch, and Formstecher.

32. DAT, 186–206. In other contexts Agus deals extensively with the thought of Ahad Ha-Am. See, *inter alia,* 2MJH, 357–66; TJQ, 108f.; MPJ, 39–53; and GMJ, 145–48 and 151f. On Krochmal, see MPJ, 33–39; and GMJ, 99f. On Dubnow, see 2MJH, 373–79.

33. DAT, 206–9.

34. DAT, 210–16. On Agus' further evaluation of the thought of Yehezkel Kaufmann, see also EJT, 15–16; 1MJH, 93f.; and 2MJH, 350ff.; on Baron, see 1MJH, 186f.

35. DAT, 225.

36. Ibid., 223.

37. Ibid., 237–40.

38. 2MJH, 481; cf. GMJ, 148, 224.

39. GMJ, 214–15.

40. Ibid., 188–91.

41. EJT, 417–20.

42. "The Future of Jewish Messianism" (1981), in TJQ, 249–60.

43. TJQ, 259f. More extensively on Jewish messianism, see 2MJH, 269–80; DAT, 329–39; and GMG, 431ff.

44. DAT, 579f. This essay is dated 1959. See also GMJ, 164f.

45. On the recent demographical findings regarding the rate of intermarriage among American Jews, see the Council of Jewish Federations' *Highlights of the CJF 1990 National Jewish Population Survey* (New York, 1991), 13.

46. 2MJH, 476.

9

JACOB B. AGUS AND THE CONSERVATIVE MOVEMENT

Mordecai Waxman

THE DEFINING ERA of Conservative Judaism in the United States was the two decades after the end of the Second World War. This was the period in which the movement of the Jewish population to new neighborhoods and particularly to the suburbs took place. Thus new Jewish communities were formed and new institutions created, the most common and typical of which were the synagogues. These were generally established by young Jews, many of whom had no prior significant synagogue association or were seeking something different from the synagogues in which they had grown up. Typically, they were breaking with the East European–style shuls with which they were familiar and seeking a form and a style that were adapted to the American scene. The major beneficiary of these developments was the Conservative movement, which now became the largest of the Jewish denominations, followed by the Reform and with a much-weakened Orthodoxy in third place. However, the major change in American Jewish identification was asserted by synagogue identification, rather than the loose folk Jewishness and Judaism, still heavily based on European roots and background, that had characterized the preceding decades.

It was in this period and context that Jacob Agus made his notable contributions to Jewish life. While these were by no means confined to the Conservative movement, Agus' active involvement in the movement as a congregational rabbi and as an intellectual force had a very great impact. It is to his role in Conservative Judaism that this chapter is devoted.

Agus began his career as an Orthodox rabbi. Born in Poland in 1911, he pursued his education there and subsequently in Israel, and finally at the Yeshivah Rabbi Isaac Elchanan, where he was ordained as a rabbi. As an Orthodox rabbi he held pulpits in Cambridge, Massachusetts, and Chicago, Illinois. However, from the very beginning of his rabbinate he took liberal positions on matters of Jewish law and belonged to the *Judisches Wissenschaft* school, which accepted the idea that Judaism, as well as the Jewish people, had a history and therefore had changed. Thus it was quite easy for Agus to identify himself with the outlook of Conservative Judaism and to move from the Orthodox ranks into membership in the Rabbinical Assembly.

In this respect Agus was not unique. Others who were graduates of Orthodox institutions, either in the United States or abroad, were making the same transition. Indeed, the bulk of the Jewish Theological Seminary student body at that time consisted of young men who had their earlier training in Orthodox institutions.

By the time that Rabbi Agus came to Dayton, Ohio, he was a member of the Rabbinical Assembly, and he took a Conservative pulpit. The increasingly liberal tendency in his theological and halakhic thinking that had already manifested itself in Chicago continued to develop, so that by the time he settled in Baltimore, he had made the bent of his thinking abundantly clear. In Baltimore's Congregation Beth El he served a membership that, on the whole, shared his point of view and that was attracted by his personality and his intellectual achievement.

Rabbi Agus took an active role in the affairs of the Conservative movement from the very beginning of his affiliation with it. His abilities were widely appreciated, and almost immediately he was elected to the Executive Council of the Rabbinical Assembly and a variety of other committees and offices. However, his primary involvement was as a very vital factor in the law committees over the course of the years and as an intellectual force and resource in the debates that raged within the assembly in the 1950s and the 1960s about the character and direction of the Conservative movement. These debates, which sometimes involved rump sessions at conventions, were largely centered on questions of Jewish law in the context of the changing American Jewish scene. In the situation that then prevailed, where there was a clear division of the assembly into right, center and left, Rabbi Agus belonged to what might be called the left-center. He was joined in this position by an exceptional group of colleagues who largely shared his point of view and who were simultaneously articulate spokesmen for the Conservative movement and molding forces for it. Among them were contemporary figures such as Morris Adler, Ben-Zion Bokser, Theodore Friedman, and Robert Gordis who, like Agus, enjoyed a rich halakhic background and wide-ranging intellectual interests and who were engaged in the active rabbinate and confronting the problems of the American Jewish community in their daily activities.

Agus' vital involvement in the Conservative movement was manifested in a variety of ways, both great and small. Apart from his very active role in the Law Committee of the Rabbinical Assembly, he served as chairman of the assembly's Continuing Conference on Conservative Ideology. He was a frequent contributor to the magazine *Conservative Judaism* and a member of its board of editors. For some years he gave his services to the Conservative Cavalcade, which was a project designed to bring leading spokesmen of the Conservative movement to small, isolated congregations without cost and which involved plane-hopping to four or five communities in the course of a week. In later years Agus was professor at the newly formed Reconstructionist Rabbinical College, even though he was not fully committed to Reconstructionist ideas. His general liberal approach to Jewish life led him, as it did many others, to join the Reconstructionist Fellowship prior to the time when Reconstructionism became a separate movement. Like many others, he valued Reconstructionism as an element within the Conservative movement, but he was not prepared to endorse the separation. Agus meanwhile appeared in other forums as a representative Jewish spokesman. He was significantly involved in interfaith dialogue and in a highly controversial dialogue with Arnold Toynbee, who in his multivolume *Study of History* had characterized the Jews as a fossil.

However, the principal contributions of Jacob Agus to Conservative Judaism were as a scholar and an articulate expositor on a philosophy of Jewish life, and as a man with a rich halakhic background who was concerned with the changing role of Halakhah under the conditions of modern life and how it might constructively be applied to the American Jewish community. These are the subjects to which the balance of this chapter is devoted.

A PHILOSOPHY OF JUDAISM

Jacob Agus was a prolific writer on Jewish themes. Possessed of a rich Jewish background that embraced an excellent knowledge of Halakhah and an extensive training in philosophy, he merged the two bodies of knowledge in nine books and a host of articles and essays. He began his writing in a period before the rich Jewish literature in English that now exists was available, before general publishers were willing to publish works on Jewish themes, and at a time when chairs in Jewish studies were confined to seminaries. This meant that his scholarly and literary work had to be undertaken while he was pursuing an active career as a congregational rabbi. It is a testimony to his industry and rich scholarship that he was so productive.

Precisely because Agus was in the active rabbinate, however, his work reflected the perceptions and outlook of someone who had to cope with the problems of contemporary Jewish life. As a result, his writings deal with contemporary Jewish religious movements and philosophies, with theological questions, with Jewish ethical principles, and with the history of Jewish philosophy or the philosophy of Jewish history. All of his works seem intended to establish the meaning of the Jewish tradition and philosophies for the contemporary Jew rather than to undertake a purely scholarly study of the subjects. Agus was working in the frontlines of Jewish life rather than dwelling in an ivory tower, and his works were addressed to the general, intellectually minded Jewish public. Indeed, his writings were notably and happily lacking in extensive footnotes.

Basically, Agus' works reflect the underlying ideology of Conservative Judaism, which was born out of the confrontation with new conditions of Jewish life in the Western world and validated by the *Judisches Wissenschaft* scholarship of the nineteenth century. This approach was carried on in the American scene by the teaching and scholarly work at the Jewish Theological Seminary, which was the central institution of Conservative Judaism. The basic doctrine was that both Judaism and the Jewish people had a history and that Judaism had changed over the course of the centuries in relation to new circumstances and the needs of the Jewish people.

Agus' works, which had a heavy philosophical and theological emphasis, were dedicated to illustrating this thesis: in philosophy in *The*

Evolution of Jewish Thought; in a philosophy of Jewish history in *The Meaning of Jewish History;* and in the philosophy of Jewish ethics in *The Vision and the Way.* All of these explorations, as well as Agus' examination of Jewish ideologies in several books and his theological essays on *The Jewish Quest,* were founded on the meaning of the intellectual, historical, and religious tradition for the contemporary Jew and for contemporary Judaism. Agus was seeking to define appropriate paths for Judaism and the Jewish people in the revolutionary age that followed the Holocaust, the creation of Israel, and the dramatic new role of the American Jewish community. He therefore, in *The Jewish Quest,* defines revelation "to be not the conveyance of concrete information, but an awareness of the numinous and the sublime that develops into a hunger for wisdom, a dedication to goodness and an intensified sense of the holy."[1] He sees this view of Jewish thought and life reflected in Conservative Judaism, and he goes on to say that "the exposition of Maimonides' philosophy of continuous creativity" and the concepts of what he calls "Neo-maimonism" are demonstrations that the roots of Conservative Judaism are in the rationalistic current of Jewish philosophy.

In seeking, then, to define the Jewish role in what he describes as a postideological age, in which the earlier ideologies on "which we continue to feed" had been fulfilled as well as frustrated, Agus was concerned both with theological objectives and with the patterns of Jewish life, law, and organization that might further them. His theological view, expounded in a variety of ways, was that "the Jewish quest is to make oneself and the world fit for the indwelling of the Divine Presence; theologically speaking, it is a yearning for the 'Kingdom of Heaven.' " Solomon Schechter called attention to the aspects of this goal, an "invisible reality in the hearts of people . . . and the universal dimension of messianism."[2]

The value of Agus' writings and expositions to the general public was that they served as an authoritative and lucid expression of Jewish thought and ideology applied to a consideration of the contemporary situation. To his colleagues Agus represented an attempt to cope intellectually with what he designated as the "cult of ambiguity" in Conservative Judaism. He pointed out that vigorous dissent with this ambiguity was voiced chiefly by men serving in the active rabbinate and by what he characterized as intellectuals of the school of Mordecai M. Kaplan. Since Agus' earlier work was undertaken in a period when Conservative

Judaism was undergoing remarkable growth and seeking to redefine itself, his formulations had a significant impact. For his colleagues this impact was heightened by the fact that Agus was vitally concerned with how Conservative ideas could be transformed into guidelines for Jewish behavior and by his involvement in and creative contribution to the debates that were raging within the movement about the nature and treatment of Halakhah.

HALAKHAH AND CONSERVATIVE JUDAISM

Precisely because Conservative Judaism is committed to the principle that Jewish law is central to Judaism, the true test of one's definition of the Conservative ideology is in the treatment of Jewish law. It was in this area that Jacob Agus made a major contribution on both a theoretical and a practical level.

On a practical level, in a paper delivered at the 1958 convention of the Rabbinical Assembly Agus discussed three stages or emphases that grew out of one another in the Conservative approach to Jewish law.[3] The first stage he characterized as classical Conservatism, which negated Reform and adopted a basic Orthodox position, with, however, some major reservations. One such is that there are "areas of freedom" in the law that permit new interpretations or enactments. A second reservation is that there are different orders of importance in the law: biblical, rabbinic, and later enactments and customs. Tactics for the preservation of Jewish life may dictate treating laws differently. Third, and of great importance, is the recognition that there are principles in Judaism as well as laws, and at times the principle must be set above the law. And fourth, the history of Jewish life has shown that in effecting change by interpretation, the rabbinic authority was great, and the same tactics might be exercised today.

However, Agus points out, once "you digest the thought that the literalist version of the revelation at Sinai is not to be taken as historic fact but as a postulate of Faith . . . the whole foundation of classical conservatism collapses." This acceptance of history, says Agus, led to a second stage, the Reconstructionist position, an outlook that proposed the idea of ethnic folkways, "setting the people as the base instead of the dogma of revelation at Sinai. This conception was both naturalistic and nationalistic, calling attention to the rootedness of Jewish law in the realities of life. It was a good interim approach, helpful in an age of transition and congenial to the spirit of the age twenty years ago [i.e., 1938]." Agus thought it a hopeful outlook, oriented to a vision of the future, but with major drawbacks.

The third stage as he discerned it is the liberal Conservative position. Agus contends that the inadequacy of folkways as a basis is that they do not capture "the spiritual momentum contained in our sacred tradition." People, Agus asserts, give their lives for faith, not for folkways. The essentially secular character of folkways, he asserted, would be made manifest by the development of new folkways in Israel. This prediction, made in 1958, has indeed been borne out in Israeli life.

The liberal Conservative position that Agus espouses emphasizes law as standard, rather than as Halakhah with reservations or as a folkway. In an era in which *mizvot* are neither consistently practiced nor universally observed, the concept of standards may be the most effective form of education and of inducing commitment. Agus sees standards as equivalent to the idea of *Takkanot* (rabbinic ordinances) in Jewish legal thought. In essence, he contends that the doctrine and the principles of Judaism that embody the spirit behind the laws are the things to be sought. Yesterday's Aggadah must be the basis for today's Halakhah. The *taamei hamizvot*—the reasons and rationales for laws—must be considered in determining which elements of the Halakha will be fruitful and valid in our day. It is out of that sort of evaluation that the standards for observance must be built.

Agus applied this thinking—the respect for the spirit of the law, the *Aggagah,* and an examination of the reasons for the commandment—to the question of whether the Conservative movement, as a result of the establishment of Israel, should advocate the abolition of the Second Day of Festivals. His minority responsum (available in the Rabbinical Assembly files) recognizes that the uncertainty of communication is no longer a proper reason for adding a second day, but simultaneously notes that a continuing major Diaspora cannot take Israeli practice as normative for itself. Asserting that every festival is an instrument of Jewish piety, Agus proposes to retain the second day as a standard and validates it as conforming to the spirit of the law, rather than as a law whose reason has disappeared. He therefore recommends stressing the flexibility of the tradition and enriching it with fresh meaning. Specifically, he proposes to turn the Musaf service into a study period, with emphasis on the ethical and intellectual aspects of the festival. While the specific proposal is scarcely radical, what is important in the Agus analysis is the emphasis on flexibility and on finding new and positive meaning for old practices.

For Agus, the decisive recognition of what he characterized as the liberal Conservative approach came with the formulation of the "Responsum on the Sabbath," which was produced by the expanded Law Committee, designed to represent all segments of the movement, and presented to the Rabbinical Assembly Convention, but not voted on, in 1950. In their majority responsum, Rabbis Agus, Adler, and Friedman made a decisive break with the thinking and limited action of previous law committees. They thereby established the role and the thinking of the Law Committee as committed to what Agus described as liberal Conservatism. While Rabbis Gordis and Bokser did not agree with the majority conclusion, the general line of their own thinking was such as to establish the liberal Conservative outlook as the majority portion within the Rabbinical Assembly. Once the position of classical Conservatism had been set aside, the way was opened for the Conservative movement to implement its theoretical position that Jewish law could be changed. The new *Ketubah,* attempts to facilitate the giving of a get (Jewish divorce) and subsequent decisions on divorce, eventual decisions on the calling of women to the Torah and on counting them in a minyan, and the whole history of Conservative law rulings thereafter were based on and couched in the spirit of majority "Responsum on the Sabbath."[4]

The responsum addressed itself to the questions of travel on the Sabbath and the use of electricity. It analyzed the problems of observance on the American scene and proposed a program for the revitalization of the Sabbath by the united actions of all arms of the Conservative movement. However, it further advanced the thesis that "we must learn to adjust our strategy to the realities of our time and place in keeping with the realistic genius of the great builders of our faith." In this spirit the responsum permits riding to the synagogue on the Sabbath when necessary, to fulfill the *mizvah* of public worship, and permits the use of electricity as necessary in modern life for the normal comforts of living and therefore contributing to enhancing the enjoyment of the Sabbath.

Legal analysis of course underlay the responsum, but at a later date (1958), Agus made the broader point that classical Conservatism and Orthodox doctrine were untenable theoretically, as was the doctrine of Torah *min ha-shomayim* (Torah literally "revealed from heaven"), once you assume the validity of historical research. "From the study of Jewish law as developed in research, then from the study of Jewish laws as developed in Talmudic times and thence to evolution in Biblical and pre-Biblical times, no arbitrary limit is possible."[5]

In formulating the principles of what he called liberal Conservatism, Agus was not really proposing a radical doctrine. The thesis that Judaism had changed over the course of the centuries and that it was responsive to historical and sociological circumstances was, after all, the premise on which Conservative Judaism had been built. However, the question of the impact of this outlook on the doctrine of Torah *min ha-shomayim* had largely been avoided in relation to the Bible but was largely accepted in relation to the Talmud and the entire theory of the oral law. Nonetheless, classical Conservatism, while asserting the right to change Jewish law, had by and large avoided doing so.

The "Responsum on the Sabbath" represented the first major translation of a widely held theory into action. It was this propensity to face the theoretical issues and to implement them that characterized liberal Conservatism. However, the responsum and subsequent developments were an outgrowth of the restructuring of the Law Committee in November 1948. Twenty-three members were appointed to the committee on the assumption that, as a result, all the points of view about Jewish law in the Rabbinical Assembly were represented. The principles to which the majority of the committee were committed were presented after a year of study by the chairman, Rabbi Morris Adler, and included the statement that "change is a significant and characteristic property of Jewish Law. The Halachah was born out of a meeting of a people with life." Adler went on to say "such a conception of the Halachah introduces possibilities of amendment beyond the strict and formal procedure traditionally followed in effecting change." However, it was emphasized that change must be effective in creating opportunities and sensitivity for positive Jewish living.

Agus, as I indicated, was an active member of this new Law Committee, and the "Responsum on the Sabbath" that articulated the principles enumerated by Adler was his work, along with Adler's and Theodore Friedman's. While the Sabbath responsum reflected Agus' general feeling that Jewish law should make Jewish living more feasible, some of his individually composed responsa demonstrate the nuances in his thinking.

For instance, Agus considered the question of whether it is proper to have a candle-lighting ceremony at an Oneg Shabbat on Friday night if the candles have been lit earlier by the janitors. His decision was that "we should treat the established patterns of our faith with reverence, and not allow them to be misused at will. A candle-lighting ceremony in the synagogue when no candles are lit, using the blessing intended for this purpose at home, is self-contradictory. *No innovation which contains its own contradiction can possibly serve any noble or edifying purpose.*"[7] Agus then proposed an alternate form of celebration without the *brochah*. Here, as in the case of the Second Day of the Festivals, he took a more traditional position than did many colleagues who shared his liberal Conservative outlook. Nonetheless, because he recognized that the life situation did raise questions, he proposed alternate solutions."

In contrast, Agus permitted the taping of a service on the Sabbath on the general principle that in the current conditions of Jewish life, ceremonies such as bar mitzvah have a special lifelong impact, and therefore recording them is desirable. While stressing the psychological reason, Agus offered an interesting legal theory. He wrote, "I consider it possible that the rabbis defined the prohibited categories of work in the archaic terms of the building of the *Mishkan* (Tabernacle) in order to allow a certain latitude for future generations." Agus took the point further by proposing that distinction in purpose rather than manner of performance should be decisive, citing the talmudic passage *Shabbat* 103: "If it is to serve your desire, it is forbidden; if it is to serve the purposes of your Maker, it is permitted."[8] To create a basis for accepting and implementing this practice, Rabbi Agus called for the adoption of a *Takkanah* by the Rabbinical Assembly.

The idea of *Takkanah* as a means of dealing with problems in Jewish law was central to Agus' halakhic philosophy. In discussing a "Theological Foundation for the Halachah" (*Jewish Quest,* 198), Agus cites Maimonides to assert that not all Halakhot are born equal: "We have to study their origin in history, their justification in philosophy, their pragmatic consequences, their merit in terms of the primary interest of faith." The living community of Israel, as a result, has developed different schools of interpretation. According to Agus, Conservative Judaism is one such school and is characterized by the attitude that the "Halachah is a starting point, not a blueprint, and it is one of the given components of our tradition, not the whole of it."

Asserting that Conservative Jews are not literalists and therefore do not accept revelation in the Torah or in the oral law word for word, and denying the binding quality of custom, Agus lays the foundation for defining a means of changing Jewish law. He rejects the method of individual interpretation founded by some of his colleagues as leading to anarchy. He proposes instead a system of *Takkanot* in which the sense of communal enactment is provided by the Law Committee and by congregational endorsement. Further asserting the doctrine of *Klal Yisrael,* defined as the consensus of the concerned, Agus suggests that the rabbinate does not totally exhaust the category of those whose opinion should be weighed in formulating Jewish law today. He points to others who help to shape the Jewish mentality, including academic philosophers, scholars, educators, social workers, writers. Moreover, as the domain of religion is progressively contracted to the synagogue, associations of the synagogue come closest to representing the religious fellowship of Israel and to providing authoritative endorsement of *Takkanot.* Just how much latitude Agus is prepared to allow the collective synagogue in endorsement is not clear. Presumably, he would limit himself to those who accept the Halakhah as central to Judaism and thus limit himself to the *Klal Yisrael.* Yet in an essay on liberal Judaism, Agus, while asserting that Reform Judaism denies the worth of laws governing the domain of religious life, expresses his expectation that in the future it, too, will accept standards of Jewish observance.[9] He argues therefore for the continuance of diversity in ritual but for "the emergence of a common ideological platform of Liberal Judaism which would deal with the major issues of the Jewish world."

Nonetheless, while the remarks on liberal Judaism were a recognition that there was a need to seek Jewish unity on the basis of ethical and spiritual principles, rather than only through ritualistic and liturgical expressions, Agus was primarily concerned with a forceful treatment of Jewish law by the Conservative movement. He contended therefore that the Sabbath responsum should not be regarded as a *hetair* (a permissive ruling) but rather as a *Takkanah* through which the movement asserted its willingness to grapple with the problem of Jewish life in relation to the conditions of life and took deliberate and collective positive action to find an answer. Agus was not disposed to suggest that the citing of legal sources, precedents, and interpretations was irrelevant, but he sought an activist approach to Jewish law by the consensus of the Rabbinical Assembly and the collective congregations represented in the United Synagogue and by the the free employment of the *Takkanah.* Indeed, he extended his concept to propose that the tradition develops by new *Takkanot,* which he defined as ordinances of conduct initiated by the elite; *aggadot,* as new ideas which arise either out of Judaism or out of universal culture; and *minhagim,* as customs initiated by the people and concurred in by the elite.[10] In essence, he said, "our entire sacred tradition is the compendium of *takkanot* in previous generations. The living traditions that we shall leave to the future will consist, in effect, of the *takkanot* we institute in our lifetime."

Agus' ideas on the nature of Conservative Judaism were not unique. They were circulating within the group that he referred to as the liberal Conservatives. In the Rabbinical Assembly of the late 1940s, the 1950s, and the 1960s, this group constituted the central and majority group that incorporated and harmonized the thinking of the classical Conservatives on the right and the Reconstructionists on the left.

In summary, Agus' contribution to the dominant group was, first, that he gave its ideas significant and authoritative theoretical and lucid expression. Second, he participated actively in the work of the legal and ideological bodies in the Rabbinical Assembly and was a major factor in formulating decisive responsa, most notably the Sabbath responsum, that initiated a new and activist era in dealing with Jewish law in the Conservative movement. The methods of dealing with *Agunah* status, with the role of women in the synagogue, and with the ordination of women as rabbis and cantors all stemmed from the change in approach involved in the reorganized Law Committee and the Sabbath responsum. Third, because Agus was a practising pulpit rabbi and a productive scholar, he, like several of his contemporary colleagues, brought the realities of American Jewish life into the courts of law and translated the new approaches into the life of the community.

"One generation goes and another generation comes," and it is highly probable that a younger generation of the Conservative rabbinate and lay leadership does not know of its indebtedness to Jacob Agus. But perhaps they unknowingly quote his words, live by his ideas, and follow his rulings.

NOTES

1. Jacob Agus, *The Jewish Quest* (New York, 1983), vii.
2. Solomon Schechter, cited by Jacob Agus in *The Jewish Quest,* vii.
3. *Proceedings of the Rabbinical Assembly, 1958* (New York, 1958), 81.
4. Mordecai Waxman, ed., *Tradition and Change* (New York, 1958), 348.
5. *Proceedings of the Rabbinical Assembly, 1958,* 112.

6. Ibid., 70.

7. This responsum will be found in the files of the Rabbinical Assembly.

8. Rabbi Agus' full discussion of these issues will be found in the files of the Rabbinical Assembly.

9. *Dialogue and Tradition* (New York, 1971).

10. See Jacob Agus, *The Jewish Quest,* 199.

10
JEWISH LAW AS STANDARDS
Elliot N. Dorff

JACOB AGUS was among the first to develop a philosophy of Jewish law distinctive to Conservative Judaism. Zacharias Frankel had long since argued for the legitimacy of change within Jewish law while still maintaining loyalty to it, and others such as Alexander Kohut and Israel Friedlander had subsequently continued and expanded that line of argumentation. Solomon Schechter had called attention to the role of "catholic Israel" in defining the content of the law, although not with much clarity or depth. Louis Ginzberg, Louis Finkelstein, and many others at the Jewish Theological Seminary of America had written essays and books about specific topics within Jewish law, but none had seriously and thoroughly tackled the philosophical questions inherent in the historical approach they were taking in their scholarship. Mordecai Kaplan was the sole exception, but his view of God in deistic terms as the power in nature that makes for salvation forced him to interpret Jewish ritual law as mere folkways, a view that was destined to split off from the Conservative movement and become Reconstructionism.

In the late 1940s and the early 1950s, though, several factors made it imperative to formulate a distinctly Conservative philosophy of law. The Holocaust had just wiped out the eminent rabbinical seminaries of Europe. That meant American Jews could no longer depend on, and were no longer constrained by, European rabbinic scholarship. On the contrary, American Jewry had suddenly become the largest Jewish community in the world, a place it occupies to this day. American rabbis, then, had to take on the responsibility of shaping Judaism in the last half of the twentieth century. Since the vast majority of America's Jews were affiliated with the Conservative movement—still the largest religious movement in North America—that task was especially critical for Conservative rabbis. Boaz Cohen, Robert Gordis, and others leaped into the fray in what must have been an immensely exciting and heady time.[1]

It was precisely in this context that Jacob Agus wrote the philosophical essays that were to become the cornerstone of his later work in Jewish law. They were first published in the journal *Conservative Judaism* in close succession: "Torah M'Sinai" (February 1947), "Law in Conservative Judaism" (February 1948), and "Laws as Standards" (May 1950). Those essays, together with his seminary lecture "Pluralism in Law" (summer 1953), subsequently appeared as chapters 6, 7, 8, and 9 of his 1954 book *Guideposts in Modern Judaism*.

In these writings Agus managed to develop what was arguably the most thoroughgoing philosophy of law for the Conservative movement. More than anyone else (with the possible exception of Robert Gordis), Agus spelled out not only what the Conservative approach to Jewish law was and should be but why one should adopt it. This required him to articulate not only an approach to Jewish law but also a theory of revelation and, ultimately, a theology. On each of these topics Agus' arguments combine the latest in modern scientific theory with the knowledge we have gained through a historical approach to the Jewish tradition. As such, Agus quintessentially preserves all three of the characteristics that became the hallmarks of Conservative Judaism: a theistic, personal God who commands; a historical approach to understanding the Jewish tradition, including its legal texts and practices; and a willingness to integrate those first two principles in concrete legal decisions.

This chapter, then, concentrates on the essays listed above while noting relevant material in Agus' later philosophical works that expanded on his vision of Jewish law. We will also see how Agus applied his perception of Jewish law to several concrete cases he addressed in responsa for the Conservative movement's Committee on Jewish Law and Standards. In doing so, we hope to recapture an approach to Jewish law that, in this author's opinion, has much to teach us today.

THE SOURCES OF AUTHORITY FOR JEWISH LAW: REASON AND REVELATION

Following a long line of Jewish philosophers, Agus speaks of two "pillars" that form the foundation of Judaism: reason and revelation. He argues against those who would base Judaism on either one alone.

Revelation cannot be the exclusive source of Jewish law's authority, according to Agus, because "there can be no inner correspondence between our present feeling and the events of several thousand years ago."[2] That is, even if we want to believe that verbal revelation took place amid thunder and lightning at Sinai, our own experience does not give us warrant for that belief, for we now do not experience such a revelation. The Passover liturgy wants us to identify with that event when it proclaims, "In every generation a person must see him/herself as if s/he left Egypt," but even that liturgy recognizes the best it can hope for is that contemporary people *see* (that is, imagine) themselves *as if* they had left Egypt. Thus immediate experience will not provide the necessary ground for Judaism for contemporary Jews, even if it did so for those who stood at Sinai.

Moreover, reason is necessary for faith if one "is to escape the manifold pitfalls of unbridled superstition and unmitigated fanaticism." The religious bent in people is that which recognizes human limitations and dependence on factors beyond human comprehension and/or control. Keen awareness of those elements in our experience makes for passivity, acceptance, and thankfulness. Religious people are therefore all too prone to accept superstitions as absolutely true and to acquiesce to fanatic and sometimes downright immoral actions, based on blind faith in what is presented as religious truth—often on the basis of some interpretation of the religion's official revelation. Reason, then, is necessary to counteract these inclinations.

Reason is also necessary to balance another common religious tendency, namely, the emphasis on inwardness. In some forms of mysticism, for example, one turns inward to find God, either with the help of revelation or as a substitute for revelation. Often this is accompanied by a disdain for reason and a denial of the reality of the physical world. For Agus, though, genuine piety requires a dialectic from subjectivity to objectivity, and vice versa. One must balance inner perceptions and emotions with reason and experience focused on the world outside us, "for the life of the spirit is not a static reflection and crystallization of the Truth, but a dynamic apprehension of it from every changing angle, in the ceaseless change of perspective from subjectivity to objectivity, and back again. . . . To condemn objective piety [based on reason] on the grounds of inwardness is therefore to betray the marks of spiritual astigmatism."[3]

And finally, Agus notes, in our day revelation cannot justify propositions that are not supported by reason, even if there are no compelling proofs to the contrary and even if such propositions are deemed necessary for one's salvation. That is, revelation cannot fill in gaps left by reason. That is because "the dogma of 'Torah M'Sinai,' in its fundamentalist interpretation, is no longer a 'live' proposition to those who have made their own the spirit of Western culture and the modern methods of research in the history of religions."[4] In the past, Jews—perhaps even large numbers of them—may have believed that the manuscript of the Torah we have in hand is the literal word of God at Sinai and therefore supercedes all other forms of knowledge in its authority and, indeed, sets the criteria for what will count as knowledge from any other source. In the modern world, however, that is no longer true. Western culture has all but totally triumphed among Jews, and therefore even religion must submit to the canons of intersubjective reason for its analysis and validation. In such a context, Agus asserts, basing the authority of Jewish law on a literalist interpretation of the Torah *in the absence of* rational grounds for believing what it says is no longer even what William James would call a "live" option for contemporary Jews. Where reason seems to contradict propositions affirmed on the basis of the Torah, revelation would lose even more credibility in the eyes of moderns.

However, Jewish law's claims to authority, according to Agus, should not be based on reason alone. When one does this, as many nineteenth-century Jewish thinkers did, "the Law is stripped of every vestige of authority, the whole range of tradition is denied any inherent truth-value, and worship becomes a mere human exercise in mnemonics";[5] for if reason is the sole source of authority, everything else—law, beliefs, story, revelation, poetry, custom, history—becomes handmaiden in its service, demonstrating or re-enforcing rational principles in some way. This strips Jewish law of its inherent authority, making whatever sanction it has a derivative of reason.

Reason cannot sustain such a burden, and Agus provides four reasons to demonstrate why.[6] First,

> religious consciousness is a realm of unique values, *sui generis,* even as art and music, so that in it the concepts of ethics and esthetics acquire a special tone and substance. Beauty is transmuted into a feeling of the Divine, duty is viewed as self-orientation to the Divine Will and the measure of right and wrong is construed as the judgment of God.[7]

That is, even where reason can help us understand phenomena such as moral principles or aesthetic qualities, those phenomena, when viewed by reason, appear in its specific light. They take on a completely different coloration and meaning, however, when experienced in the context of religion. If one's view of these phenomena is going to be adequate to their substance, then, one must use both reason and other avenues of knowledge appropriate to the specific phenomena to know and understand them. In the case of Jewish law, the other appropriate approach is through revelation, as Jewish sources themselves attest.

Second, within religious consciousness all objects are seen as dependent and creaturely, functions of a higher power. That is, religious people view our finite world as limited in its power and dependent on that which goes beyond it. This perception is not a reasoned inference but rather "an immediate intuition of the transcendent." One recognizes such a perception of our finite world as appropriate without creating a rational argument to claim so but rather as soon as one experiences it. It is like the experience of trying on a pair of eyeglasses: one knows immediately whether or not the view of the world they give is right. If asked to do so, one may be able to supply some arguments to demonstrate that a particular view of the world is suitable, but such arguments are not the basis of one's conviction that the eyeglasses give a proper vision of the world; that comes from the experience itself. Reason is therefore not the sole ground of our religious knowledge.

Third, religion in general and religious law in particular develop organically. They are not the product of abstract truths applied in some ivory tower; they grow instead out of the continuing experiences of a community that affirms a religion's truths and lives by its laws. Because this is so, reason is really incapable of capturing much of the substance of Jewish law. Reason, after all, is universal in its nature, while Jewish law is peculiar to the Jewish people. Furthermore, a rational argument is, at least in theory, valid or invalid forever, while Jewish law is subject to changes over time. Jewish law may derive some of its authority from the rational and moral purposes it serves, but the particular and developing qualities of Jewish law prove that those purposes cannot be the whole story.

And finally, fourth, "revelation is an actual phenomenon, not merely a euphemism, and Judaism is a revealed religion." In other words, any interpretation of Judaism that denies the revelational base of it in favor of reason alone is to that extent distorting Judaism.

Agus defines revelation as "the belief that truth and creative vision may come to man from God, thru *[sic]* channels other than the physical senses." He distinguishes three stages of revelation: (1) the intuition of the objective validity of ethical values; (2) experiencing the highest levels of religious feeling, designated "the feeling of the holy," "when the awareness of Divine mystery and majesty is the supreme note in man's consciousness," prompting one to dedicate oneself to God in the moral forms revealed in the first stage of revelation; and (3) "the covenant or destiny experience," when one acquires new insight and creative energy, such as the revelations that led to the appearance of Judaism in the midst of the pagan world. All people are recipients of the first two levels of revelation if they open themselves to receiving it, but the third stage is the possession of only a privileged few.

Just as the second stage of revelation includes and fortifies the first, so, too, the third stage proves "its authenticity by the intensification it affords to the first two phases of revelation. . . . Religion, in the specific or Jewish meaning of the term, is thus seen to be inherently related to the ethical ideal, as the roots of the tree are to its fruits." Agus in fact takes it as a specific mark of "the Conservative conception of the authority of Jewish law" that the higher phases are to be judged for their authenticity by their effect on the lower levels,

> for whereas the higher states of revelation gain in inspiration and in creative power over the lower ones, they decrease correspondingly in the quality of objectivity. . . . Thus, concerning every form of piety, it is legitimate to inquire whether it conduces to the good life of ethics, and in regard to every claim of Divine inspiration, it is necessary to employ the yardsticks of genuine piety, as we know it.[8]

Deuteronomy, the fifth book of the Torah, suggests two criteria for determining whether a revelation is true. Chapter 13 says that if the prophet tells you to worship other gods, that proves she or he is a false prophet. Chapter 18 makes prophetic authenticity depend on whether the prophet's predictions come true. Agus' criterion of moral rectitude is neither of these, but it is closer to the first, for in both Deuteronomy 13 and in Agus' approach, true prophets are to be recognized by the content of their words. Deuteronomy 13, though, makes the judgment depend on the theological correctness of the prophet's words, while Agus focuses on their moral rectitude.

LAWS AS STANDARDS

Agus is not simply restating the obvious when he makes the law depend on the combination of reason and revelation. As we have seen, his commitment to reason forces him to deny an Orthodox, literalist understanding of the Torah, which would locate the authority of Jewish law—ultimately, at least—in revelation alone. In contrast, he also finds it necessary to show why reason cannot be the exclusive source of authority for Jewish law either. Probably the hardest battle he had to fight within the Conservative movement, however, was against three popular conceptions of Jewish law that base its authority on historical and sociological factors.

One such theory is that proposed by Mordecai M. Kaplan, to wit, that Jewish law consists of moral demands and of folkways. Agus points out that conceiving of many of the commandments as folkways robs them of legitimacy as commandments and of authority to command unto death. Folkways lack historical legitimacy to obligate, for Judaism from its very roots denied parental folkways in order to attain patterns of action that reflect divine truth:

> Is the nostalgic reverence for parental practice to be glorified as an absolute imperative? Such a consummation would indeed offer a strange climax to the great adventure of Judaism, which began with a revolt against established customs and parental mores, as expressed in the command given to Abraham, "go, thou, from thy land, the place where thou wast born and from the house of thy fathers."

Furthermore, philosophically, folkways lack the power to bind, which, for Agus, can come only from a deep conviction that Jewish law articulates divine truth:

> Why should we strive with might and main to preserve folkways? . . . The motivation of Jewish piety was actually derived from a deep conviction in the truth of Israel's religious heritage, and the consequent common sense preference of eternal reward for temporary bliss. In this interpretation [of Jewish laws as folkways], however, the glory of Jewish martyrdom for the sake of Divine truth and the soberness of its mentality would be interpreted as the senseless stubbornness of a clannish people, fanatically isolating itself from the ways of the world, forebearing all mundane goods and spiritual values for the sake of mere tribal customs.

Interpreting Jewish laws as folkways, Agus is convinced, could appeal only to a transitional generation that lost the purpose but retained the sentiment of group survival for no good reason that it could give.[9]

A second conception of Jewish law, that of Ahad Ha'am, views law as a bulwark to preserve Jewish national identity in the Diaspora. This approach, Agus acknowledges, is widespread among the American rabbinate and laity; it is invoked whenever there are appeals to preserving the "Jewish way of life." Historically, however, Jews obeyed Jewish law out of religious conviction; the survival of Jewish nationality was an effect, rather than a cause. Indeed, it is not at all clear that the survival of every branch of a biological or historical group must be regarded as a supreme end in itself; the Nazi experience, at least, should call into question any philosophy that puts ultimate value in blood and folk. And finally, if preserving Jewish nationhood is the only reason to obey Jewish law, it should become obsolete now that the State of Israel has been established, at least for those who live there, and even for those who choose to bask in its reflected national glory while living elsewhere.

A third understanding of Jewish law to which Agus objects goes to the very roots of the Conservative movement, appearing as it does in the writings of Zechariah Frankel and Solomon Schechter. It is the idea, propounded by the "historical school" and rooted in nineteenth-century romanticism, that Jewish law is the product of the national psyche (soul), which developed over time, and that it therefore must be maintained, even if—perhaps, especially if—it is irrational. Here again, though, "what is to prevent historic processes that functioned relatively well in the past to function poorly in the present, or even to cease functioning altogether?" Moreover, how can historical processes "be regarded as sources of absolute value, sufficient unto themselves?"[10]

These sociological and historical views, then, cannot provide a source of validity for Jewish law. They speak to the body of the law, not its soul. But if Conservative Jews are not, for reasons of historical accuracy, going to see the Torah, much less later Jewish law, as the direct transcription of God's word, how can they understand Jewish law in a way that preserves its authenticity and authority? Agus articulates his task in this remarkably candid way:

> Let us begin our analysis then with a frank and clear rejection of the literalist Orthodox position. We do not believe that God dictated the Torah to Moses, as a scribe to a pupil, and that He had transmitted to Moses all the comments, interpretations, and inferences relating to it that were later recorded in the Oral Law. Having taken this step, we find ourselves still profoundly convinced of the importance of the Law and its supreme significance. But if these vague sentiments of reverence are to serve as the enduring foundations for Judaism of the future, they must be envisaged in all clarity as proven true in terms of the contemporary situation and as rooted firmly in the eternal scheme of things. How then shall we think of Halachah?[11]

He outlines five elements of a viable answer to this challenge: it must acknowledge, first, that "the relationship of the Jew to God is the incontrovertible starting point" of any theory of Jewish law that preserves the self-understanding and motivation Jews have had historically in obeying it. Second, the commandments historically have been authoritative not only because they were seen as the word of God but also because they purified human beings morally and served as worthy instruments of piety. Third, the authority of the commandments traditionally has rested not only on the conviction that God commanded them but also on their acceptance by the Jewish people. (Thus, according to rabbinic legend, "the Torah was offered to the other nations, but it is not for them obligatory since they never accepted it.") Fourth, in addition to the moral-legal basis of Jewish law, the Jewish people's historical memory also played a major role in affording authority to Jewish law. We all were at Sinai, and we all, along with our ancestors and descendants, agreed to become part of the covenant with God. Fifth, and finally, the precepts of the law constitute the minimal standards of the community; the good person must rise above its demands and act beyond the letter of the law.[12]

These tenets together, Agus maintains, lead to a conception of Jewish law as "standards," or "divinely imposed disciplines of the Jewish people." Agus stresses that the authority of Jewish law rests on both components of that formula, namely, God and the Jewish people.

In theological language, the authority of Jewish law derives from the love of God. Agus describes God as "the Pole of the Absolute, Ideal Personality"; using the language of physics, God is the ultimate point in the field of reality. In the love of God, then, "all moral and esthetic values are fused together into a new and creative unity." God thus functions dynamically as both the source and the goal of all human ideals, and the goal of all Jewish law "may be viewed as being motivated by the one sustained attempt to incorporate the love of God as a living reality in every phase of public and private experience." But it is not God alone who is the source of authority of the commandments, for love must be mutual. Therefore, Jewish law is both "Divinely inspired and self-imposed."[13]

Furthermore, it is multiple in character. Agus proposes that we think of Jewish law as a threefold ladder leading to God, corresponding to the three pillars of Jewish faith: Torah, worship, and good deeds. This model accurately describes both the accomplishments and the remaining challenges of those who climb high on one ladder while remaining on the lower rungs of the other ladders, and it "permits us to regard all Jewish groups, seeking sincerely to elevate the level of spiritual life, as falling within the pattern of one common endeavor."[14] Thus, conceiving of Jewish law as three sets of standards enables us to understand and appreciate what we and others have done in striving for the divine goals of morality and piety, thereby engendering feelings of pluralism and cooperation within the Jewish community while still depicting what we all have yet to do in seeking the ideal.

TRADITION AND CHANGE

Legal expressions of piety are the body that enables the soul of piety—and derivatively, of ethics—to become part of our lives. Without such concrete manifestations of ethics and piety, our claims of commitment to the latter would be empty:

> Religious seeing . . . is not only perception, but dedication and action as well. Thus, the original insight of Judaism was never simply Knowledge of the One God, but a consecration to the service of the One God. . . .

> Halachah is for us the way in which God's word is progressively being shaped into ways of life.[15]

Therefore such legal forms must be preserved. Since they are easier to grasp than the abstract goals of morality and piety, though, laws tend to be conservative in nature, evidencing little room for changing the specific way in which they embody the moral and pious elements at their core. Therefore, while Agus is careful to say that legal forms must be maintained so that revelation in both its moral and religious aspects can enter our lives meaningfully, he also makes it clear that, in his opinion, laws are "identified as instruments" and must always be subject to evaluation according to the objective goals they are designed to advance. Put succinctly, morality and piety trump laws whenever the latter get in the way of the former or cease to further them:

> The revealed character of Jewish legislation refers to the general subconscious spiritual drive which underlies the whole body of Halachah, not to the details of the Law. The vital fluid of the Torah-tree derives from the numinous soil of the Divine, but the actual contours of the branches and the leaves are the product of a variety of climatic and accidental causes.[16]

At the same time, "it is necessary to beware of the kind of changes that destroy the spell of the Law." Even if a given law begs to be changed because it violates our sense of morality or piety, Agus says, rabbis must take care not to change a specific law in a way which undermines respect for the law as a whole. "The new must be so delicately grafted upon the old that the health of the tree as a whole will not be affected."[17]

This, of course, complicates matters. However difficult it may be to recognize when a given law sufficiently offends our sense of morality or piety to require change, it is even harder to balance such considerations against the need to preserve the integrity of the corpus of the law. Judging the law by the objective standards of morality and piety entices one to change the law, or at least to be ready to do so. Concern for preserving the integrity of the law, in contrast, prompts one to be wary about any change. In Agus' terms, morality and piety, which are "objective" in that they are shared by everyone, come into conflict with the "subjective" ways individuals and groups have traditionally expressed them in practice.

But that is precisely Agus' point: a Conservative position must find a way to balance both of these impulses, just as it balances reason and revelation. In contrast to the Reform position, which focuses on reason and change at the expense of revelation and continuity, and in contrast to the Orthodox position, which does the reverse, the Conservative position affirms both elements of these two pairs equally: reason *and* revelation, tradition *and* change. This subjects the Conservative Jew to the tension inherent in doing so; the simplicity, clarity, and confidence of those who embrace one or the other of the extremes are not available to him or her. For Agus, though, the price is worth the gain, for the Conservative position is the only one that preserves both truth and Jewish authenticity:

> The life of the spirit is a ceaseless movement between the two poles of objectivity and subjectivity. He who would keep his soul turned to the rhythm of truth must forever be on the move. He cannot stop at either pole and embrace the whole truth in his bosom; back and forth, he must move between the subjective and objective poles of the spirit, if he is not to petrify in static, sterile self-admiration. For reason and faith imply and fructify each other. . . .
>
> Coming now to the problems of Judaism proper, we maintain that our employment of a two-fold evaluation in the assaying of laws and ceremonies is true to the inward nature of piety. On the one hand, we accept the Halachah subjectively; on the other hand, we subject specific halachic precepts to criticism by means of the objective standards of piety and the good life that derive from the *yetzer tov* [good inclination] of modern thought and civilization. Both approaches are integral to the life of the spirit; we cannot afford to give up either one without forfeiting the soul of our faith.[18]

LEGISLATION AS A METHOD OF CONSERVATIVE JEWISH LAW

Agus, though, does not have the usual notions in mind when he affirms the necessity to preserve Jewish law. On the one hand, he thinks that much more must be done than "business as usual" to engender observance of the law; he envisions, in fact, a vigorous campaign to make it a priority for the Jewish masses. On the other hand, though, he thinks that the process of applying Jewish law in our day also cannot be "business as usual"; it must instead be done using much more aggressive legal techniques. What marks both of these contrary moves—the one toward tradition, the other toward change—is balance and vigor, two characteristics that pervade Agus' thought.

First, on the side of tradition, Agus asserts that Conservative Judaism must not be characterized exclusively by the ways in which it has broken away from Orthodoxy. That would be to cast it in a solely negative light, defining it according to what it does *not* do. Instead, the Conservative movement must devote itself with enthusiasm and energy to stimulating knowledge, observance, and piety among its adherents, so that it is characterized by what Conservative Jews *do.* Toward that end, the movement "must undertake a campaign for the stimulation of a minimum of religious observances among our people, stressing in particular those precepts which contribute decisively and directly to the cultivation of the spirit of piety, such as the acceptance of regular weekly worship and study periods."[19]

Agus clearly would have liked more than "a minimum of religious observances," but he was enough of an educator to discern the difference between the ideal and the possible and to recognize the need to begin with something that could clearly be accomplished. Others of his colleagues apparently agreed with his assessment of the educational realities and with this aspect of his approach to Jewish law, for his idea of a campaign to engender observance was soon to be embedded in the "Responsum on the Sabbath," approved by the Law Committee, that he coauthored with two other rabbis. Whether or not one agrees with his strategy, it clearly indicates that Agus wanted to shift the momentum within the Conservative movement from what it denied to what it affirmed, and his campaign to engender observance among the many Jews affiliated with the Conservative movement was one aspect of Agus' understanding of a Jewishly serious movement.

While dedication to observance must be one mark of the Conservative movement, another must be its readiness to modify the content of Jewish law in order to achieve its moral and religious goals. Agus maintains that the Conservative movement's Law Committee, as constituted at the time, is "insufficient" to the task at hand. If the Conservative movement sees itself authorized only to interpret and apply traditional law, it will never get beyond the claims of the Orthodox to be the only authentic form of Judaism, for that is precisely what they do. Even if Conservative responsa generally prefer the lenient option within the traditional materials, the movement will not be distinctive in character and, worse, will always feel itself undermined by the learning and zeal of the Orthodox. Moreover, such an approach is based on an exaggeration of the degree of freedom embedded in traditional Jewish law, and if the Conservative movement does nothing else, it should not, as a movement dedicated to historical Judaism, misrepresent what the historical sources say.

The way out of this problem, according to Agus, is for the Conservative movement to have the courage and creativity to act on its own principles. What Jewish history does reveal is that various Jewish communities over time went beyond the interpretive method and legislated laws *(takkanot)*. Sometimes these represented changes in what had been traditional practice, and sometimes they were simply positive law to address community needs not covered in the received law. In like manner, Agus asserts, "we need a law making body, not a law interpreting committee."[20]

Why have the Orthodox rejected such an approach? In large part, Agus avers, because they have an exaggerated sense of the deference that must be paid to earlier sources. They are, indeed, stymied by the authority they attribute to previous generations, who, by that very fact, are for the Orthodox greater in wisdom and knowledge than any contemporary person or group could be. Such an approach, though, is not necessitated by the sources themselves, which demand that we have respect for previous generations but that judges in each generation decide matters "according to what their own eyes see." Therefore, the Orthodox methodology represents a *choice* as to how to read Jewish sources, and it is an arbitrary one at that, for it flies in the face of some of those very sources. Furthermore, the automatic Orthodox preference for the earliest decisions is "a mechanical principle of selection" of what should count in determining the law, rather than one based on the merits of any particular case. As such, it does not hold much promise for wisdom in applying Judaism to modern circumstances:

> If we follow the principle that the rabbis of our own days are incompetents and that the rabbis of the past were all-knowing, we undermine the very basis for development and growth in religion, even while we presume to speak in the name of religious progress. Obviously, the past cannot of its own momentum effectively progress in the contemporary world. Again, if we deny Divine sanction to the "Rishonim" [rabbis of the tenth to the sixteenth centuries] and grant it to the masters of the Talmud [completed ca. 500 C.E.], or if we deny it to the Amoraim and

> Tannaim [the rabbis of the first through the fifth centuries C.E.], reserving it for the prophets [who lived between the ninth and the fifth centuries B.C.E.], we should be operating with a mechanical principle of selection, for which there is no basis in our philosophy of Judaism. . . . From our viewpoint, then, the present is more determinative than the past, and the immediate past more authoritative than the remote past.[21]

Agus proposes, then, that the Conservative movement make extensive use of the method of legislation *(takkanah).* He is careful to point out that this is a perfectly traditional way of doing Jewish law, evidenced in Jewish history from at least as early as the first century C.E. (indeed, arguably from the time of Ezra in the fifth century B.C.E.) and continuing throughout the Middle Ages and the modern period to contemporary times. The corpus of legislation includes measures that embodied far-reaching sociological change, as, for example, in the *takkanot* of Rabbenu Gershom (ca. 1000 C.E.), which decreed monogamy and the need for a woman's consent to a divorce. Thus Agus thinks that there is ample precedent for using legislation as a legal method in our own time.

Moreover, that method is definitely needed now, for, as Agus asks rhetorically, "is not our time and circumstances so strikingly new as to justify the creation of new precedents?"[22] As we shall see, he has in mind not only the needs of contemporary Jewish society to make changes in the law but also—and perhaps, primarily—its need for legislation to reenforce practices that Jewish law already mandates.

In addition to these historical arguments, Agus supports the use of legislation on legal and philosophical grounds. Legally, as he points out, legislation was justified on the basis of Deuteronomy 17:11: "You shall act in accordance with the instructions they [the judges of your generation] give you and the ruling they hand down to you; you must not deviate from the verdict they announce to you either to the right or to the left." The "you must not deviate" *(lo tasur)* clause in the verse Agus calls "the magna carta of rabbinic legislation," and it is indeed the source of authority that the rabbis of the Talmud and thereafter used to stretch the law considerably in all directions.[23] If, on the one hand, the Conservative movement is not going to restrict itself to the legal method of interpretation, and if, on the other hand, it is not going to abandon Jewish law altogether, then, according to Agus, it must embrace the method of legislation "or else disappear from the scene, as a movement."[24]

Philosophically, says Agus, "this principle [of *takkanah*] is fully in accord with our dynamic conception of revelation."[25] He elaborates on his own concept of revelation at length in another essay included in his 1954 book *Guideposts in Modern Judaism* and in a subsequent book (published in 1983) as well,[26] but in referring to "our dynamic conception of revelation" here, he undoubtedly has in mind any of the concepts of revelation within the Conservative movement, many of which were stated explicitly only after Agus made his proposal. Even so, Agus clearly realized by 1949 that, by definition of "Conservative Judaism," all Conservative concepts of revelation would have to take into account the historical development of the Torah and would understand revelation as continuing in our day through the work of contemporary rabbis and thinkers.[27] That tenet of continuous revelation, Agus maintains, also argues for contemporary rabbis to use the legal vehicle of legislation as they discern the will of God in new ways, of which only some can be reasonably derived from interpreting previous elements of the tradition.

PUTTING THE METHOD OF LEGISLATION INTO PRACTICE

Legislation, then, is one mode of applying Jewish law that the Conservative movement must embrace. In the past, Jewish legislation has enjoyed two sanctions, "one deriving from the most sensitive conscience and the most creative scholarship of the age, the other deriving from the democratic principle of 'the consent of the governed.' " Accordingly, Agus proposes the establishment of two bodies: a "Jewish Academy," similar to the French Academy of Napoleon's time, consisting of selected rabbis, scholars, and laypeople; and periodic, joint special sessions of the United Synagogue and the Rabbinical Assembly, empowered to accept or reject *takkanot* proposed by the academy.

Agus deliberately calls the first body "the Jewish Academy" and *not* "the Sanhedrin" so as to rule out from the beginning any pretensions to the authority that the ancient Sanhedrin had (at least, apparently) on its own: Agus' academy would instead act like "the upper house" of a legislature, whose actions would still need the confirmation of "the lower house," that is, the special joint assemblies he describes. Unlike the British Parliament, however, the academy would take the primary role in studying issues and initiating suggestions for legislation. As such,

> it should consist of the greatest men in our movement, those who have achieved distinction in the fields of scholarship, rabbinic leadership, Jewish education and social welfare. Like the [French] Academy, too, appointments should be made for life or for long terms—such appointments constituting the highest marks of recognition in our movement.[28]

The academy would, in Agus' proposal, discuss not only matters of Jewish law but also "principles and dogmas of faith, the latest developments in various fields of study bearing upon the philosophy of religion and ways and means of dealing with specific problems."[29] It thus, in his vision, would function not only in the role of the current Committee on Jewish Law and Standards but also in place of the Commission on the Philosophy of Conservative Judaism, which produced the first movement statement of Conservative ideology, and perhaps also in place of some of the other current committees or commissions dealing with specific problems within the movement (for example, the Conservative Movement Council, which exists nationally, in the Pacific Southwest region, and perhaps in some other regions, consisting of the presidents or their representatives of all the arms of the movement, and which is used for joint planning purposes). While Agus' proposal may be institutionally too cumbersome, demanding much too much of any one group of people, it has the theoretical advantage of making it clear at the outset that within Conservative Judaism, law, ideology, and social policy are to be seen not as disparate, independent entities but rather as part of an integrated whole, each affecting the other. This certainly has been a distinctive mark of much of what the Conservative movement has done in practice in the decades since Agus made his proposal.

Two points should be made about the membership of this body. First, in speaking of "the greatest *men* in our movement," Agus was probably simply using the language of 1948, when this was written, to refer to people of either gender. Female rabbis did not exist within the Conservative movement until 1985, and so he could not have known of that possibility, but he certainly knew of other women leaders within the movement, and he generally was supportive of expanding women's rights.

Second, it is interesting that Agus would include as members of the academy not only scholars and rabbis but also "laymen."[30] In practice, the Committee on Jewish Law and Standards did not begin to include lay representatives until 1990, and then only as nonvoting members and only as the result of political pressure brought by the United Synagogue. Agus would have included lay leaders in his proposal forty years earlier, presumably as voting members. While he does not justify that suggestion specifically, he presumably thought that the primary group to be responsible for shaping the beliefs, practices, and policies of the movement should include at least some representatives of the masses in whose name such pronouncements were being formulated. The Commission on the Philosophy of the Conservative Movement also had lay representatives—this time as full members—but there again, they were added only after the rabbis and scholars had had time to begin the work on their own. As a member of both committees, I can attest that Agus was right long ago, for the lay members' contributions to the discussions of both groups have been both insightful and valuable.

Agus considers and answers several possible objections to the establishment of such an academy. In response to the worry that using legislation as a legal tool will lead to antinomianism, especially in the context of the large gap between rabbinic and lay patterns of Jewish observance within the Conservative movement, Agus points out that the initial *takkanot* need not be negative; that indeed, "there is no need for 'takkanot' to sanction non-observance, but there is great need for 'takkanot' to raise the level of observance." Accordingly, the academy's "first task shall be to lead and guide our movement in a nationwide 'tshuvah' [return] effort, calculated to reestablish a minimum of observance among the members of our congregations . . . so that membership in a synagogue shall not be purely a financial transaction." It is only after this has been achieved that legislation would be considered to correct certain abuses in Jewish life, such as the refusal of a man to grant a writ of divorce (a get) when there is no good reason for his unwillingness.[31]

Furthermore, as Agus points out, the principle of "catholic Israel," embedded in the Conservative movement by Solomon Schechter, would guard against any changes considered too radical by the Conservative community. Agus' proposal, in fact, gives that community a clear voice in the process of determining Jewish law, a voice laypeople lack when the law is established exclusively through rabbinic interpretation.

Another possible objection to such legislation is the dissension it might cause among the movements and within the Conservative movement itself. Agus dismisses the first as a serious concern on both practical and theoretical grounds. Practically, "uniformity of observance among Jewish people today is out of the question," and to wait for such agreement "would be tantamount in practice to the utter bankruptcy of our religious leadership." Theoretically, there is no reason to expect such uniformity, for the ways in which the Reform, the Orthodox, and the indifferent understand Jewish law bespeak convictions radically at odds with each other and with that of Conservative Judaism.[32]

The possibility of conflict within, and even defection from, the Conservative movement Agus takes much more seriously. The academy he proposes, he says, should not dare try "to make up with one fell blow for a century of arrested progress." Caution and careful deliberation will be needed. However, he is convinced that the Conservative movement must adopt the way of legislation if it is to live out its ideological roots and if it is to do what must be done in our time to make Judaism a dynamic, living religion, rather than a "desperate holding action" or merely a "way-station" to assimilation:

> The question raised by this objection, therefore, is a very fundamental one—to wit, is there room on the American scene for a Conservative movement, as distinguished from a Conservative way-station? To phrase the question is to answer it. There is not only room, but crying need, for a Conservative movement. If there were no such steadily emerging movement, it would have had to be created. For our time calls for a bold constructive approach, which neither Reform nor Orthodoxy can give—the former thriving on the growing decay of tradition, the latter reduced to a desperate holding action.[33]

In sum, then, the academy's purpose would be to function in *both* capacities that Agus demands of a living Jewish legal system: seriousness of purpose on the part of both the institutions and the individual members of the Conservative movement, as manifested by at least a minimum of observance of Jewish law, and, simultaneously, readiness to enact legislation to make the substance of Jewish law grow in appropriate ways to meet the needs of contemporary times.

AGUS' OWN RESPONSA

Agus wrote several responsa for the Conservative movement's Committee on Jewish Law and Standards that illustrate his principles in concrete form. Undoubtedly the most famous of them is the "Responsum on the Sabbath," which he coauthored with Rabbis Morris Adler and Theodore Friedman. It secured the support of a majority of the Law Committee in 1950, and it has been the subject of much debate within the Conservative movement ever since.

One immediately sees Agus' theory at work in the responsum's call for a program for the revitalization of the Sabbath. The campaign does not demand total observance but rather has "as its immediate goal the acceptance on the part of the people of . . . basic indispensable elements of Sabbath," which the responsum articulates in detail. The emphasis is on creating Agus' "minimal standards." These include elements of traditional Jewish Sabbath observance, such as preparation for the Sabbath and the traditional Friday-night home rituals. The responsum does not demand all things required by Jewish law, however, and even those it includes are stated with room for individual adjustments. So, for example, attendance at public worship should happen "at least once on the Sabbath"; "one should refrain from all such activities that are not made absolutely necessary by the unavoidable pressure of life and that are not in keeping with the Sabbath spirit, such as shopping, household work, sewing, strenuous physical exercise, etc."; and "the type of recreation engaged in on the Sabbath should be such as is calculated to enhance one's spiritual personality in its intellectual, social, and esthetic aspects." The tone is clearly one of encouragement rather than one of obligation, and the content is explicitly directed at achieving the Sabbath's spiritual goals rather than asking for a blind obedience of the law as law.

The most controversial parts of the responsum, however, concerned riding to the synagogue and the use of electricity. The authors urged people not to use a motor vehicle on the Sabbath as an aid to both one's own repose and to keeping the family together, but they also said that "where a family resides beyond reasonable walking distance from the synagogue, the use of a motor vehicle for the purpose of synagogue attendance shall in no wise be construed as a violation of the Sabbath but, on the contrary, such attendance shall be deemed an expression of loyalty to our faith." The authors assert that because most Jews no longer know how to pray at home or to study Torah on their own, "were it not for synagogue attendance on the Sabbath, there would be no prayer for most of our people," and no Torah study either. Furthermore, "in the spirit of a living and developing Halachah responsive to the changing needs of our people, we declare it to be permitted to use electric lights on the Sabbath for the purpose of enhancing the enjoyment of the Sabbath, or reducing personal discomfort or of helping in the performance of a mitzvah."[34]

The responsum itself announces three principles "implied in this program," principles in which Agus' philosophy is clearly evident. First, despite the "cynical skepticism" that some may have about such a program of reconsecration, there have been many such efforts in the past, so that what we learn from history is that "the Jewish religion does not favor the emotional excesses of the Christian 'revivalist' movements, but it fosters the principle of voluntary acceptance of a pattern of life." At the same time, the authors say, rabbis must be realistic in their demands of their community, for, as the classical rabbis said, "to overreach is to court failure" *(tafasta m'rubah lo tafasta),* "it is better to build a fence of ten handbreadths that is likely to stand than one of a hundred handbreadths that is liable to fall" *(tov assarah t'fahim v'omed mimeah t'fahim v'nofel),* and "it is better not to say a thing which will not be heeded" *(mutav shelo lomar davar sheaino nishma).* All of these features of this principle are vintage Agus: creating a positive program for rededication; rooting one's approach in what Judaism has been historically; basing the authority of Jewish law, at least in part, on the voluntary acceptance of the people; and creating minimal standards that have a reasonable chance of being accepted, rather than adopting an "all-or-nothing" attitude.

Second, the community power to enact ordinances is "virtually unlimited, provided its ordinances are made with consent of the resident scholars and provided further that they be inspired by the purpose of 'strengthening the faith,' " and such enactments should be made jointly "through their spiritual leaders and lay representatives." This is clearly Agus' program for using the legal vehicle of legislation *(takkanot)* to accomplish desired ends. Here the authors apply it to riding to the synagogue on the Sabbath and the use of electric lights, both of which they justify in this responsum not only on narrow, legal grounds but also on principled grounds of enhancing the joy of the Sabbath *(oneg shabbat)* and, primarily, of enabling Jews who would otherwise be unable to observe the Sabbath to do so.

Third, "The power of communities to make special enactments in behalf of the faith, through their spiritual leaders and lay representatives, is in turn a corollary of the principle of development in Jewish Law."

This development has historically included creating new practices and repudiating old ones. As the authors demonstrate through reference to a number of talmudic and medieval sources, the authority for that development is based, at least in part, on the necessity for the community to accept the law voluntarily in order for it to be valid; God's command is not enough. As we have seen, these principles are deeply rooted in Agus' view of Jewish law.[35]

These decisions were not, however, grounded only in considerations of morality, aesthetics, or piety; they also follow on an extensive analysis of the specific legal issues involved in riding and using electricity. Thus the theory used by the three authors was not to replace legal reasoning but rather to weave it into a broader consideration of how to accomplish the goals of the law in a contemporary setting. Since most Conservative congregants drove and used electricity in any case, though, skeptics commonly interpreted the responsum as simply a way of giving retroactive sanction to the laity's practice and prospective sanction to those rabbis who wanted to do these things as well, rather than as part of a concerted effort to revitalize Sabbath observance based on a serious reading of Jewish sources.

Agus himself complained bitterly about the fate of the responsum within the movement when it was again discussed by the Law Committee eleven years later (1961). Any rabbi by himself, he points out, and even the rabbis together as a group could not possibly launch the revitalization effort on their own; from the very beginning it was to be a movementwide effort:

> Our central agencies [by which he apparently means the lay organizations of the Conservative movement] ignored this effort altogether, with the result that the Sabbath Revitalization effort remained merely an intra-Rabbinical Assembly project. . . . It would have been far better for the movement if the Sabbath Responsum had been directly endorsed by the Rabbinical Assembly [and not merely by the majority of the Law Committee] and freely accepted by the United Synagogue and its affiliates. We should then have had truly autonomous legislation, bearing potent ethical-spiritual influence.

Agus notes that some rabbis objected to the self-declared status of the responsum as a *takkanah,* preferring that the Conservative movement restrict itself to the more common method of interpretation. He thanks the leadership of the Rabbinical Assembly for preventing a vote, intended to nullify the responsum's classification as a *takkanah,* from being taken on the floor of the Rabbinical Assembly Convention, and he argues that, in our time, legislation is in fact the *preferred* way of achieving united action, because it prevents the anarchy inherent in individual opinions:

> Actually, the sole difference between a *takkanah* and an interpretation is that the former is a *communal* enactment and the latter is a private opinion. It is clear that a conscious policy of limitless commentary, allowing free interpretation by individual rabbis, borders on anarchy. On the other hand, a communal enactment is likely to restrain arbitrary and extremist policies and to frame new enactments in the spirit of the tradition as a whole and of previous precedents.

There is still plenty of room for individual rabbis to make legal decisions based on their authority as the local rabbi (*mara d'atra,* literally, "teacher of the place"), Agus maintains, but that is properly restricted to whether this or that bottle of wine is kosher, not whether, as a community, we are going to declare a principle that governs such decisions invalid in our day. That is, he draws the line "between *general* rules and *individual* applications," holding that in the former, the way of legislation is the only one that prevents anarchy.

Agus says, however, that the Committee on Jewish Law and Standards should get involved in setting *policy* for individual applications of the law, especially when the issues at hand occur on a regular and frequent basis. So, for example, it is proper that the Committee discuss whether this Sabbath responsum permits driving to a synagogue other than one's own to attend a bar or bat mitzvah (which Agus thinks is perfectly proper) or to visit the sick (which Agus thinks should be done only in an emergency). Given this, one wonders whether Agus has, in effect, vacated the status of the communal rabbi to make decisions; he certainly has limited it considerably.

Agus argues against those who object to the responsum on the grounds that it widened the rift between the Conservative and the Orthodox. If ecumenism within Judaism is the issue, he points out, then relationships with the Reform movement should occupy the attention of Conservative leadership at least as much as ties with the Orthodox. Moreover,

> unity is neither desirable nor attainable by way of squeezing all of Jewish life back into "the four ells of Halachah," as it took form in the *Shulhan Arukh;* nor it is either desirable or attainable by way of fostering a rank anarchy of individual interpretations behind a facade of official loyalty to the *Halachah;* nor is it either desirable or attainable by way of negotiations between "spiritual statesmen on the summit" on a *quid pro quo* basis. . . .
>
> To me, the only kind of religious unity which is salutary is the one that derives from the recognition of the distinction between the ethical-spiritual core of faith and the ritualistic-historical expressions of it. Hence, it is only in the growth of the liberal spirit that we can eventually attain the goal of creative unity.[36]

When Agus addressed the problem of "the chained woman" *(agunah)* in another responsum, his belief in the preferability of using legislation as a legal technique prompted him to object to the proposal put forward by Rabbi David Aronson that the rabbinic court, based on the talmudic principle that the rabbis have the right to annul marriages, should issue a writ of divorce if the husband refuses to grant one for reasons that the court finds insufficient or if the husband is absent. Agus claims that such an approach requires rabbis to issue a writ that says the opposite of what is in fact the case (namely, that the husband voluntarily divorces his wife, when he does not), and it misunderstands the talmudic principle in the first place to be a condition of marriage instead of what it really is, namely, an assertion of the rabbinic prerogative to govern marriage law and to institute new procedures when necessary. "On this view, we have the right to analyze the problem of divorce and the 'agunah' in basic terms." Agus does precisely that in suggesting a number of measures to deal with the various kinds of "chained women," including some suggestions openly based on the desire to equalize the status of men and women in marital law. In saying these things Agus was objecting to a bold proposal, on the part of another liberal Conservative rabbi, on the grounds that there are clear limits to our ability to interpret precedents responsibly in order to achieve the results we need and want to achieve, and that legislation is a much more honest and desirable method for doing so.[37]

Finally, it is interesting to note that Agus maintained his principles to the very end of his life. In his responsum titled "The Mitzvah of Keruv" (1982), dealing with how the Conservative movement should balance its objections to intermarriage with its desire to attract the non-Jewish spouse to convert to Judaism, he advocates communal action to assert the firmness required to resist intermarriage, for in a democratic country people will not accept the authority of an individual rabbi but will understand and respect communal standards:

> So long as the spirit of anarchy is kept within bounds, legal adjustments, even if far-reaching in character, may be enacted, without damaging the structure of authority within the movement.
>
> We live in a democratic age, where the supreme authority of a *mara d'atra* [local rabbi] is likely to be disregarded, if not resented, while the collective authority of a national or world-wide body of representative rabbis, scholars and laymen is generally acceptable. A people, so religiously mature that it could glory in Rabbi Joshua's triumph over the mystical *bat kol* [voice from heaven] with the slogan, *lo bashamayim hi* ["The law is not in heaven"], can certainly be trusted in our day to understand that laws can be divine, when they are man-made. But, they are not likely to tolerate the arbitrary tyranny of the resident rabbi or scholar, acting on his own judgment.[38]

AFTERWORD

Rabbi Jacob Agus, arguably more than any other Conservative rabbi of his generation, clearly and thoroughly articulated a philosophy of law appropriate for the Conservative movement, rooted in both reason and revelation, reflecting the developing history of Jewish law and its inherent values, and embracing both tradition and modernity in a conscious and serious way. One cannot help but admire the honesty and erudition of his approach, as well as its concern for preserving tradition while making it vital for contemporary Jews. With the exception of his "Responsum on the Sabbath," however, his responsa were not endorsed by the majority of the Law Committee, and his proposal to use the legal technique of legislation has not been widely adopted by the Conservative movement. If anything, the movement has shied away from taking such steps, preferring instead to justify its actions as much as possible within the more commonly used legal technique of interpretation.

In our own time, though, some of Agus' proposals have effectively been adopted, although without citing him as their ideological progenitor. The decision to ordain women, a major point of conflict within the movement, was not handled by the Committee on Jewish Law and

Standards alone but rather entrusted to a movementwide commission, which took testimony from Conservative Jews in a number of cities. That commission ultimately reported to the Rabbinical Assembly Convention, which directed its Membership Committee to accept applications regardless of gender once the Jewish Theological Seminary of America ordained its first woman rabbi; and the faculty of the seminary had to vote to do so before the actions of either the commission or the Rabbinical Assembly took effect. But clearly, Agus' proposal that such significant actions be taken by the movement as a whole found expression in this rather convoluted process. It also was evident in the process by which the Conservative movement framed its first ideological platform, *Emet Ve-Emunah: Statement of Principles of Conservative Judaism,* for that was written by the Commission on the Philosophy of Conservative Judaism, with representatives from all arms of the movement. This was actually closer to Agus' model, for the commission did not have to gain the approval of any the movement's arms for its document. And finally, although I proposed in a responsum for the Committee of Jewish Law and Standards that there be a movementwide commission to study areas of human sexuality—including, but not restricted to, the issues raised by homosexuality—with its recommendations reported to all of the arms of the movement, only the Rabbinical Assembly chose to take up the idea, and so it created a Commission on Human Sexuality with a mandate to study such issues and to report its findings to the Law Committee.[39]

None of these is quite what Agus wanted, but they all have elements of his proposals. He, however, laid the ideological groundwork for such an approach much more clearly than any of the initiators of these actions, and he did it thirty years before they did! We may yet see the Conservative movement develop much more aggressively in ways he foresaw long ago.

NOTES

1. Mordecai Waxman collected and translated some of the relevant essays by Zacharias Frankel, Abraham Kohut, Moshe Davis, Solomon Schechter, Louis Ginzberg, Mordecai Kaplan, and Robert Gordis in his book *Tradition and Change: The Development of the Conservative Movement* (New York, 1958). Boaz Cohen's essay on the shaping of Judaism, "Towards a Philosophy of Jewish Law," first published in 1949, has been reprinted in his book *Law and Tradition*

in Judaism (New York, 1959), 1–38. Some of the early material on the conservative approach to Jewish law (including one of Agus' essays) is reprinted along with some later essays in Seymour Siegel, ed., *Conservative Judaism and Jewish Law* (New York, 1977).

In February 1980, George Nudell wrote an unpublished class paper titled "The Clearing House: A History of the Committee on Jewish Law and Standards." It describes the vicissitudes of the committee to that point, together with the arguments that produced those fluctuations. The paper is available through the Rabbinical Assembly Office, 3080 Broadway, New York, NY 10027.

2. Jacob Agus, *Guideposts in Modern Judaism* (New York, 1954), 279. Agus does not use the Passover liturgy to illustrate this point, as I do in the next several lines, but I think it is in keeping with his meaning.

3. Ibid., 301, 302.

4. Ibid., 280.

5. Ibid.

6. In a later passage (301), Agus indicates why reason cannot be used exclusively to account for *any* area of life:

> The pole of reason or objectivity must be constantly replenished with subjective insights, if it is to keep from degenerating into a hollow mockery of itself. First, it must assimilate the subjective feeling of trust in reason itself. Second, it must operate with the subjective intuitive valuations of the sanctity of the human person, the validity of the goal of the Good or the validity of the moral law and the perception of beauty and harmony. Third, it renews itself and ascends to a higher level only thru *[sic]* periodic intuitive insights, that is, periodic reversions to the pole of subjectivity.

In religion, for Agus, revelation provides the pole of subjectivity, and hence with regard to religion he argues specifically for the need of revelation. As this passage indicates, though, Agus maintains that reason would need some such element of subjectivity in other areas of human experience as well, for the reasons he mentions.

7. Ibid., 281. All citations in the next few paragraphs, in which I explain Agus' arguments for why reason is not a sufficient ground for Jewish law, come from *Guideposts,* 281–82.

8. Ibid., 282, 285, 288–89.

9. Ibid., 323–35; reprinted in Siegel, ed., *Conservative Judaism,* 30–31.

10. Ibid., 329; in Siegel, ed., *Conservative Judaism,* 35.

11. Ibid., 322; in Siegel, ed., *Conservative Judaism,* 29.

12. Ibid., 332–33; in Siegel, ed., *Conservative Judaism,* 37.

13. Ibid., 333–35, 340–41; in Siegel, ed., *Conservative Judaism,* 38–39, 42–43.

Agus develops his point-field analysis of the meaning and existence of God in chapters 4 and 5 of *Guideposts.*

14. Ibid., 341–42; in Siegel, ed., *Conservative Judaism,* 44–45.

15. Ibid., 295, 297.

16. Ibid., 298; see 292 for his statement on the need to preserve the law as an instrument of attaining morality and piety.

17. Ibid., 299.

18. Ibid., 300, 303. Agus applies this analysis to every aspect of life, as the passage quoted in n. 6, above, indicates. The objectivity represented by reason is necessary for, and must be balanced by, the subjectivity proper to the particular area of life in question.

19. Ibid., 304.

20. Ibid., 309.

21. Ibid., 311–12. I have embellished Agus' argument here, emphasizing the choice involved in the Orthodox interpretation of Jewish sources and adding the citation from B. *Bava Batra* 131a that a judge must decide according to what his own eyes see, but I think this line of argumentation is very much in keeping with both the letter and the spirit of the arguments Agus himself makes.

22. Ibid., 316.

23. See, for example, Elliot N. Dorff and Arthur Rosett, *A Living Tree: The Roots and Growth of Jewish Law* (Albany, N.Y., 1988), 402–20.

24. Agus, *Guideposts,* 317.

25. Ibid., 312.

26. Agus, *Guideposts,* part 2, sec. 2; see also Jacob B. Agus, *The Jewish Quest: Essays on Basic Concepts of Jewish Theology* (New York, 1983), 43–86.

27. For a survey of the varying doctrines of revelation within Conservative Judaism, Agus' included, see Elliot N. Dorff, *Conservative Judaism: Our Ancestors to Our Descendants* (New York, 1977), 110–57.

28. Agus, *Guideposts,* 313.

29. Ibid.

30. Ibid.

31. Ibid., 313–15.

32. Ibid., 316.

33. Ibid., 317–18.

34. Morris Adler, Jacob Agus, and Theodore Friedman, "A Responsum on the Sabbath," in *Proceedings of the Rabbinical Assembly* (New York, 1950), 122–23, 130; reprinted in Waxman, ed., *Tradition and Change,* 361–62, 368; and, in part, in Dorff, *Conservative Judaism,* 168–69.

35. Ibid., in *Proceedings,* 124–28; in Waxman, *Tradition and Change,* 362–66; in Dorff, *Conservative Judaism,* 169–71.

36. The above description of Agus' 1961 reevaluation of the Sabbath respon-

sum comes from his paper "Reevaluation of the Responsum on the Sabbath," which is stored in the Rabbinical Assembly Archives as an unofficial paper submitted to the committee—that is, a paper on which the committee did not take a vote. I thank Rabbi Gail Labovitz, administrative assistant of the Committee on Jewish Law and Standards in 1991–1992, for making this responsum and the one cited in the next note available to me.

37. Jacob Agus, "Re Agunah," an undated and unofficial responsum in the Rabbinical Assembly Archives.

38. Jacob B. Agus, "The Mitzvah of Keruv," in *Proceedings of the Committee on Jewish Law and Standards of the Conservative Movement, 1980–1985* (New York, 1988), 147.

39. My responsum, titled "Jewish Norms for Sexual Behavior," was validated by eight members of the Committee on Jewish Law and Standards at its meeting on March 25, 1992. The Rabbinical Assembly, meeting in convention in May 1992, passed a resolution directing its officers to establish such a commission, which would report its findings to the Law Committee within two years. Both my responsum and the assembly resolution will be published: the former in the collection of Law Committee responsa for 1990–1995 and the latter in the *Rabbinical Assembly Proceedings* for 1992; in the meantime, they are both available from the Rabbinical Assembly Office, 3080 Broadway, New York, NY 10027.

The Commisssion produced two documents. One is a report to the Law Committee indicating the issues in human sexuality that have yet to be analyzed halakhically by the Committee and recommending that the Committee reexamine the entire issue of homosexuality. The other is an educational booklet to be used by teenagers and adults to learn the import of the Jewish tradition for matters of sexuality, namely, Elliot N. Dorff, *"This Is My Beloved, This Is My Friend": A Rabbinic Letter on Human Intimacy* (New York: Rabbinical Assembly, 1996).

The chancellor of the Jewish Theological Seminary and the president of the United Synagogue both refused to get involved in the Commission, on the grounds that this was a matter solely within the province of the rabbis. Agus would forcefully disagree!

11
JACOB B. AGUS AS PULPIT RABBI

Mark Loeb

HAD HE BEEN BORN thirty years later than he was, it is quite likely that Jacob Agus would never have become a pulpit rabbi at all. His scholarly proclivities would probably have led him to become a professor of Judaic studies, an option not readily available in the 1930s, when he began his career. Notwithstanding the fact that he had a genuine interest in working with people in normal societal configurations (as opposed to exclusively inhabiting the world of academia), it seems fair to say he would probably have found the scholarly life hard to resist. However, reality won out, and the pulpit rabbinate became his principal vocational arena.

EARLY RABBINATE

After being ordained at Yeshiva University's Rabbi Yitzchak Elchanan Theological Seminary, the preeminent training ground for Orthodox rabbis in the country, he began his rabbinate—with the encouragement of Rabbi Bernard Revel, the President of Yeshiva University, who had high hopes that Agus would become an articulate voice for modern Othodoxy—by serving a congregation in Norfolk, Virginia. After a brief stay there, he enrolled at Harvard University to earn his doctorate in the history and philosophy of religion, studying with the great scholar Harry Austryn Wolfson. His studies focused on Jewish medieval philosophy, especially that of Maimonides, which, combined with an appreciation of the historical and contextual evolution of religious thought, apparently wrought a significant change in his understanding of Jewish historical development. One major consequence was a liberalization of his attitudes toward Jewish law and practice and a tendency toward a more philosophical piety.

While at Harvard, Agus continued to be a pulpit rabbi, simultaneously serving a congregation in Cambridge, Massachusetts, and completing his studies. In 1940, at the suggestion of Rabbi Bernard Revel, Agus moved to Chicago to serve yet another Orthodox congregation. It was there he met a man he would later describe as "the most luminous spiritual personality" he had ever encountered, Rabbi Solomon Goldman. His friendship with Solomon Goldman would prove to be of far-reaching consequence.

In those days, Solomon Goldman was one of the leading spokesmen for the then rapidly growing Conservative movement. He was also a figure with a national reputation in the organized Jewish community, having served as president of the Zionist Organization of America and as co-chairman of the United Jewish Appeal. Himself a product of the Yeshiva University world, he became a major influence on the young Jacob Agus and thus helped impel him to consider moving into the world of Conservative Judaism, something other defectors from Orthodoxy were doing at an increasing rate. Nonetheless, after his brief sojourn in Chicago Rabbi Agus accepted a call to yet another Orthodox community, this one in Dayton, Ohio, where he served for the next seven years as the rabbi of Beth Abraham United Synagogue, which had been created out of three smaller congregations. However, it was during this period that Agus moved toward formal identification with the Conservative movement, which was then in a dynamic stage of development. This move to the "left" (religiously) was also influenced by a growing collegial familiarity with a number of the major figures in the Conservative world, including Mordecai M. Kaplan, with whom he had corresponded in the 1930s and on whose work he, as a budding scholar, had written both appreciatively and critically in Jewish journals of the day.

In the 1940s, Agus' affiliation with the Rabbinical Assembly, the international association of Conservative rabbis, formalized his break with Orthodoxy. It was a personal choice that had the air of inevitability about it, given his intellectual predilections. His affiliation seems to have provided him with some genuine gratification even in the face of criticism from former Orthodox allies and the consternation of some members of his extended family. (His brother Irving Agus, for example, served on the faculty of Yeshiva University for many years and probably did not share Jacob's perspective. Yet another brother, Dr. Chaim Agus, a highly respected physician in the Orthodox community, was fully accepting of his brother's choice.) Agus' encyclopedic grasp of Jewish sources caused Rabbinical Assembly leaders to place him on the prestigious Committee on Jewish Law, where he rapidly achieved substantial status and influence. As a result, within a relatively few years his stature grew in Conservative circles as he earned an increasingly important reputation as a halachically progressive voice in the movement. He was elected to an officership in the Rabbinical Assembly, though the Law Committee remained his favorite venue.

In 1948, along with Rabbis Morris Adler and Theodore Friedman, Agus coauthored a groundbreaking responsum that permitted the use of the automobile to drive to the synagogue on the Sabbath. In later years he extended his liberal instincts by supporting the abolition of the requirement of *Hatafat Dam* for previously circumcised male converts, even against such opinions as that of Saul Lieberman, the renowned Talmudist and rector of the Jewish Theological Seminary. This liberalism also was reflected in later years, after Agus became a rabbi in a Conservative synagogue, when his synagogue's service was characterized by the excision of verses regarding the restoration of the sacrificial system of the Temple; the use of the Triennial Cycle of the Torah long before it was widespread in the Conservative movement; the abolition of the designation of Kohen and Levi, and any attendant privileges that those designations implied; and the granting of aliyot to women long before most congregations did so.

CONSERVATIVE JUDAISM AT LAST

In 1946, Agus joined the Rabbinical Assembly of the Conservative movement, and Beth Abraham United became a member of the United Synagogue federation. In 1950 he moved to a recently organized Conservative synagogue in Baltimore, Beth El Congregation, which at that time was looking for its first rabbi. Beth El was the first congregation in Baltimore to be founded as a Conservative congregation and had been organized by an impressive group of lay leaders, many of whom were of substantial intellectual inclination. As a sign of their thoughtful style, they had chosen to utilize the services, on a rotating, interim basis, of some of the leading luminaries of the Conservative rabbinate of that day, including Israel Kazis, Solomon Grayzel, and, by chance, Solomon Goldman, friend to a layman who had himself thought of studying for the rabbinate. Solomon Goldman thought Jacob Agus would be an ideal match for the new Conservative congregation, given its scholarly and somewhat liberal inclinations. (In fact, as an expression of that philosophical direction, the masthead of the Beth El bulletin bore for some years the superscription "Conservative Judaism is the expression in our time and on the American scene of the eternally vital, liberal current within Jewish tradition.")

Thus it was that, after a careful deliberative process, the leaders of Beth El Congregation elected Jacob Agus to be their first rabbi, despite some moderate disagreement on the Search Committee as to whether he was really equipped to serve their needs. The lack of unanimity reflected an understandable concern that Agus might be too traditional; after all, he was Orthodox by upbringing and training and had not studied at the Jewish Theological Seminary (as had Rabbi Israel Goldman, then rabbi of Chizuk Amuno Congregation, Beth El's "sister" congregation). Also, some thought him too inward and reserved, lacking the instinct for gregariousness. Notwithstanding this ambivalence, he was elected rabbi and received with solid respect and friendship. Thus began a relationship that lasted for thirty years of his service as rabbi of the congregation and six years as rabbi emeritus, until his death in 1986.

Thinking of what Beth El's leaders might have done, one is impressed by their instinct, for in Jacob Agus they had selected a man of distinction rather than charm, a person of erudition rather than glibness, and a rabbi of reserved dignity rather than one obsessed with a need for the public spotlight—an obsession that would presumably redound to the prestige of the congregation. As it evolved, the synagogue's relationship with its rabbi (and, by extension, in later years with its cantor, educational directors, and executive directors) was characterized by mutual appreciation and respect, leading to a proud heritage of stability. Four decades later, many at Beth El believe the quality of this heritage is a function of the relationship forged between the first rabbi and the first generation of the Beth El laity.

Rabbi Agus enjoyed a significant measure of personal autonomy in terms of the programmatic direction in which he wanted to take Beth

El. Even when there was disagreement—and occasionally there was—the congregation always showed respect for his learning and his sincerity. Yet it is fair to say that his general instinct was highly congruent with the instincts of the congregation.

THE EDUCATION OF ADULT JEWISH LEARNERS

If anything was fundamental to Agus' pulpit rabbinate, it was a concern for adult education. Few rabbis have immersed themselves so deeply into programs directed toward the intellectual growth of the adult laity of their synagogue. In one area he became the longtime guide to the membership on matters of faith and temporal interest, namely, through his weekly bulletin columns in the congregation's newsletter, *The Voice.* In his first column, he set forth his task: "I propose to discuss every phase of Jewish thought and life, in particular, the philosophy of Conservative Judaism and the ideology implied in the slowly unfolding program of our Congregation. . . . In the course of time these columns will add up to a fully-rounded analysis of modern Jewish life and thought."[1]

Jacob Agus also became the spiritual adviser to the Mens Club of Beth El, which established a weekly Sunday-morning series of worship services, each followed by breakfast and a public forum. Each week more than two hundred men would gather for the fellowship of prayer and study. More often than not, the lecturer was the rabbi of the congregation. Notwithstanding the modest Judaic background of some in his audience, the rabbi consistently addressed himself to thoughtful topics. For example, in the 1961–1962 program year he spoke on "The Dead Sea Scrolls and the Messiah," "Synagogue and Church—When Did They Separate?" "Controversies between Hasidim and Hellenists," "Between Israelitism and Canaanitism," "Gamliel, Saul of Tarsus and Saint Paul," "Arnold Toynbee's Philosophy of History," and other topics of similar ilk. Clearly, Jacob Agus did not "talk down" to his congregation.

Yet Agus also spoke on matters of contemporary interest in the political world and offered stimulating reviews of newly written books. At the end of each lecture, there was a period of open dialogue with the speaker. Questions came from the floor, some challenging and illuminating. Those who shared in those forums still recall them as basic to their sense of Jewish commitment, inasmuch as Jacob Agus' unspoken message was that Judaism was a faith of intellectual depth that could provide a meaningful intellectual challenge to the kind of educated Jews who were then coming to the fore in American Jewish life.

A second dimension of Agus' involvement in adult education was his annual participation in the Jewish Laymen's Institute, conducted for nearly forty years at Camp Wohelo over a long Shabbat weekend. At Camp Wohelo, cosponsored by Beth El and Baltimore's other two Conservative congregations, Rabbi Agus became the intellectual center of the enterprise, while his colleague, Rabbi Israel Goldman of Chizuk Amuno Congregation, was the dynamic organizational force behind the encampment. Such luminaries as Mordecai Kaplan, Abraham Joshua Heschel, Robert Gordis, Abraham Halkin, Harry Orlinsky, and H. L. Ginsberg, along with many others, served as visiting faculty at Camp Wohelo, providing an opportunity for intimate communion with major scholars.

Rabbi Agus also taught for thirty-five years at Baltimore's Inter-Congregational Institute for Adult Jewish Studies. For years his was the largest class, as he elucidated the pathways of Jewish philosophy, ecumenical relations, New Testament studies, midrash, and so forth to a group of four or five hundred laypersons. This was luxury "casting" for those who had never been privileged to learn from a world-class Jewish scholar.

INTERFAITH RELATIONSHIPS

Beyond his commitment to adult Jewish education as the central thrust of his rabbinate, Agus also placed great emphasis on developing and improving relationships with the non-Jewish community, especially its clergy. For years he served as a co-chair of various clergy roundtables, some of which met in the homes of rabbis and ministers. He was especially adept at such undertakings because of his extraordinary grasp of Christian Scriptures and patristic literature. In later years he would be engaged to teach New Testament at the Ecumenical Institute of St. Mary's Seminary in Baltimore, through which he was able to establish a relationship with Lawrence Cardinal Sheehan that was of significant importance, given Cardinal Sheehan's role at Vatican II and his chairmanship of the committee that drafted the statement on the Church's relationship to Judaism and to the Jewish people.

Rabbi Agus' articulated instinct for the universal dimension of religion (versus the particularistic strain that so often dominates intercommunal dialogue on the sociopolitical level) found receptive ears and hearts over several decades. The impulse that led a Polish-born rabbi from Orthodoxy to Conservatism may also explain in part his interest in ecumenism. To him, an evolving sense of the value of religious pluralism seemed to have the potential to lead to a reduction of interreligious conflict and, even more, to the deepening of all faith traditions. Thus he wrote in *The Voice* in 1961, "Our sacred tradition as a whole has much to say concerning a world-wide fellowship of believers in God. The Jewish way of advancing this goal is distinctly relevant . . . It consists of a concept of unity of spiritual intention coupled with diversity of ritual and dogmatic practice that can be of the greatest significance for the future of humankind."[2]

However, it is clear that Agus' appreciation for the potential value of the ecumenical movement unabashedly reflected a concern for the safety of Jews. In later years especially, he expressed great concern that the "machismo-like" swagger that some Jews affected in the aftermath of the Israeli victory in the Six Day War might lead to a dangerous form of historical amnesia. He was genuinely concerned that Jews might forget the all-too-modest numbers of the Jewish people and the clear minority status implied by those numbers, as well as the urgent need for Jews to engender positive feelings on the part of gentiles.

But at the heart of Agus' philosophy of ecumenism was a passionate concern for Jewish universalism. He deeply felt the dangers of Jewish parochialism, which may also explain his leaving the Orthodox world, which seemed too constricted for him. He believed that Judaism in its classical periods of intellectual growth had been typified by a confident responsiveness to the philosophical challenges of the day, a responsiveness that had strengthened it immeasurably and further developed its inner vitality as a faith. To him, the ecumenical movement provided just such an opportunity for responsiveness and growth (and also, incidentally, implied a substantial public benefit, the reduction of anti-Semitism). This general attitude is reflected in his volume *Jewish Identity in an Age of Ideolgies,* wherein he described Jewish responses to the various philosophical challenges in the modern period, responses that led Judaism to a deeper intellectual maturity of its own.

In later years, Agus pursued this universalist instinct by participating in a "trialogue" of Jews, Christians, and Muslims, which also reflected his concern for peace in the Middle East and his belief that Islam had not yet been drawn into a "reformation" stage in its religious development, without which true dialogue could not be achieved. His activities in these areas earned him national recognition, particularly for his distinguished writings in the *Journal of Ecumenical Studies* and his participation in many national dialogues organized by the American Jewish Committee and its director of Inter-Religious Affairs, the late Rabbi Marc Tanenbaum, a good friend and a Baltimorean by upbringing.

TEACHING

Like some pulpit rabbis of his generation, Jacob Agus' scholarly interests impelled him to engage in university teaching when opportunities arose. At one time he taught at the Reconstructionist Rabbinical College and at Temple University in Philadelphia; at other times he taught at the Baltimore Hebrew College. In 1965 he spent four months teaching at the Seminario Rabbinico in Buenos Aires. His academic talents also enabled him to serve for many years as an editor of the *Encyclopaedia Britannica* while still in the pulpit.

AS RABBI OF THE CONGREGATION

Agus' rabbinic career at Beth El naturally required him to be a pastor, something to which he committed himself faithfully, even visiting nonmembers who had been his students at the various places where he had lectured. He would visit the sick in hospitals, comfort the bereaved in houses of mourning, and provide counsel to congregants when called upon. It became his predilection in all such circumstances, especially houses of mourning, to give *divrei Torah,* which more often focused on philosophical topics than on personal connection with the deceased.

Agus addressed himself to "shul business" in the mornings and usually focused on his writing in the afternoons. While he was not an administrative leader by nature, he nonetheless participated in many dimensions of the synagogue's "practical" life. For example, when the current synagogue was constructed in 1960, largely through the efforts of several talented and dedicated lay leaders, it was Rabbi Agus who provided the architectural and artistic inspiration for the building, arguably one of the most beautiful synagogues in the country. His conceptualization of the sanctuary focused on Jewish learning: a mixture of large, stained-glass "Bible windows"; "Mishnah windows," which depicted the themes of the Sedarim of the Mishnah; and "Talmud apertures," which, together with the other windows, signified the triadic unity of Jewish knowledge.

During the years of Agus' leadership, Beth El, which had originally been envisioned by its founders as a small, "family congregation" of two or three hundred families, began to grow. Many factors account for this, of course, but one principal factor had to be the rabbinate of Jacob Agus. By the time of his retirement, Beth El had grown to well over a thousand families. His luster as a teacher and as a scholar and his graciousness as a man all gained approbation for the synagogue. Yet it was clear, even in the early years at Beth El, that many members were concerned about the rapid growth of their congregation. In answer to this concern Rabbi Agus wrote:

> Our goal is a great synagogue, big only as the needs of greatness dictate. It is the program and the quality of service and the evolving pattern of synagogue life in the community, that determine the size and nature of our building program. Economy and dignity go hand in hand. When a congregation serves a large number of families, it can transmit the heritage of Judaism with the effectiveness and the impressiveness that modern Jews require. And *only* a synagogue of stature can fulfill its historic role in the American environment.[3]

Ironically enough, despite the need to speak frequently to many hundreds of people from his pulpit—something that he did with confidence and a modicum of charisma—Rabbi Agus off the pulpit was actually quite diffident and, at times, even shy. He was not of the school that luxuriates in "small talk" or intimate therapeutic consultation. To sit alone with Jacob Agus usually meant discussion about matters of current political importance or of historical relevance. Yet his reserved personality overlay a passionate set of commitments and spiritual values. For example, his sense of universalism once impelled him to engage in an atypically intense protest to the chaplain of Baltimore's Jewish hospital when he allowed a sign to be posted with the rabbinic dictum "He who saves one *Jewish* life [my emphasis] has saved an entire world." Rabbi Agus informed the chaplain that the sign had to go, first, because it was an insult to gentiles, and second, because there was an alternative reading in a talmudic manuscript that omitted the offending word. The sign came down.

He also could get deeply disturbed about the political situation in the Middle East. As others have noted, Agus was at best a lukewarm Zionist, believing that Zionism was a flawed philosophy because it reflected the nineteenth century's perverted obsession with nationalism, a force that had been infected with racism in most countries, which might well prove contagious to Jews. He was disturbed by the Israeli government's indifference to Palestinians and spoke out on the matter frequently, often to people in the most ordinary pastoral settings.

THEMES OF AGUS' RABBINATE: PREACHING IN THE PULPIT

Week after week, Rabbi Agus mounted his pulpit to address the critical issues of the day as seen through the prism of Jewish religious thinking. His universalism led some to see him as rather odd, with regard to the security issues that have surrounded the State of Israel for several decades. For example, he once opined in a sermon how wonderful it would be if Jerusalem could become an internationalized city—distinctly not a centrist view. When Golda Meir refused to acknowledge the Palestine Liberation Organization (PLO) as valid negotiators for Palestinian Arabs, Jacob Agus declared that Israel's problems would never be resolved until it accepted the fact that dialogue with the PLO was a necessity.

He also spoke against the facile phrasemaking of the organized Jewish community on many issues, including Soviet Jewry. He called for a lesser focus on rescue than federations wanted and a greater one on influencing Soviet society so that the many Jews who would remain could be sustained in their Jewishness, a stance that makes a great deal of sense today.

Agus spoke out against the glib sloganeering about Jewish "identity," seeing it as a meaningless substitution for authentic Jewish faith. He deplored the "We Are One" mentality, which he saw as both historically absurd and probably stifling of true Jewish creativity. He also denounced the tendency to see the Holocaust as a *mysterium,* as an event that stood uniquely beyond the tenets of traditional historical explanation, and he openly challenged the thinking of such writers as Emil Fackenheim and Elie Wiesel.

He also decried the Jewish organizational world's self-righteous tendency to reduce Jewish–Christian relations to a forum in which Jews could blame Christians for anti-Semitism while assuming that they had nothing to learn from Christians. While Agus did frequently speak about the persistence of anti-Semitism, he also spoke of the transformation of Christian attitudes that ecumenism was making possible.

Jacob Agus inveighed against the tendency toward "romantic" religious philosophies and made quite clear his distaste for those aspects of the Zionist message that substituted nationalistic fervor for religious faith. In his sermons he spoke about the importance of Diaspora Jewry and attacked, both orally and in a review in *Judaism* magazine, Hillel Halkin's *Letters to an American Jewish Friend,* an anti-Diaspora Zionist polemic that Agus found offensive.

As a classic Maimonidean, Agus preached a faith in God based on intellectual piety and the reconciliation of philosophy and religion. In many sermons he preached against the mentality of religious primitivism and superstition seen in Hasidic sects and childishly imitated, even by many supposedly sophisticated people. In this spirit, he also frequently attacked sermonically the mindless search for emotional gratification that led to an unsophisticated yearning for religious mysticism.

ISSUES OF RELIGIOUS PRACTICE

Like many a pulpit rabbi who was in the "front line" of Jewish life, Jacob Agus could be both intellectually consistent and inconoclastic. As a halachic liberal who endorsed egalitarianism, he suggested early on that women wear a tallit, particularly for *aliyot,* yet in the initial debates in the Rabbinical Assembly on the ordination of women, his opposition helped to kill the proposal, which he felt was inadequately thought through and not consistent with the Conservative halachic process as he understood it. His personal preference impelled him to walk to the synagogue on the Sabbath as long as he could (later, to *be driven,* when walking became difficult due to illness), even though he had coauthored the responsum permitting driving. His halachic liberalism also impelled him to introduce bat mitzvah at Beth El, the first Conservative congregation in Baltimore to establish it on a peer level with bar mitzvah.

In all cases, whether at Beth El or in national halachic debates, his profound textual grounding made him unassailable, even in more traditional quarters. Whether he was iconoclastic or not, no one was prepared to claim that he was ignorant of the sources.

INTELLECTUAL CHALLENGES

Jacob Agus' essential thrust was to speak on a high intellectual level and to welcome dialogue with other faiths and ideologies that challenged Judaism. His volume *Jewish Identity in an Age of Ideologies* reflects this proclivity for intellectual "jousting." In the 1950s, for example, he engaged in a scholarly debate with the British historian Arnold Toynbee, whose critique of Judaism as a "fossil" religion had enraged Jews all over the world. He corresponded with Toynbee, debated him, and visited with him, and a special friendship developed. Jacob Agus, as a Jew capable of self-criticism, in muted acknowledgment of one of Toynbee's points even argued in an April issue of *The Voice:*

> We have left ourselves open to the charge of 'fossilization,' because we have failed to cultivate the field of Jewish thought in accordance with the high standards of the academic world. . . . Of exponents of modern Jewish philosophy and thought, we have none or almost none in the high spheres of the university world. Why then should the society of scholars not feel that we are simply sailing on the accumulated momentum of the past?[4]

Toynbee later reconsidered *his* position and attributed his changed ideas to Jacob Agus. As part of the dialogue, Rabbi Agus invited Toynbee to lecture at Beth El. Some of the congregants were outraged, seeing Toynbee as nothing more than a sophisticated anti-Semite. Yet their respect for their rabbi remained intact. However, when the local chapter of the Zionist Organization of America threatened, in a puerile gesture, to picket Beth El, Agus changed the venue of Toynbee's talk to his own home, for a more select audience.

ESTEEM

Jacob Agus' pulpit rabbinate embraced high personal scholarship, the writing of eight serious books, university teaching, adult education programming for congregants, a dedicated pastorate, the offering of literally thousands of sermons and *divrei Torah,* communal involvement in interfaith dialogue, rabbinic service on the Rabbinical Assembly Law Committee, and the attainment of an international reputation that brought great respect to his congregation. However, yet another criterion for judging a pulpit rabbi is his personal quality as a Jewish model. To his congregants Jacob Agus was considerably more than an intellectual. He was also a spiritual standard-bearer, however obscure his message may have been to some. At one Mens Club forum, when one of his own books was being reviewed, a genuinely respectful congregant who had faithfully bought every book Rabbi Agus had written asked if *this* book at least had a few pictures in it! Yet after the review, in a telling comment, Rabbi Agus insisted that, however valuable books might be, Judaism was to be found not in books but in the hearts of living, committed Jews. That was why, he said, he was glad, after all, that he had become a pulpit rabbi—so that he could influence everyday Jews to deepen their understanding and their love of their heritage.

When his career in the active rabbinate was completed by retirement, Agus continued to participate in projects of interest, especially in the field of interfaith dialogue. In later years he struggled against illness, but he remained productive nearly up to the end. With his death the era of the founders of Beth El, the first true generation of Conservative Jews in Baltimore, came to an end, substantially defined by the contribution he had made in alliance with those men whose discriminating judgment caused them to select an unusual rabbi for a fledgling congregation.

All rabbis, especially those in the pulpit, are products both of their time and of their inner nature. Yet Jacob Agus was able to transcend the conventional borders and categories of the American rabbinate. His iconoclasm was born of intelligence, and his programmatic focus as a teacher of Judaism to Jewish adults reflected an understanding of what American Jews ought to know. Unlike many other rabbis, he offered what was needed rather than what was wanted. As a rabbi in the pulpit, many would argue that he was *sui generis.* However one sees him, it is fairly clear that he had few peers and probably no real successors.

NOTES

1. Jacob Agus, *The Voice* 1, 1 (August 18, 1950), 1–2.
2. Ibid. 9, 11 (January 16, 1959), 1.
3. Ibid. 6, 20 (January 27, 1956), 1.
4. Ibid. 5, 27 (April 22, 1955), 1.

BIBLIOGRAPHY OF THE WORKS OF JACOB B. AGUS

BOOKS

Modern Philosophies of Judaism: A Study of Recent Jewish Philosophies of Religion. New York: Behrman's Jewish Book House, 1941.

Message of Judaism. Dayton, Ohio: Beth Abraham United Synagogue Center, 1945.

Banner of Jerusalem: The Life, Times, and Thought of Abraham Isaac Kuk. New York: Bloch Publishing Co., 1946. Reissued under the title *High Priest of Rebirth: The Life, Times, and Thought of Abraham Isaac Kuk.* New York: Bloch Publishing Co., 1972.

Guideposts in Modern Judaism. New York: Bloch Publishing Co., 1954.

The Goldenson Lecture: The Prophet in Modern Hebrew Literature. Cincinnati: Hebrew Union College Press, 1957.

The Evolution of Jewish Thought: From Biblical Times to the Opening of the Modern Era. New York: Abelard-Schuman, 1959. Published in French and Spanish translations. Reissued by New York's Arno Press in 1973.

The Meaning of Jewish History. 2 vols. New York: Abelard-Schuman, 1963.

The Vision and the Way; An Interpretation of Jewish Ethics. New York: Frederick Ungar, 1966.

Dialogue and Tradition: The Challenges of Contemporary Judeo-Christian Thought. New York: Abelard-Schuman, 1971.

Jewish Identity in an Age of Ideologies. New York: Frederick Ungar, 1978.

The Jewish Quest: Essays on Basic Concepts of Jewish Theology. New York: Ktav, 1983.

ARTICLES

"The Offensive for Judaism." *Jewish Outlook* (February 1938): 7–8; (March 1938): 6–8.
"Reply to Critics." *Jewish Outlook* (September 1938): 11–12.
"Thinkers Who Came Home." *Jewish Outlook* (November 1939): 8–11.
"Democracy in Jewish Life." *Reconstructionist* 7, 10 (June 1941): 18–19.
"The Character of Jewish Piety." *Reconstructionist* 8, 5 (April 1942): 14–18.
"Nusach ha-Chaim ha-Yehudi be-Amerika u-ve-Eretz Yisrael." *Mezuda* 7 (1945): 17–30.
"Orthodox Zionism." *New Palestine* 35, 17 (June 1945): 225–27.
"The Status of American Israel—A Conservative View." *Conservative Judaism* 2, 2 (February 1946): 1–14.
"La-Hever Higayon Ha-Kabbalah." *Sefer Hashanah li-Yehuong America* 8–9 (1946): 254–79.
"Torah M'Sinai—A Conservative View." *Conservative Judaism* 3, 2 (February 1947): 23–42.
"Ish Hamistorin." *Talpiot* (Nisan 1948): 20–30.
"A Rabbi Speaks His Mind." *Congress Weekly* 14, 13 (March 1947): 5–8.
"Goals for Jewish Living." *Menorah Journal* 36, 1 (winter 1948): 1–25.
"Law in Conservative Judaism." *Conservative Judaism* 5, 1 (October 1949): 26–40.
"Ends and Means of Jewish Life in America." *Menorah Journal* 37, 1 (winter 1949): 10–36.
"Laws as Standards." *Conservative Judaism* 6, 4 (May 1950): 8–26.
"Obsolescence in Jewish Ritual Law." *Conservative Judaism* 7, 4 (June 1951): 9–19.
"Ancient Sanhedrin or Sanhedrin-Academy." *Judaism* 1, 1 (January 1952): 52–63.
"The Idea of God." *Judaism* 1, 3 (July 1952): 203–17.
"Assimilation, Integration, Segregation—The Road to the Future." *Judaism* 3, 4 (April 1954): 498–510.
"Mitzvot—Yes; Averot—No." *Reconstructionist* 21, 6 (April 1955): 9–14.
"Toynbee and Judaism." *Judaism* 4, 4 (fall 1955): 319–32.
"Can Judaism without Walls Endure?" *National Jewish Monthly* (March 1956): 14–56.
"An Answer to Rabbi Blumenthal." *Conservative Judaism* 11, 2 (spring 1956): 18–27.
"Towards a Philosophy of Jewish History." *Judaism* 5, 2 (spring 1956): 99–107.
"Nationalistic Philosophies of Jewish History." *Judaism* 5, 3 (summer 1956): 256–71.
"Mixed Pews in Jewish Tradition." *Conservative Judaism* 11, 1 (fall 1956): 32–41.

"Rebuttal of Presentation of Rabbi Lapidus and the Statements of Rabbis Silver and Soloveitchik." *Conservative Judaism* 11, 1 (fall 1956): 53–58.
"Synthesis in Current Philosophies of Jewish History." *Judaism* 6, 1 (winter 1957): 56–69.
"Polarity in Jewish History." *Judaism* 6:2 (spring 1957): 160–70.
"The Meaning of the Mitzvot: An Analysis of Heinemann's *Ta-amei Ha-mitzvot Besiphrut Yisrael*." *Conservative Judaism* 11, 4 (summer 1957): 24–34.
"Standards and the Ideal." *Reconstructionist* 24, 4 (April 1958): 18–23.
"The Nature and Task of Liberal Judaism." *Judaism* 7, 4 (fall 1958): 291–301.
"Claude Montefiore and Liberal Judaism." *Conservative Judaism* 13, 2 (winter 1959): 1 21.
"Tradition and Change." *Conservative Judaism* 13, 2 (winter 1959): 46–54.
"Toward a Philosophy of Hope." *Judaism* 9, 2 (spring 1960): 99–111.
"An Analysis of Milton Steinberg's *Anatomy of Faith,* ed. Arthur Cohen." *Conservative Judaism* 14, 4 (summer 1960): 1–4.
"Towards a Philosophy of Hope." *Judaism* 9, 4 (fall 1960): 351–65.
"Survival: Faith and Culture *versus* Blood and Politics." *Menorah Journal* 48, 1–2 (autumn–winter 1960): 1–8.
"Toward a Conservative Philosophy of Jewish Education." *Synagogue School* 19, 3 (March–April 1961): 5–15.
"Toynbee's Epistle to the Jews." *Commentary* 3, 32 (September 1961): 239–42.
"Freedom and the Judeo-Christian Tradition." *Jewish Heritage* (summer 1962): 5–11.
"Jewish Philosophy and World Tensions." *Midstream* 8, 3 (September 1962): 67–82.
"Mass Crime and the Judeo-Christian Tradition." *Minnesota Review* 3, 2 (winter 1963): 205–19.
"Chances for American Survival: The Staying Power of Religion." *Jewish Heritage* 6, 3 (winter 1963/1964): 21–24.
"Hacia una filosofía Judía." *Maj'shavot* 3, 1 (March 1964): 5–14.
"Filosofías nacionalistas de la historia Judía." *Maj'shavot* 3, 2 (July 1964): 5–23.
"God and the Catastrophe." *Conservative Judaism* 18, 4 (summer 1964): 13–21.
"It's the Mythology of the Jewish and Christian Traditions That Hinders Fruitful Communication between the Two." *National Jewish Monthly* 79 (September 1964): 20–24; 79 (October 1964): 14–18.
"A Jewish View of the Problem of War Prevention Today." *Torch* (winter 1965): 10–13.
"Case for Dialogue." *National Jewish Monthly* 81, 1 (September 1966): 26–32.
"A favor del Diálogo." *Maj'shavot* 6, 3 (November 1967): 57–67.
"Myth, Faith, and Reality in Jewish Life." In Max Kreutzberger, ed., *Studies of the Leo Baeck Institute* (New York, 1967), 179–264.

"Religious Ethics in the Contemporary Scene." *The Future of Ethics and Moral Theology.* Chicago: Argus Communications Co., 1968.

"Context and Challenge: A Response to Rylaarsdam." *Bulletin* 48, 2 (spring 1968): 35–44.

"Israel and the Jewish Christian Dialogue." *Journal of Ecumenical Studies* 6, 1 (winter 1969): 18–36.

"Jerusalem in America." In Elwyn A. Smith, ed., *The Religion of the Republic.* Philadelphia: Fortress Press, 1971, 94–115.

"Revelation as Quest: A Contribution to Ecumenical Thought." *Journal of Ecumenical Studies* 9, 3 (summer 1972): 521–43.

"Jewish Self-Definition—Classicism and Romanticism: Our Basic Alternative." *Central Conference of American Rabbis* 19 (autumn 1972): 3–15.

"The Homecoming of the Talmud." *United Synagogue Review Quarterly* 26 (spring 1973): 4–5.

"Judaism and the New Testament." *Journal of Ecumenical Studies* 13, 4 (fall 1976): 596–613.

"Perspectives for the Study of the Book of Acts." In Arthur Chiel, ed., *Perspectives on Jews and Judaism.* New York: The Rabbinical Assembly, 1978, 7–17.

"The Dialogue—Exceptionalism as Metamyth." *Central Conference of American Rabbis* 21 (autumn 1979): 3–15.

"Continuing Creativity in Maimonides' Philosophy." In A. Katsh and L. Nemoy, eds., *Essays on the Occasion of the Seventieth Anniversary of the Dropsie University, 1909–1979.* Philadelphia: Dropsie College, 1979, 11–31.

"Neo-Maimonism." In *Conservative Thought Today.* New York: The Rabbinical Assembly, 1980), 9–20.

"Six Jewish Thoughts." *Journal of Ecumenical Studies* 17, 1 (winter 1980): 110–11.

"A Theological Foundation for the Halakhah." *Judaism* 29, 1 (winter 1980): 57–63.

"The 'Yes' and the 'No' of Revelation." In L. E. Frizzel, ed., *God and His Temple.* South Orange, N.J.: Department of Judeo-Christian Studies, Seton Hall University, 1980, 215–30.

"God in Kaplan's Philosophy." *Judaism* 30, 1 (winter 1981): 30–35.

"The Religion of Ethical Nationhood." *Conservative Judaism* 34, 4 (March–April 1981): 28–33.

"The Covenant Concept—Particularistic, Pluralistic, or Futuristic?" *Journal of Ecumenical Studies* 18, 2 (spring 1981): 217–30.

Foreword to Pinchas Lapide and Jurgen Moltmann, *Jewish Monotheism and Christian Trinitarian Doctrine.* Translated by Leonard Swidler. Philadelphia: Fortress Press, 1981, 17–24.

"The Future of Jewish Messianism." In Michael D. Ryan, ed., *Human Responses to the Holocaust*. Texts and Studies vol. 9. New York: E. Mellen Press, 1981, 225–38.

"A Jewish View of the World Community." In A. Finkel and L. Frizzel, eds., *Standing before God*. New York: Ktav, 1981, 339–74.

"The Mitzvah of Keruv." *Conservative Judaism* 35, 4 (summer 1982): 33–38.

"The Messianic Ideal and the Apocalyptic Vision." *Judaism* 32, 2 (spring 1983): 205–14.

"Choosing Life." *Present Tense* 10, 2 (winter 1983): 64.

"Between Faith and Skepticism." In Jacob J. Petuchowski, ed., *When Jews and Christians Meet*. Albany: SUNY Press, 1988, 3–7.

BROCHURES

Jewish Ethics and Labor Israel. New York: American Histadrut Cultural Exchange Institute, 1965.

Syllabus for the Study of the Sabbath. Baltimore: The Week End Jewish Layman's Institute and Beth El Congregation, 1980.

BOOK REVIEWS

"Sepher Al Torah Hasod Shelanu: Major Trends in Jewish Mysticism—The Hilda Stich Stroock Lectures, Gershom Scholem." *Hadoar* 23, 37 (August 18, 1944): 719–20.

Kaplan, Mordecai M., *The Future of the American Jew*. *Jewish Quarterly Review* 39, 2 (October 1948): 181–204.

Cohon, Beryl D., *Judaism in Theory and Practice*. *Jewish Social Studies* 12, 4 (October 1950): 397–99.

Baeck, Leo, *The Essence of Judaism*. *Jewish Social Studies* 12, 4 (October 1950): 413–14.

Maybaum, Ignaz, *The Jewish Mission*. *Jewish Social Studies* 14, 2 (April 1952): 186–88.

Halevy, Jehuda, *Kuzari: The Book of Proof and Argument*. *Jewish Social Studies* 14, 3 (July 1952): 253.

Kegley, Charles W., and Robert Brettel, eds., *The Theology of Paul Tillich*. *Judaism* 3, 1 (winter 1954): 80–89.

Glatzer, Nahum N., *Franz Rosenzweig: His Life and Thought*. *Jewish Social Studies* 16, 3 (July 1954): 273.

Glenn, Menahen G., *Israel Salanter*. *Reconstructionist* 20, 10 (July 1954): 26–27.

Kohn, Eugene, *Religion and Humanity*. *Jewish Quarterly Review* 45, 3 (January 1955): 245–49.

Lieberman, Chaim, *The Christianity of Sholem Asch*. *Judaism* 4, 2 (spring 1955): 186–88.

"History and Zeitgeist: Dinur, Ben Zion, *B'Mifneh Hadoroth*." *Midstream* 1, 1 (August 1955): 100–103.

Patterson, Charles H., *The Philosophy of the Old Testament. Jewish Social Studies* 17, 4 (October 1955): 330–31.

Epstein, Isidore, *The Faith of Judaism. Jewish Quarterly Review* 46, 3 (January 1956): 278–89.

Lebowitz, J., *Torah U-mitzvot Bizman Ha-zeh. Conservative Judaism* 10, 4 (summer 1956): 47–50.

"Is Toynbee an Anti-Semite? Samuel, Maurice, *The Professor and the Fossil*." *National Jewish Monthly* (November 1956): 32–35.

Waxman, Mordecai, ed., *Tradition and Change. Conservative Judaism* 13, 2 (winter 1959): 47–54.

Blau, Joseph L., Philip Friedman, Arthur Hertzberg, and Isaac Mendelsohn, eds., *Essays on Jewish Life and Thought. Jewish Social Studies* 22, 3 (July 1960): 186–91.

Gargan, Edward T., *Intent of Toynbee's History. Conservative Judaism* 17 (fall–winter 1962–1963): 48–60.

"Reconsiderations. *Study of History,* v. 12. *Conservative Judaism* 17 (fall–winter 1962–1963): 48–60.

"Between Two Traditions: Gordis, Robert, *The Root and the Branch*." *Midstream* 10, 1 (March 1964): 109–11.

Glatzer, Nahum N., ed., *Faith and Knowledge: The Jew in the Medieval World. Jewish Social Studies* 27, 2 (April 1965): 122.

Jacobs, Louis, *Principles of the Jewish Faith. Religious Education* 60, 3 (May–June 1965): 248–50.

Kohn, Hans, *Living in a World Revolution, My Encounters with History. Jewish Social Studies* 27, 3 (July 1965): 207–8.

Efros, Israel I., *Ancient Jewish Philosophy. Jewish Social Studies* 27, 4 (October 1965): 250–51.

Gordis, Robert, *Judaism in a Changing World. Congress Bi-Weekly* 34, 6 (March 20, 1966): 15–16.

Heschel, Abraham Joshua, *The Insecurities of Freedom. Jewish Social Studies* 29, 2 (April 1967): 120–22.

Bea, Augustin, Cardinal, *The Church and the Jewish People. Jewish Social Studies* 29, 2 (April 1967): 120–22.

Neusner, Jacob, *A Life of Rabban Yohanan ben Zakkai* and *A History of the Jews in Babylonia. Judaism* 17, 1 (winter 1968): 108–13.

MacDonald, Duncan Black, *The Hebrew Philosophical Genius. Jewish Social Studies* 30, 3 (July 1968): 182–83.

Gilbert, Arthur, *Vatican Council and the Jews. Congress Bi-Weekly* 36, 2 (January 1969): 19–21.

Kohler, Kaufmann, *Jewish Theology Systematically and Historically Considered. Jewish Social Studies* 31, 4 (October 1969): 349–52.

Rosenzweig, Franz, *The Star of Redemption,* trans. William H. Hallo. *Reconstructionist* 38, 2 (March 1972): 24–29.

"Bringing Clarity into the Mystical: Scholem, Gershom, *The Messianic Idea in Judaism and Other Essays on Jewish Spirituality.*" *Judaism* 21, 3 (summer 1972): 376–83.

"A Review Essay: *The Encyclopedia Judaica.*" *Conservative Judaism* 26, 4 (summer 1972): 46–57.

Schweitzer, Frederick M., *A History of the Jews since the First Century A.D. Jewish Social Studies* 34, 3 (July 1972): 267–70.

"A Review Essay: Finkelstein, Louis, *Pharisaism in the Making.*" *Conservative Judaism* 28, 3 (spring 1974): 60–65.

"Types of Redemption: Contribution to the Theme of the Study Conference Held at Jerusalem, 14–19 July, 1968." *Jewish Quarterly Review* 65, 1 (July 1974): 52–53.

Scholem, Gershom, *Kabbalah. Jewish Quarterly Review* 66, 4 (April 1976): 242–44.

Buber, Martin, *Briefwechsel aus sieben Jahrzenten. Jewish Quarterly Review* 67, 1 (July 1976): 59–62.

"Charting the Map of Jewish Theology: Jacobs, Louis, *A Jewish Theology.*" *Jewish Quarterly Review* 67, 2–3 (October 1976–January 1977): 168–71.

"Schaeder's *Martin Buber:* Schaeder, Grete, *The Hebrew Humanism of Martin Buber.*" *Jewish Quarterly Review* 67, 4 (April 1977): 237–41.

Halkin, Hillel, *Letters to an American Jewish Friend. Judaism* 27, 1 (winter 1978): 120–26.

"Kaufmann's *Religion in Four Dimensions:* Kaufmann, Walter, *Religions in Four Dimensions—Existential, Aesthetic, Historical, Comparative.*" *Jewish Quarterly Review* 69, 1 (July 1978): 55–57.

Weinstein, Joshua, *Buber and Humanistic Education. Jewish Quarterly Review* 69, 4 (April 1979): 245–47.

Gordis, Robert, *Understanding Conservative Judaism;* Martin Bernhard, ed., *Movements and Issues in American Judaism;* Jerry V. Diller, ed., *Ancient Roots and Modern Meanings;* Norman B. Mirsky, *Unorthodox Judaism* 29, 2 (spring 1980): 248–55.

Kaplan, Mordecai M., *The Religion of Ethical Nationhood. Conservative Judaism* 34, 4 (March–April 1981): 28–33.

"Diamond's *Philosophy and Religion:* Diamond, Malcolm L., *Contemporary Philosophy and Religious Thought.*" *Jewish Quarterly Review* 72, 1 (July 1981): 53–56.

Alexander Altmann Festschrift: S. Stein and R. Loewe, eds., *Studies in Jewish*

Religious and Intellectual History. Jewish Quarterly Review 72, 2 (October 1981): 132–39.

Thoma, Clemens, *A Christian Theology of Judaism. Jewish Quarterly Review* 72, 4 (April 1982): 312–16.

Goodman, Lenn Evan, *Monotheism. Judaism* 32, 3 (summer 1983): 367–68.

Siegele-Wenschkewitz, Leonore, *Neutestamentliche Wissenschaft vor der Judenfrage. Journal of Ecumenical Studies* 20, 4 (fall 1983): 696–97.

Mendelssohn, Moses, *Jerusalem. Jewish Quarterly Review* 75, 2 (October 1984): 192–94.

A. R. C. Leaney, *The Jewish and Christian Worlds. Journal of Ecumenical Studies* 23, 2 (spring 1986): 318.

LETTERS AND REPLIES TO LETTERS

"The Rabbinical Assembly and Jewish Law." Open letter to the editors. *Reconstructionist* 19, 6 (May 1953): 26–28.

Response to letter from Bernard Heller. *Conservative Judaism* 15, 3 (spring 1961): 40–41.

Letter to the editor. *Conservative Judaism* 15, 3 (spring 1961): 42–44.

Response to letter from Werner Steinberg. *Conservative Judaism* 27, 3 (spring 1973): 84–85.

"The Jackson Amendment." *Present Tense* 2, 1 (autumn 1974): 2.

"Old Testament." Response to I. Franck on Spinoza's onslaught on Judaism. *Reconstructionist* 44 (fall 1979): 27.

SYMPOSIA

"The Jewish View of Man and the New Democratic Order." *Proceedings of Seventh Annual Convention of the Rabbinical Council of America* (June–July 1942): 20–29.

"The Meaning of Galut in America Today." *Midstream* 9, 1 (March 1963): 5–9.

"The Quest for Jewish Values: Questions for Thinking Jews." *Jewish Heritage.* (spring 1965): 21–34; (summer 1965): 28–43.

"The State of Jewish Belief." *Commentary* 42, 2 (August 1966): 73–76.

"The Holocaust: Summation of the Colloquium." Paper delivered at Dropsie University, Philadelphia, 1973, 50–52.

"The Congregational Rabbi and the Conservative Movement: Ten Questions." *Conservative Judaism* 29, 2 (winter 1975): 9–10.